Praise for *Influencing Powerful People*

"I would definitely recommend this book to others. Having worked for such powerful people in my past experience, I learned the hard way many of the lessons Dirk Schlimm has been able to capture in his book. He has clearly articulated the challenges and offers practical insight for effectively managing, and ultimately influencing, these type-A personalities. A must-read for all business school graduates looking to advance their careers."

—Joel Schulman, Senior Director, Strategic Sourcing,
Genzyme Corporation, Cambridge, Massachusetts

"In the business world, often the most creative entrepreneurs have strong personalities and prove very difficult, if not impossible, to work for or with. However, to successfully grow their businesses, these very talented entrepreneurs almost always need a strong counterbalance—someone with unique skills to be a positive interface and make an impact. Dirk Schlimm has the experience and success in this capacity, and his book offers invaluable help to others in this type of environment."

—John Doddridge, former Chairman and CEO,
Intermet Corporation; former Director, Penske Corporation;
and former President, Magna International

"Dirk Schlimm's book provides a compelling analysis of people in power and what it takes to deal with them. Whether you are an emerging senior executive, an experienced director of a publicly traded company, or a fundraiser—knowing how to deal with powerful (and self-absorbed) people is a key to success."

—David Beatty, Conway Chair
of the Clarkson Centre for Business Ethics and Board Effectiveness,
Rotman School of Management, University of Toronto

"Having seen the effectiveness of Dirk Schlimm's methods firsthand in a tenuous situation, I can say only one thing: buy this book!"

—*Daniel Marks, President,*
Stonehouse Capital Management, Toronto, Canada

"I wish I had read Dirk Schlimm's book twenty years ago! There are many powerful leaders in Europe, and I had to find out the hard way many of the lessons Dirk shares in his book. His book certainly would have put me on a steeper learning curve."

—*Tom Haak, Group Director Human Resources,*
ARCADIS, Arnhem, The Netherlands

"The ability to work with and influence key decision makers becomes more critical as executives move higher on the corporate ladder. Dirk Schlimm's insights will prove invaluable for both those aiming for the top of the pyramid and those who just want to do well where they are. These skills are transferable across continents and extremely important in a globalized business world."

—*Katherine Zheng, Director,*
Greater China, Spencer Stuart, Beijing, China

"Influencing powerful people is an art. It is a mix of technical skills, experience, instinct, empathy, and creativity. It may be difficult but, in the end, also very rewarding, both intellectually and professionally. There are many biographies or business cases regarding powerful people, but it is rare to find a book that helps you deal with them, influence them, and prevent the risk of being too complacent. Dirk Schlimm's book is a survival manual that is both interesting and very useful."

—*Giuseppe Addezio, Head of Human Resources and Organization,*
Pirelli Tyre and Part Group, Milan, Italy

"Working with powerful people, no matter if entrepreneurs or top leaders of corporations, is a great experience. It is a hard learning curve, however. While individually these people are all different, they do share many characteristics, such as intelligence, vision, and instinct. Having had the chance to work with many powerful people, I wish I had been better prepared. *Influencing Powerful People* is not another management or leadership book but a unique guide for all people who will experience these situations."

—*Volker Neuber, President,*
Ettlinger Kunststoffmaschinen GmbH, Königsbrunn, Germany

"Most people during exit interviews say they leave an organization for better prospects. In reality, most good people leave because of their managers or poor management. If there was a strategy to understand how to influence or, at best, work better with demanding people, we would start to empower these individuals who are valuable intellectual assets. Dirk Schlimm's book is both timely and of great value to every one of us who has had to deal with overbearing individuals and not been able to put in place an effective strategy in overcoming these adversities."

—*David Tan, Program Director,*
Trenium, and Program Founder, Camp Discovery

"Dirk Schlimm is a noted author and speaker on issues related to power and politics in organizations. He has distilled a wealth of knowledge gained from years of engaging a wide array of leaders from different cultural backgrounds into a book that will prove indispensible to practitioners and students keen on learning the 'soft skills' necessary to engage powerful people. This is an extremely relevant work that meets a long-standing need for a readable and comprehensive view of the practical methods for influencing those in power."

—*Leonard C. Sebastian, Associate Professor,*
S. Rajaratnam School of International Studies, Singapore

"*Influencing Powerful People* provides a unique perspective and fills a gaping hole for anyone responsible for improving organizations and their performance. With his insights and recommendations, Dirk Schlimm delivers the guide to making leadership effective, especially in organizations that overflow with powerful egos."

—*Friedrich Blase, Director, Strategic Initiatives,*
Holland & Knight LLP, New York, New York

"*Taming of the Shrewd* may be a more apt title for this must-read book for those trying to channel the energies of a difficult boss. Dirk Schlimm's well-presented case studies provide valuable insights to optimize any working relationship."

—*Bruce Haas, Partner,*
Fitzpatrick, Cella, Harper & Scinto, New York, New York

INFLUENCING
POWERFUL
PEOPLE

ENGAGE AND COMMAND
THE ATTENTION OF THE
DECISION MAKERS TO GET
WHAT YOU NEED TO SUCCEED

DIRK SCHLIMM

New York   Chicago   San Francisco   Lisbon   London   Madrid   Mexico City
Milan   New Delhi   San Juan   Seoul   Singapore   Sydney   Toronto

The McGraw·Hill Companies

1 2 3 4 5 6 7 8 9 10 11 12 13 14 15 16 17   QFR/QFR   1 9 8 7 6 5 4 3 2 1

ISBN 978-0-07-175286-2
MHID   0-07-175286-2

This publication is designed to provide accurate and authoritative information in regard to the subject matter covered. It is sold with the understanding that neither the author nor the publisher is engaged in rendering legal, accounting, securities trading, or other professional services. If legal advice or other expert assistance is required, the services of a competent professional person should be sought.
> —*From a Declaration of Principles Jointly Adopted by a Committee of the American Bar Association and a Committee of Publishers and Associations*

Library of Congress Cataloging-in-Publication Data

Schlimm, Dirk.
    Influencing powerful people : engage and command the attention of the decision makers to get what you need to succeed / by Dirk Schlimm.
       p.   cm.
    Includes bibliographical references and index.
    ISBN 978-0-07-175286-2 (alk. paper)
    1. Persuasion (Psychology).   2. Influence (Psychology).   3. Leadership.
 I. Title.

BF637.P4S35   2011
658.4'092—dc22   2010042698

For my wife and best friend, Jennifer

Contents

Foreword

Throughout the course of my career in the worlds of international business, academia, competitive sports, and not-for-profit endeavors, I have worked with and for many powerful people. While their backgrounds and the actual challenges involved varied greatly, building strong working relationships was crucial to success in every instance.

As a leader of a large international packaging enterprise, I saw first-hand the challenges of dealing with business executives in different cultures; wrong assumptions about power, politics, and people could easily derail otherwise sound strategic plans. My role as an academic included preparing business students for the real world—a world that is often different from what is described in leadership books professing how the world should be. As a corporate director and board chair, I interfaced with strong-willed business founders—people who had built multinational enterprises and now had to get used to the rigors and constraints of dealing in a public corporation. I also had more than my share of experience with professional consultants, be they lawyers, accountants, or investment bankers who were serving their powerful clients.

I have dealt with powerful people whom I respect and even admire greatly for their accomplishments, can-do attitude, and confidence to lead and create world-leading organizations. In the process, I learned that you need to know who you are dealing with and how to approach them in the best way. The closer you get to the really powerful people, those in the larger-than-life category, the more you have to ask yourself whether you are making a contribution to them and their enterprise. If you're not, there really is no point being there. As far as my students were concerned, I would remind them that very often they would not choose their boss but that he or she would choose them; therefore, it was up to them to make the relationship work.

I will freely confess that I learned some lessons the hard way.

I first met Dirk when I joined the board of a publicly traded global company. Dirk had been there as an executive for some years and, in addition to many other responsibilities, served as secretary to the board. I soon came to rely on Dirk to facilitate the relationship between the various company stakeholders, who included its strong-willed founder, independent directors, executives, and other advisers. He had the ability to get the president's attention on key issues and, from my perspective, soon became the best conduit for dealing with him. Dirk had a true appreciation for what needed to be done and employed practical solutions to deal with the reality as it was. His actions were always guided by the best interest of the company, the direction provided by its leader, and the needs of other stakeholders. His integrity and influencing skills helped greatly with achieving business success, moving forward in alignment, and forestalling the occasional crisis.

I was therefore excited when Dirk approached me with his book idea, and we quickly realized that his insights would be of tremendous value in a broad set of circumstances. New graduates entering the workforce, middle managers, senior executives, consultants, board members, academics, and not-for-profit leaders all will benefit from Dirk's practical and systematic approach to the topic of dealing with powerful people. This approach will allow you to avoid pitfalls, become more effective, and intentionally build an important skill. If I had had access to the material Dirk shares with us in this book early in my career, it would have affected many of the decisions I had to make. It would certainly have focused me on the challenges I was facing, and I believe it would have given me the insight I needed to confront and deal with issues earlier rather than later.

Influencing Powerful People is a book that needed to be written. The practical situations described in the pages that follow are very common; in fact, I believe them to be universal. My sense is therefore that you will enjoy this book and place it on the shelf by your desk for handy reference. Dirk's "rules" for dealing with powerful people will no doubt have a significant impact on you as you move upward on your ladder of success.

—Lawrence Tapp (1937–2011)
Dean Emeritus, Professor Emeritus
Richard Ivey School of Business
University of Western Ontario

Acknowledgments

Throughout my career, people have told me that I should "write a book." It sounded like a really great idea. It is fun to recount great stories, toss around concepts, discuss ideas, and put it all into a big banker's box filled with file folders. But at some point, you have to settle on an outline that makes sense, answer the question "who cares?" and, believe it or not, sit down and get something written. The last part is a lot less glamorous than it appears from afar and requires quite a bit of tenacity. That's when writing a book can become a lonely affair consisting of being holed up in an office—especially when a ghostwriter or cowriter isn't an option.

Given the loneliness-of-the-writer syndrome, getting a book written requires two things in spades: encouragement and accountability. That's why my biggest thanks go to my wife, Jennifer, who has provided both in ample measure over the years, even and especially at times when it was otherwise in short supply, and to our two sons, Quinn and Christian, who had to live with Dad hiding in his office over extensive periods.

What also helps is a role model, someone admired for his or her strong character and good reputation. I found that in Jim Collins. When I told Jim that, after leaving my corporate career, I wanted "to do what he does"—write books, teach, and learn—he put me to work right away. Jim challenged me to "aim high," and he generously shared his ideas and experience with the book-writing process. More about that in the Introduction.

Another close companion in the writing journey was Larry Tapp. Larry took a practical interest in the project from day one, acted as a critical reader, and agreed to write the Foreword. Again, it was great to have his encouragement and to write a book that Larry assured me needed to be written.

A special thank-you also goes to my other critical readers (some were actually quite critical), and I owe a lot to them. They are Frank Cioffi (President at Greater Burlington Industrial Corporation), Richard J. Crofts (Senior Vice President, Legal Affairs and General Counsel at Bentall Kennedy), Ian Crookston (Director, Energy/ Sustainability and Maintenance at Sobeys), Rev. David Daniels (Senior Pastor at Grace Baptist Church), Governor Howard Dean (Chairman Emeritus of the Democratic National Committee), Bruce Haas (Partner at Fitzpatrick, Cella, Harper and Scinto), Peter Jewett (Partner at Torys LLP), Professor Michael Koch (Professor at the Technical University of Ilmenau), Michael McKendry (Vice President, Corporate Services and General Counsel at Husky Injection Molding Systems), David Nirenberg (Founder and CEO at SKR Partners), Jim Reid (Vice President, Organizational Development at Husky Injection Molding Systems), and Bernard S. Sharfman (Adjunct Professor at George Washington University School of Business). They all provided great insight and did not tire of the project; on the contrary, they kept on challenging and cheering on. Richard Crofts made the additional contribution of detailed editing.

And, of course, I want to thank all my Husky friends who in many ways have provided the inspiration for this book. First and foremost is philanthropist and Husky Injection Molding Systems founder Robert Schad. Robert is a generous man who took me under his wings and exposed me to the world of powerful people. To be sure, he did not coddle me but through his own unique way of doing business and life challenged me to grow and take on new responsibilities. Were it not for "Husky University," as it became known around the dinner table, this book would not exist. I also need to mention Husky's current chief executive and long-time colleague, John Galt, and former Husky board members David Beatty, Mike Cardiff, David Colcleugh, John Doddridge, Robert Gillespie, Bob Rae, David Richardson, Richard Roswech, Eric Russell, Elizabeth Schad, and of course Larry Tapp. Bob Gillespie became a much-needed fatherly friend during the Husky years, and he continues to generously share his experience and wisdom in our regular meetings. David Beatty, who taught me much about corporate governance and board dynamics, has opened new doors and keeps providing valued guidance. Larry Tapp, who shared his life's lessons generously, sadly and unexpectedly passed away while this book was in production. I also extend my gratitude to Andrée Brière, the previously mentioned Mike McKendry, and Derek Smith, with whom I worked very closely during my closing years at Husky. I hope these former teammates will one day consider me a role model for them.

Final thanks go to John Willig (President, Literary Services), as well as to Gary Krebs (Vice President and Group Publisher, Business, for McGraw-Hill Professional) and Ron Martirano (Project Editor at McGraw-Hill Professional). John's extensive experience in representing business authors helped me to position the project properly. It was great to have Gary's personal interest, attention, and challenge to broaden the scope of the book (as well as his confession that he has powerful people in his life who need influencing). Ron is a true professional; he immersed himself in the project and challenged my logic with great precision. I would also like to thank all those at McGraw-Hill who worked on the production of the book—Susan Moore (Editing, Design, and Production Supervisor), Pam Juárez (Senior Production Artist), and Denise Duffy-Fieldman (Production Artist)—and copyeditor Karen Schenkenfelder, proofreader Lisa Stracks, and indexer Sharon Duffy.

As I conducted my research for the book, I discovered many valuable stories and insights in the biographies and autobiographies of powerful people as well as in the works of other authors. They are referenced in the notes, and I would like to acknowledge the most critical ones here as well. They are Rick Atkinson (*Crusade*), Sally Bedell Smith (*In All His Glory*), Claire Berlinski (*There Is No Alternative*), Gwenda Blair (*Donald Trump*), Otto Preston Chaney (*Zhukov*), David D'Alessandro (*Executive Warfare*), Michael D'Antonio (*Hershey*), Eric Eyck (*Bismarck and the German Empire*), Robert Greene (*The 48 Laws of Power*), Caroline Van Hasselt (*High Wire Act*), Kitty Kelley (*Oprah*), Wayne Lilley (*Magna cum Laude*), Jean Lipman-Blumen (*The Allure of Toxic Leaders*), Bethany McLean and Peter Elkind (*The Smartest Guys in the Room*), Ferdinand Piëch (*Auto.Biographie*), Jeffrey Pfeffer (*Managing with Power*), Colin Powell (*My American Journey*), Ted Rogers (*Relentless*), H. Norman Schwarzkopf (*It Doesn't Take a Hero*), Richard Siklos (*Shades of Black*), Blema Steinberg (*Women in Power*), Rita Stiens (*Ferdinand Piëch*), and Michael Wolff (*The Man Who Owns the News*). Additional reporting and perspective came from writers of the business and academic press. The most outstanding are Nanette Byrnes and Roger Crockett of *Bloomberg/BusinessWeek*; Peter Elkind of *Fortune*; Peter Frost and Sandra Robinson of *Harvard Business Review*; Marc Gunther of *Fortune*; Dacher Keltner, Deborah Gruenfeld, and Cameron Anderson of *Psychological Review*; Adam Lachinsky of *Fortune*; Betsy Morris of *Fortune*; and Ralf Neukirch of *Der Spiegel*. In addition, I express my appreciation to all other authors, reporters, and experts whose work I have referenced.

Introduction

He who gets fired gets nothing done.

—JEFFREY PFEFFER, THOMAS D. DEE II PROFESSOR OF
ORGANIZATIONAL BEHAVIOR, STANFORD UNIVERSITY

Midlife is a good time for personal reflection. When I left the rigors of an executive job in 2008, I was able to look back on almost three decades of experiences that had encompassed the military, academia, judicial service, the not-for-profit sector, and life in a global corporation. In the process, I had the opportunity to encounter a fascinating diversity of people with varied personal and professional backgrounds from the Americas, Europe, and the Asia-Pacific region.

Now that it was time to chart a new course, my friend and mentor Jim Collins challenged me to write down "everything I had learned." It is good to have a mentor or coach, especially when he or she is asking us to do something that is important but would otherwise easily fall victim to the tyranny of the urgent or to our own laziness. Having that request come from a person with some profile is helpful, too, as we don't want to embarrass ourselves. In my own executive-coaching practice, I have found that the combination of questioning, challenging, and making my clients accountable is just as important as giving them good advice. In fact, it's probably more so.

To write down everything I have learned seemed like an amorphous task to start with. It required some thinking and clarification in order to get to a concrete work plan I could actually implement. Fortunately, as we will see, powerful people have quite a habit of making high-level "visionary" pronouncements and requests that need extensive translation in order to become operational, so I have considerable experience with this type of activity. I quickly determined that the best way to make Jim's assignment concrete was to create a number of headings under which I could categorize my learning. These headings included things like business strategy, human resources development, corporate governance, ownership succession, international negotiations, business communication, and legal policy.

After reviewing these categories with me, Jim informed me (politely) that although my learning in these areas was valuable, it was perhaps not earth-shattering. However, he picked up on one category that was buried in the fifteen or so I had listed. The heading was "How to Deal with Powerful People."

Interestingly enough, this topic had been a focus of mine for a long time. I learned my first lessons on the topic in the military, hardly a place of "participatory leadership." I had lodged a complaint over a colonel's disparaging remarks of the intellectual abilities of combat troops with the parliamentary ombudsman of Germany's armed forces, which yielded little in return. At the same time, it had been possible to engage in a constructive dialogue with commanding officers of my company, which led to a modification of senseless drill practices. I learned that influencing powerful people was a better and more effective route than complaining about them. Later, my work for university professors and judges, people who had a lot of status and stature, taught me new lessons.

I had my first exposure to "larger-than-life" leaders in politics and industry as a fellow of the Konrad Adenauer Foundation, an organization that provides scholarships for university and doctoral studies. In fact, one of the foundation's goals was to expose us to such people so that we could learn how to engage them better. In particular, such exposure taught us how to manage stressful circumstances, keep our balance, and communicate with precision and utmost clarity at all times. All of this proved invaluable when it became my job to interface with entrepreneurs, professional executives, board members, strong-headed managers, and other powerful people. It was also the competency I needed most to survive, make a contribution, and progress within a global corporation.

A key insight—the one I believe makes this book both necessary and useful—is that working with powerful people is not straightforward. You cannot just walk into their office, tell them what is needed, and expect that they follow your logic. Why not? Because they have their own logic. Further, if they are impulsive enough, which many of them are, they may have already judged you before you even got your first word out. Their judgment may have been wrong, but that matters little. Of course, much has been written lately about emotionally intelligent, participatory, and authentic leadership, and the world would be a better place if more people would embrace these concepts. But the reality is that many powerful people simply are not that way and will not become that way anytime soon. Yes, they may be full of charm, drive, and brilliance (some more than others, of course), but they can and will be equally as domineering, demanding, and temperamental. And you certainly cannot tell them what to do. So instead of engaging in wishful thinking (*I wish my boss would listen, would appreciate what I do, was more reasonable, etc.*), you must face the brutal reality as it is. You must adapt and make things work. You can do so by learning to effectively influence those who are your boss, superior, or otherwise in charge. Waiting for them to change, in contrast, will be just as futile as an all-out power struggle.

The ability to influence powerful people is a critical skill in a large variety of settings. As I alluded to earlier, it is needed in business, the military, academia, politics, not-for-profit organizations, and pretty much every other arena. In addition, it has become even more indispensable in the context of global business, which involves different cultures, personalities, and management styles. Consider how progress in the following situations requires influencing powerful people:

» **Dealing with a powerful boss.** This is the most obvious category. If your boss is strong-willed, demanding, and has a bit of a temper, you must counter that with superior influencing skills. There are things you can and must do to increase your chances of getting the job, keeping it (the revolving door is a constant theme with many powerful people), and progressing in it. Examples in this book will introduce you to people who were out the door as soon as they got in and others who rose to positions of tremendous influence.

» **Working in a diffuse power structure.** Organizational power structures have lost a lot of their clarity and definition with the arrival of the "flat" organization, especially if they are global. Clear hierarchies have been replaced by a matrix where geographic managers work (or compete) at the same level as product and/or functional leaders. In that environment, you are often accountable to more than one boss in addition to "internal customers," and you may have to influence quite a few other people—many of them more powerful than you are—to get the resources you need and deliver the results your organization expects. These people include sales and marketing directors, vice presidents of finance, purchasing managers, and a whole host of strong-willed managers at various levels. For example, you may need budget approval from a corporate finance chief, customer support resources from an overseas manufacturing operation, or buy-in for a compensation policy from a subsidiary with foreign laws. You may not have authority, but you do have responsibility for results. The power structures in the world of politics and not-for-profits can, of course, be just as byzantine. There is no question: people who can navigate such environments will be in high demand.

» **Dealing with powerful clients.** Influencing skills are a must for professional service providers and other advisers. I have seen lawyers, accountants, and other consultants lose clients because they did not understand the dynamic of a powerful personality. I have seen others relate in the right way, act without presumption, and communicate with great effectiveness. As a result, they increased their influence and were called upon in a much broader range of circumstances. The powerful people they worked with valued someone who understood them much more than someone who (just) had brilliant technical expertise.

» **Sitting on boards of directors.** This can be an extremely tricky category. Conventional wisdom says that the board has all the power and that the chief executive serves at the board's pleasure. But the reality can be quite different. Your chief executive may be a major shareholder or have star power that makes him or her indispensable and irreplaceable, or there simply may be no one else to do the job—and the CEO well knows it. Instead of the directors governing the CEO, he or she may actually think that they work for him or her. Superior influencing skills will go a long way in managing this situation, leaving power struggles as a last resort, if that.

To provide structure to the key insights—I have called them rules—that describe how to influence powerful people, I have ordered them in the following way: Rules 1 and 2 deal with some general attributes of powerful people, that is, what they are like as a type and how they perceive us, the less powerful. To be effective, you have to know who you are dealing with. Rules 3 to 9 focus on building a working relationship with powerful people. That relationship becomes critical to managing the inevitable ups and downs and, of course, the occasional crisis. Rules 10 to 15 look at specific things you may be doing for and with powerful people. Once the relationship and your influencing skill progress, you may be doing much more than your regular job. You will be called upon as a facilitator, counselor, and even counterweight; as you'll discover, powerful people occasionally need protection from themselves. Rule 16 addresses the fact that you will likely have some power of your own and that there are things you can learn from your dealings with powerful people in order to make more effective use of your power.

Many of the illustrations, examples, and case studies in this book come from well-known powerful people. They describe real instances as reported in a variety of media. I have found this approach compelling for a number of reasons: My research of powerful characters confirmed that many of them have common traits and that the "rules" have worked in practice across a much larger spectrum than my own experience. It also confirms the breadth of application, as the illustrations span business, politics, and the military. Further, it allows a look at some very high-impact people and situations. Whether you find yourself in exactly that situation or deal with circumstances that are not quite as dramatic, the range of examples should help you prepare for your biggest challenges. Some of the powerful people I have referenced include Steve Jobs of Apple, Rupert Murdoch of News Corporation, William Paley of CBS, General Norman Schwarzkopf, Donald Trump, Oprah Winfrey, Canadians Ted Rogers (Rogers Communications) and Frank Stronach (Magna International), Britain's Conrad Black (formerly of Hollinger) and Prime Minister Margaret Thatcher, and Germany's Ferdinand Piëch of Volkswagen and Chancellor Angela Merkel. I have chosen their stories because I believe all of them deserve admiration for their accomplishments, all seem to be demanding personalities who could never be accused of coddling people, and a few of them had their share of controversy. In the following chapters, you will also meet real people who have done an outstanding job at engaging them and helping them and their enterprises succeed, all while building great careers and profiles of their own. Others have suffered shipwreck, and you must learn from them as well.

In addition, other examples will relate to working with "everyday" powerful people." Clearly, the rules for influencing powerful people apply far beyond interaction with high-profile characters. Depending on where you are, the managing director of your local subsidiary, the head of your finance department, the influential member of your board, the critical donor in your charity, or the owner of your small business may be just as powerful in your setting as a corporate tycoon in someone else's. Thus, exercising smart influence as detailed in the pages that follow will be critical to making your best contribution, earning respect, and progressing toward greater achievement and responsibility.

Get Ready for a Potent Mix of Brilliance and Drive

Tenacity and perseverance are the way to success.

—TED ROGERS, FOUNDER AND CEO, ROGERS COMMUNICATIONS

I f you want to learn how to influence powerful people, you must first understand where their power comes from. It is way too simple to assume that power is simply conferred by position. Within any business organization or government, there may be people with impressive-sounding titles who are mere figureheads. Others may hold unassuming positions yet wield great power; you must have them on your side if you want to get anywhere or move ahead with your priorities.

In that regard, there is much to learn from larger-than-life characters who did not simply have position bestowed on them, but made it to the top while others—who might have had equal potential—fell by the wayside. When you then deal with the powerful person in your specific circumstance, it will be wise to assume that these qualities are present at least in some measure.

Brilliance

A few years back, I worked with a senior political staffer who was incredibly adept at making things happen through influence. His first insight to help him do his job was that his boss, a U.S. governor, was smarter than he was. That assumption served him extremely well. It reflected great humility and unbiased assessment of reality.

A review of the accomplishments of larger-than-life characters easily reveals that many of them are indeed brilliant and that this quality has contributed in no small measure to their rise to power. What makes these "geniuses" especially powerful is that they have much more than just technical or subject-matter expertise. From the basis of knowing their business inside and out, they are able to derive unique insight and intuition regarding the development of an entire industry. This insight can even extend further to become a catalyst for change that affects global business, society, and culture at large. The following are but a few examples:

» Ferdinand Piëch, the chairman of auto giant Volkswagen, may not have inherited the last name of his famous grandfather Ferdinand Porsche, but he is nonetheless an exceptionally gifted car designer. From a very early age, his life revolved around automobiles. Piëch can sketch a complete engine or drive system in freehand, and his design innovations on a napkin are reported to be many. Unlike most engineers and designers today, he certainly does not need a CAD (computer-aided design) workstation. Piëch is equally skilled at orchestrating the high-stakes acquisition and turnaround strategies that have propelled Volkswagen to become one of the world's largest car companies with the ongoing ambition to take the top spot from rival Toyota.

» Steve Jobs, cofounder and chief executive of Apple, is, of course, the brilliant inventor of Apple's many computers and gadgets, the latest revelation of which is always a highly anticipated occasion. Jobs is a master at design and has an incredible ability not just to package products but also to reinvent the way they are used—the ultimate fusion of form and function. Beyond that, the business press around the world ascribes huge cultural influence to Steve Jobs, as when *Fortune* crowned him CEO of the decade.[1] The German weekly *Der Spiegel* writes that, as the "philosopher of the 21st century," Jobs has convinced humankind that Apple products make their lives (and modern life at large) cool and easy. In fact, he has made us "want to need" his products. We need an iMac desktop for the office, a MacBook for the road, an iPod for jogging, an iPad for education, and an iPhone to stay connected. We couldn't imagine life without these devices.[2]

» In the world of publishing, Rupert Murdoch, the creator, chairman and managing director of media juggernaut News Corporation, perfected the art of tabloid journalism and knows how to make newspapers profitable. While being incredibly hands-on, Murdoch also was the first to develop the vision for expanding news delivery beyond a single medium (in his case, the newspaper) and created a multisource news corporation. The takeover of the venerated *Wall Street Journal* was probably his most triumphant achievement as a deal maker. Lately, Rupert Murdoch has taken the lead in revisiting the practice of free news content delivery over the Internet.[3]

» Conrad Black, whose media empire once included the *Chicago Sun-Times*, Britain's *Daily Telegraph*, and the *Jerusalem Post* and who remains embroiled in an epic battle with the U.S. judicial system, remains known for his tremendous intellect. His command of the English language is legendary, as is his incredible on-the-spot brilliance and encyclopedic knowledge of world history and current affairs. His biographer Richard Siklos wrote of a meeting with British Prime Minister Margaret Thatcher at which Lord Black was easily able to enlighten the head of the Tories on the nineteenth-century history of her party. He did it without any sort of preparation and simply based on his vast knowledge at hand, all the while conversing in a pleasant and fascinating manner.[4] That was no easy feat at all and left an impression on Thatcher.

» Frank Stronach, the Austrian-Canadian chairman of auto parts powerhouse Magna International, proves that innovation and change leadership can be just as effective in established (some may say old) hardware-oriented industries. A tool-and-die maker by trade, he built his auto parts empire outward from its North American roots and continued to thrive while the former Big Three carmakers found themselves mired in a fight for survival. Most notably, he understood early on that automotive industry leadership was not just a matter of racing to lower costs; rather, the industry needed low cost *and* innovation. Therefore, Stronach continued to invest in research and development while others only cut costs. His simple yet extremely powerful mantra is to deliver "a better product at a better price."

What makes these geniuses so powerful is not ground-level exper-tise *or* vision. It is the fact that they have both; they are equally capable of and comfortable with micromanaging and dreaming up a large-scale, big-picture vision.

Sometimes the Genius Is Alone

However, the genius's vision is not always obvious to those who are supposed to follow. In fact, powerful people can find themselves alone with the pursuit of an idea yet be unprepared to give it up. An episode involving Ted Rogers illustrates the point. Ted Rogers was the founder, chief executive officer, and controlling shareholder of Rogers Communications, one of Canada's largest media conglomerates and communications companies; he has been described as "Canada's version of Steve Jobs."[5] In the early 1980s, Rogers Cablesystems, the forerunner of Rogers Communications, was heavily in debt. At the same time, Rogers became interested in wireless telephone technol-ogy. Colin Watson, the president of the cable company, thought that under the circumstances, entry into the cellular business would be crazy.[6] However, Rogers had become convinced that the technology would become the next big thing. Objections from bankers invok-ing debt covenants were no obstacle for him, of course. He presented the board with his request to invest $500,000 in wireless telephones. At the board meeting, the directors backed the cable executives, not Rogers. Every board member, even Rogers's wife, voted against the wireless investment in a vote that ended up being sixteen-to-one. Undaunted, Rogers proceeded on his own. In his memoirs, he wrote, "They forced me to put my own money on the line, which I did. I just knew that wireless was the next big thing, and I wasn't about to miss it."[7]

The rest of the story is history. Wireless eventually became the big-gest part of the Rogers empire—bigger than radio and cable, which were the origins of the company. The wireless venture was also criti-cal to solving the company's persistent cash needs and making it investment grade.

In a similar fashion, the strategy of building company-owned retail stores, which is integral to Apple today, was derided at the time as a risky cash drain. According to *Fortune* magazine, Steve Jobs pursued it with "a nervous board," but he knew it was what customers wanted.[8]

This leads to a crucial lesson that you have to keep in mind when working with a brilliant boss. While the boss's intellect is the foundation for creating tremendous wealth, progress, and employment, there is a price to pay for those of us who work with the genius. The genius, who sees opportunity with outside-the-box ideas, gets easily frustrated if he or she feels surrounded by others who only see obstacles. A powerful person with a big idea is likely to feel that he or she is right and will grow impatient with naysayers.

> *Start with the assumption that you are working with people who are smarter than you.*

Certainly, you should not be fooled into believing that overruling Ted was a regular occurrence at Rogers Communications board meetings. Therefore, doubting the vision of a powerful leader is a delicate endeavor, as we will see in subsequent rules.

The Universal Genius

The experience of their own brilliance also reinforces powerful people's desire to contribute to all areas of the company or organization, whether or not they are subject-matter experts on every area. People who are firmly in charge potentially have an interest in anything that is going on and more than likely have an opinion on what can be done differently or better. In that sense, whether they are aware of it or not, powerful people see themselves as being like Leonardo da Vinci, who excelled as a scientist, mathematician, engineer, inventor, anatomist, painter, sculptor, architect, botanist, musician, and writer. They feel they can master anything—and sometimes it seems as if they can. The fact is that powerful people often are desirous and capable of a large spectrum of contribution; they are not just a "genius," but a *genius universalis*.

Thus, as Peter Elkind tells us, Steve Jobs not only is a "co-inventor" on 103 separate Apple patents, but his contributions cover everything from the user interface for the iPod to the support system for the glass staircase used in Apple's dazzling retail stores. He is personally responsible for the creation of the latest computer gadget and the selection of the chef in the company cafeteria. He even injects his sense for aesthetics—one of his critical talents—into the realm of contract drafting.[9]

This sense of being renaissance men and women has to be recognized as much more than mere idiosyncrasy; it has very practical implications for business strategy, corporate governance, and daily interaction. For example, it is possible an employee may make a statement about a certain specialized hobby he has and imply that he has a certain expertise on that rather remote subject. The powerful person, who has genuine knowledge of that topic, would pick up on that and get into a detailed discussion—only to discover that the employee's knowledge was not deep at all. "You don't know what you're talking about" would be the inevitable conclusion, and it would influence the powerful person's opinion of that individual.

> *Never profess to have expertise or knowledge (of any subject) unless confident that you are on solid ground.*

There may be broader implications here as well, especially for those who have a high level of responsibility, such as board members. Frank Stronach, the founder and chairman of the Magna automotive empire is famous for his management philosophy of "fair enterprise." Part of Frank's genius was to recognize the value of employee share ownership early on, as well as giving tremendous autonomy to Magna's plant/general managers. Rather than just putting in place a profit-sharing or employee share purchase plan, Stronach crafted Magna's "corporate constitution," which declares Magna to be a "fair enterprise corporation" and publicly "declares and defines the rights of our employees, investors and management to participate in our profits and growth." This declaration, which assigns predetermined portions of profits to the various groups, makes it difficult to challenge compensation policies.

In true renaissance fashion, Stronach also made a foray into Canadian politics and contributed innovative ideas for the redesign of government institutions; he launched his own business publication, *Vista*, to disseminate "education, information and provocation";[10] and he undertook a virtual takeover of the Austrian soccer league.[11] The most formidable da Vincian strategic decision was, of course,

Stronach/Magna's entry into the world of horse racing, which started with the acquisition of the storied Santa Anita Park racetrack in California in 1998.[12] All of this makes for interesting board meetings!

Not every single one of these ventures turned out to be successful. Frank Stronach never became Canada's Silvio Berlusconi, and Magna Entertainment had to apply for bankruptcy. But one should be equally cautious about following the suggestion of leadership scholar Jean Lipman-Blumen that too many "visions of charismatic leaders are hastily wrought and ill conceived."[13] The fact is that many powerful people successfully overcome conventional wisdom and have the resources to keep their initiatives alive. Most important, one must accept as fact that outright dismissal of the genius is rarely an effective strategy for dealing with their ideas.

At the same time, we should not leave the topic of brilliance without a word of caution. All of the leaders discussed here provide evidence that brilliant, no-nonsense leadership can be highly effective and result in great accomplishments. But it may not lend itself to *all* industries, circumstances, or phases in an organization's development. The genius, however, may tend to think that his or her management philosophy is truly universal—for all times, circumstances, industries, and situations. All of this boils down to the following conclusion: you cannot be a blind follower either, no matter how brilliant the leader might be.

> *Even if you are the expert in your field, don't expect or ask to be left alone to do your job.*

Relentless Drive

The second major trait of powerful people is their relentless drive. Jeffrey Pfeffer, Stanford professor and author of the superb treatise *Managing with Power*, believes that energy and physical stamina are the true sources of power, not great genius or intellect.[14] Pfeffer cites the energy of powerful public servants to make his point. He tells us that Maine senator Edmund Muskie was notorious for wearing down opponents in marathon meetings, that Lyndon Johnson started his day early and was still up after most others had gone to bed, and that New York's "master builder" Robert Moses would extend working hours by early-morning and late-night travel between New York City and the state capital, Albany.[15]

Rupert Murdoch's biographer Michael Wolff seems to be in full agreement with this assessment. He does point to the commonly held belief that empires like the one Murdoch created are built on some structural advantage, a monopoly, a financing strategy, a technology, a unique idea, some marketing genius. But then he goes on to say that Murdoch has none of these. At the end of the day, Wolff asserts, what really built Murdoch's empire may have just been "freakish relentlessness and opportunism."[16]

We do not need to decide whether genius or drive comes first. The reality is that having both provides a very potent combination. The point is that the relentlessness that Wolff observes as a very exceptional quality in Murdoch is, in fact, a commonality among the people who are the prime exhibits of our study.

Ted Rogers, for example, could not have provided a clearer summary of the essence of his personality when he called his autobiography *Relentless*. Rogers defined himself by his drive and determination more so than by his product or business. And one of the fundamental lessons Ted learned in business was that "tenacity and perseverance are the way to success."[17]

That drive is not reserved to men. In her biography of TV celebrity and media entrepreneur Oprah Winfrey, Kitty Kelley stresses that Oprah's "stratospheric" success was motored by her incredible drive and ambition. As a self-propelled whirlwind of industry, Oprah was unmatched by anyone in her ambition and determination to succeed; she slept only four to five hours a night, kept a grueling schedule of work and travel, and rarely relaxed.[18]

Powerful People Are Incredibly Demanding

The tremendous energy of powerful people is sustained by a deep-rooted drive to succeed, especially against the odds and in the face of real or perceived obstacles. In other words, powerful people are highly competitive. At the same time, powerful people love what they do, and for them, work is an enjoyable activity that adds even more energy. Wayne Lilley, for example, tells us that Frank Stronach's energy expands with every challenge.[19] Kitty Kelley writes that Oprah's work fills her soul, "giving her the greatest pleasure in life."[20]

All of this makes powerful people extremely demanding. In their own perception, however, they are not asking anything of others that they would not ask of themselves. But therein lies the crux of the problem: their own expectations are sky high, and they live, breathe, and eat work. Thus was the case with William Paley, the chief executive who built Columbia Broadcasting Systems (CBS) from a small radio network to one of the foremost radio and television network operations in the United States. We read that Paley had a restless energy that propelled his every move. He never sat on the beach; he was always *doing something*. Even playing golf was a pursuit. William Paley's energy often produced extraordinary results, but "it also took an extraordinary human toll."[21]

Ted Rogers described his father as a man filled with perseverance and credited his mother with a relentless drive to make sure these qualities came to the fore in him. Again, with that DNA came sky-high expectations of others. He explained that nothing in business drove him crazier than people coming to him with a list of why things couldn't be done. Instead, especially in the case of highly paid executives, Rogers felt they were richly rewarded not to put up obstacles but "to tell him how things can be done."[22]

Ferdinand Piëch is 100 percent on the same page. His perspective is that people with higher pay earn more in order to produce more. He goes on to say, "When that does not happen, I quickly take action. I would rather send a less capable executive into early retirement than to risk thousands of jobs on the shop floor."[23] Or, as his biographer puts it, "He wants it all, he wants it his way, and he wants it now."[24]

Transferring the founder's own energy to the entire enterprise is part of the secret behind Magna's success. Even his otherwise critical biographer acknowledges that Frank Stronach was true to his credo that "only perfection is acceptable."[25] To fulfill his customers' needs, Stronach demanded the same commitment to excellence in his employees, gaining their confidence by giving them the opportunity to manage autonomously, unfettered by bureaucracy. He also gave them a strong incentive in the form of a share of the profits for which they were directly responsible.

Even old age does not seem to diminish the energy of powerful people. Ted Rogers worked almost to his dying day at age seventy-five. In the year before his death, he ordered a major overhaul of the company: "I can afford to do this now," his biographer Caroline Van Hasselt quotes him as saying. "I think we're very fortunate and I think we've got great people and I acknowledge them. Having said that, *I'm dissatisfied with almost everything. I'm going to fix the company now.*"[26]

Rogers is certainly not alone. We read in *Fortune* that at age seventy-seven, Bill Marriott Jr. calls retirement a "disease" and loves going to work in the morning.[27] He walks on his treadmill four nights a week and is said to have taken up Pilates training when his daughter told him he seemed to be getting shorter. *Slate* magazine's list of the "top eighty over eighty" contains an impressive ensemble of people, including characters like Kirk Kerkorian and T. Boone Pickens, who launched major ventures late in life and wouldn't even dream of slowing down. The phenomenon has even attracted its own technical term; such people have been labeled "nevertirees."

> Fasten your seatbelt and get ready for competitive intensity, relentless drive, and huge demands.

Powerful People Are Resilient

Their unbridled energy gives powerful people a remarkable ability to bounce back. Steve Jobs returned to Apple after being ousted by John Sculley. At that point, Jobs hadn't lost a battle; he had lost an "entire war," which became the beginning of his "wilderness years."[28]

Frank Stronach kept his cool after a major effort to acquire the European Opel unit of General Motors failed because GM's board had changed its mind. The reversal came after many months of multiparty negotiations that involved GM, Opel unions, the German government, and Russian financiers. The deal would have fulfilled Stronach's dream of owning a full-fledged car company, yet all he had to say in public was, "Life goes on; you take it as it comes and you go on and look for other opportunities."[29] Of course, the fact that GM was Magna's largest customer helped with the somewhat philosophical response.

Margaret Thatcher, the British prime minister who broke the entrenched power of trade unions and fought off Argentine generals in the war over the Falkland Islands, demonstrated tremendous resilience after she abandoned her quest for reelection as party leader in light of stiff opposition and slipping fortunes in 1990. After informing the queen and her cabinet of her decision to resign, she addressed Parliament that same afternoon. Her last speech as prime minister was a brilliant performance in which she asserted herself once again as an iconic world figure of historic importance.[30] It even caused some of her internal foes to wonder whether ousting the Iron Lady had really been a wise decision.

Conrad Black even found new purpose during his incarceration through an arrangement with "his gracious temporary hosts" (the U.S. correctional facility in Coleman, Florida). He tutored other inmates in English. In his letters from prison, he noted, "This unbidden sojourn has given me a taste of the rewards of teaching. It pains me to verge on platitudes, but life's rewards sometimes come in strange and unexpected places."[31] Obviously, he had not lost his wit. What is more, he had not lost his fight either. He won an astounding victory in front of the U.S. Supreme Court, which cut his prison sentence short (albeit on bail at the time of this writing) and set the stage for striking back at his enemies.[32]

> *Never underestimate the resilience of powerful people. Don't count them out too early, and don't expect a fight to be over until it's over.*

Explosive Energy

We would not be realists if we failed to acknowledge that, more often than not, powerful people express themselves in an explosive manner rather than a measured one. The terms *balance* and *restraint* rarely come up as descriptors of powerful people or are cited as reasons for their success. When energy and drive take over, the focus is on the challenge at hand. Obstacles, real or perceived, are to be moved out of the way, and pushback can easily ignite a volatile situation. In these circumstances, there is little room for the virtues of social or emotional intelligence or compassion. Instead, powerful people will be utterly direct, to put it mildly, and tempers will flare. Interestingly, this reality is not lost on the powerful persons themselves. For example, in their autobiographies, both Ted Rogers and Desert Storm hero Norman Schwarzkopf specifically mention their respective tempers.

To get the picture, though, you must appreciate that we are not simply talking about someone raising his or her voice. Colin Powell, who was Schwarzkopf's counterpart in Washington during Operation Desert Storm, describes Norman Schwarzkopf as a volcano with a progressively building temper.[33] Rick Atkinson adds more color in his account of the campaign and how those who encountered the commander-in-chief developed their own terminology, from "going ballistic" to being "clawed by the bear."[34] If we add the confined space of an underground bunker to the scenario, we can start to imagine the physical and emotional toll such temperamental behavior may take on the recipient. How you need to handle these situations is covered in detail in the chapters that follow.

What to do when . . .

. . . you are joining your first big meeting

You are starting your new job working for a powerful person, and you're attending your first big meeting.

Especially if you are a junior person, it is critical that you not start off on the wrong foot. If possible, get some advice from a veteran regarding potential pitfalls. If you arrive when there are still many empty chairs, be sure to understand unspoken seating arrangements. Don't be the first to walk over to the refreshment cart if there is one; maybe it will be better to skip that move altogether. Instead, be ready to take notes, watch how others behave, and carefully follow the conversation. Don't consult your BlackBerry; be ready to be questioned at any moment. If you feel you have something to contribute to the discussion, do. However, asking a question will often be smarter than making a statement.

Know How to Manage the Supremely Confident

He played by his own rules, which he kept changing.

—SALLY BEDELL SMITH, DESCRIBING WILLIAM PALEY,
CHAIRMAN AND CHIEF EXECUTIVE OFFICER, CBS[1]

A second precondition to influencing powerful people is a thorough understanding of how they see themselves and how they see those who are less powerful—that is, you and me. There may be those who feel that, deep down, domineering powerful people are insecure. But that idea is only speculation; those who wield power don't come across as insecure, and treating them as insecure is certainly no way to manage them. The fact is that their view of themselves is one of supreme confidence. Again, a look at some well-known personalities provides colorful illustrations of what that means and offers an excellent starting point for understanding and managing this power dynamic.

L'entreprise c'est moi (I am the enterprise)

Larger-than-life leaders can hold a tremendous sway over their enterprises. In fact, in some cases, one can even say that such leaders *are* the enterprise. That phenomenon will not surprise anyone who considers the case of Oprah Winfrey. At Harpo Productions ("Harpo" is Oprah spelled backward), the star really is the owner, the product, and the enterprise in one person. Another obvious example is Donald Trump, who in many ways has perfected and exploited the fusion of the person and the enterprise as a brand. Thus, the Trump name alone is a significant factor in increasing the value of real estate assets, and it has been used to market an amazing variety of products bearing his name. The list includes bottled water, vodka, signature ties, steaks, fragrances, and, of course, his TV show, "The Apprentice."

Even beyond these examples, we find the phenomenon with amazing consistency. In her biography of CBS chairman William Paley, Sally Bedell Smith writes, "William Paley had led CBS for 60 years. To a select few he was Bill, to most of them Mr. Paley or the Chairman. But to everyone in the room *he was CBS*. He is to American broadcasting as Carnegie was to steel, Ford to automobiles, Luce to publishing, and Ruth to baseball."[2] It is worth noting that this characterization of CBS as being Bill Paley was made at a time when his ownership stake had dropped to just over 8 percent; there also was no dual-class share structure in place that would have allowed him to impose his control.

Today, Steve Jobs's position at Apple is described in a similar fashion. *Fortune* writer Peter Elkind reckons that the chief executive officer of the corporation at the head of *Fortune*'s list of America's Most Admired Companies has never been more personally identified with the day-to-day affairs of his business."[3] Or as another commentator put it: "Mr. Jobs is inextricably tied to Apple's brand."[4]

All of this is reminiscent of Louis XIV, the French Sun King, who famously quipped that he was the state: "L'état c'est moi." The motto of many powerful (business) people today might well be "L'entreprise c'est moi" (I am the enterprise). At least, as we have just seen, this is very much the conclusion of the world around them.

In that sense, a man who understood well for whom he was working was Robert Gruber, a former Austrian banker whom Frank Stronach had hired as managing director of Magna Europe. Wayne

Lilley tells the story of how Gruber approached one of his first tasks, which was to find a European headquarters: "He [Frank] told me, 'Look for a nice property close to Vienna,'" Gruber recalled.[5] Knowing his boss, Gruber found *schloss* Oberwaltersdorf, a 400-year-old castle on 247 acres south of Vienna. And as we are further told by Lilley, contrary to the experience of the previous owner, Magna's municipal approvals for such additions as a golf course, training center, personal living quarters, and an artificial lake were reportedly issued in record time.

Before you relegate this experience to the realm of exceptional characters, it is important to realize that such an absolutist perception is actually quite normal. In a study on the effects of power, psychologists from the University of California, Berkeley, and Stanford University have found that even people with much more modest levels of power (you and I) have a high opinion of themselves.[6] It is simply a consequence of their (our) repeated exercise of power. Thus, when you are dealing with the owner of a small business, the managing director of a local subsidiary, or the head of a company department, it is safe to assume that those individuals will likely have a bit of a Sun King or Queen in themselves as well. That's what their perception is, and that's what those around them frequently confirm.

> *Remember that powerful people identify greatly with their work and their enterprise. They expect the same from you. Show them that you take your work seriously and that you are striving to make a contribution, rather than just do a job.*

Image Matters

Powerful personalities can also be image conscious and sensitive to criticism. If you directly or indirectly report to such an individual, you need to recognize that this leader will view everything you do or don't do as a reflection of him or her personally. In addition, you are a reflection of their enterprise. Don't be surprised if this executive ascribes significance to seemingly minor missteps; there is rarely a detail that would not be worthy of perfection. Also, comments or feedback that might express or imply criticism—no matter how subtle or inadvertent—will be magnified in that person's eyes.

There are numerous obvious examples of image-conscious powerful people who love attention and the camera; Oprah Winfrey and Donald Trump come to mind again. It is also useful to review a couple of specific business examples and demonstrate how they affected the people involved. Wayne Lilley reports that Frank Stronach cooperated with no less than three writers to pen his biography. Yet according to Lilley, all versions were found to be inadequate, and the projects were abandoned.[7] In a now-famous story that hit the news in 2005, Steve Jobs banished all books published by John Wiley & Sons from the shelves of Apple's 105 retail stores because of Wiley's plans to publish the book *iCon: Steve Jobs, The Greatest Second Act in the History of Business*.[8]

The Rules Do Not Apply

Powerful people sincerely believe that the rules do not apply to them (at least not *all* of the rules). In fact, as we will see later on, telling these people they can't do something will often invite a defiant response. Sally Bedell Smith describes the phenomenon in CBS Chairman Bill Paley in one sentence: "He [Paley] played by his own rules, which he kept changing."[9] In a similar vein, we are told by Conrad Black's biographer, Richard Siklos, that the erstwhile media mogul had this to say when writing about his personal hero, the legendary press baron William Randolph Hearst: "All his life, Hearst had a conviction, often outrageous but sometimes magnificent, that the rules that applied to others did not apply to him."[10]

The reality is, of course, that especially in the case of a business owner, those in power can make many of the rules that affect their enterprise. And often, these "rules" or ways of doing things can be the very reason for the success of the enterprise. At the same time, powerful people will often want to decide issues based not on existing across-the-board policies but on the merits of the case. Thus, in an employee-related matter, the first question will often be how well an individual performs; that will have a bearing on whether a (favorable) exception from the rules is warranted. Furthermore, freedom from rules allows for making decisions unencumbered by what might have been done or said before. Thus, as *Fortune*'s Peter Elkind reports, Steve Jobs would say, "We are doing what is right today."[11]

This last point is a critical insight I have seen applied in many instances. When you work with powerful people, you simply cannot assume that previously decided issues are set in stone. Every day is a new day. For example, you cannot have a person in power look at a project plan, product design, or written document and ask for input only on the new elements. If you decide to put something in front of such a person, be prepared for wholesale review and change. Powerful people will see anything less than perfection as compromise. They will do what is right today.

Founders of big businesses tend to have an unassailable sense of ownership, even if the organization becomes a publicly traded company or is owned in part or whole by others. Ted Rogers clearly felt that, as the founder, he had a special role in his company. In his memoirs, he wrote that his first conviction was that he wanted to see the Rogers family keep control of the company that he had worked so hard to build. His second conviction was that there should be someone in charge of the controlling-shareholder position. "There has to be an individual controlling shareholder to whom the board of directors and the chief executive officer can turn when needed," he said.[12] Clearly, Ted Rogers did not see any need to apologize for the company's dual-class share structure, which afforded him absolute voting power. He saw it as foundation for the success of the enterprise.

When interacting with powerful people on a more mundane level, you have to be ready for a wide range of feedback that goes well beyond the business at hand. One of my favorite examples involves Margaret Thatcher. In her analysis *Women in Power*, Blema Steinberg tells the story of how, while seated at the cabinet table, Thatcher ordered the chancellor of the exchequer, Nigel Lawson, to get his hair cut.[13] This is hardly the way one would expect a chancellor to be treated, but nonetheless, Thatcher had no qualms about providing grooming advice. In similar fashion, reports *Fortune*'s Betsy Morris, PepsiCo's CEO Indra Nooyi told one of her senior employees that he "dressed like a bum." That wardrobe might have been acceptable while he was working in the IT department, but he did get himself a new wardrobe when he moved to corporate strategy. We are told that Nooyi actually told him where to shop![14]

In the previously mentioned study, psychologists from UC Berkeley and Stanford confirmed that, in the case of the more average boss, nonobservation of social conventions is by far more common than one might think. Their key observation, as reported by the American Psychological Association, comes from an experiment in which groups of three individuals were presented with five cookies after a tedious meeting. Consistent with the prediction, the higher-power individuals were more likely to take a second cookie. When watching videotapes, researchers also observed that these higher-power subjects chewed with their mouths open and got crumbs on their faces and on the table. Maybe not surprisingly, male participants in particular ate in less inhibited ways. (I should hasten to add that something like this would never, ever occur with Lady Thatcher.) The study's conclusion was that "elevated power increases the likelihood of socially inappropriate behavior."[15] In other words, don't be shocked when it happens to you.

> *Realize that powerful people like to play by their own rules and change them if necessary. Remain flexible, and don't get flustered easily. But remember that the rules do apply to you!*

Power Does Have Pitfalls

Despite the apparent freedom described so far, leaders can't get away with doing anything they want, especially in a publicly traded company. Some rules do apply—and with good reason. As we have seen, a founder or controlling shareholder who owns a majority of the company or has majority voting rights will sometimes take on the role of an absolute owner, especially if the individual has put his or her entire creativity and life at the service of the enterprise. This person is likely to be convinced that the enterprise's resources are and should be at his or her disposal at all times, because this leader is at the disposal of the enterprise at every waking moment.

I'm not referring to intentional fraudsters and malicious swindlers such as Kenneth Lay or Bernie Madoff. These people do not deserve any respect, and we should get away from them as far and as quickly as we can.

Rather, the issue is with people who genuinely believe they are serving the enterprise and do not see any (clear) dividing line between their own person and the company. Thus, Richard Siklos writes that Conrad Black, as a proprietor, felt he was in a different league than a professional chief executive who had been hired to run a company.[16] In fact, I have heard professional chief executives acknowledge without jealousy that they had special respect and admiration for people who had founded and built successful businesses. But that different view of the dividing line can lead to collision with those who insist on the rights of public shareholders.

This is the attitude that opened Conrad Black up to attack. As an example, the special committee charged with investigating Hollinger took issue with Black spending $9 million of Hollinger's funds on papers and other memorabilia associated with Franklin D. Roosevelt, the subject of a massive and well-received biography penned by Black.[17] One can see how the media baron would see such an acquisition as being in the interest of the company, rather than a personal expense. But his critics and adversaries added the point to their long list of violations of the rules of corporate governance, which they put in front of the Chicago jury on their case.[18]

Thus, when you are working with powerful people, part of your responsibility may be to remind them of the rules or of how others might interpret them and to ultimately protect these people from themselves (if they let you, of course). In that context, you must remember that, while such people are in all their glory, the power they wield does feel absolute to them and to many of those around them. It is a deep-rooted perception of the way things are and should be. At a minimum, you must guard against getting caught up in that same perception and the whirlpool of potential trouble.

Others Are "Helpers"

Despite all their brilliance, energy, and confidence, powerful leaders can't reach the heights of accomplishment alone. They need help.

The most obvious class of helpers for towering businesspeople are senior executives and midlevel managers, though all levels of staff can be brought into this circle. These helpers are often described as "lieutenants"—people who are paid to get things done and to turn the grand vision into reality. The names bestowed upon these lieutenants are sometimes inspirational monikers representing teamwork. Sony's Howard Stringer, for example, calls his key executives "the four musketeers."

Whether the helper is a lieutenant or a musketeer, it's clear who is in charge and that the inner circle—no matter how high up the ladder—is there to serve the powerful leader, execute that person's strategies, and help win his or her battles. For an interesting example, consider the decision made by German Chancellor Angela Merkel, then considered the world's most powerful women, to receive the Dalai Lama. Foreign-policy advisers had opposed the meeting because it would strain Germany's relations with China. But Merkel's closest adviser, Beate Baumann, realized that the Dalai Lama was popular with the people and the electorate would applaud the decision. Thus, the influential weekly *Der Spiegel* concluded that Baumann "did not see Germany but saw the Chancellor"[19] and defined global policy issues according to her interest. Thus, if you work for a powerful person, your leader is likely to be working out how you can be a personal helper as much as you are thinking about your job description.

> *Understand that powerful people think of others as their helpers first and foremost. Let them know that this is what you are there to do. However, don't let the helper paradigm stifle your creativity and ambition to lead.*

Whether you work for a larger-than-life figure or your average boss, making the boss look good will always be part of your job and, if handled correctly, it can pay major dividends.

One of my favorite, albeit extreme, examples in that regard is the story of René Vietto. Vietto was the youngest rider on the French team in the 1931 Tour de France. He was ahead of the pack on the descent after a grueling climb up the French Pyrenees. But when word came that his team leader had crashed, Vietto heeded the call of duty and rode back up the mountain to deliver his bike to the boss, the great cyclist Antonin Magne, who went on to win the tour.

CAN A HELPER BECOME A FUTURE LEADER?

Given this emphasis on assigning helpers, some have concluded that powerful leaders seldom build great management teams. The helpers become helpless once the genius is removed. Jim Collins provides the example of Eckerd Corporation, which was founded by Jack Eckerd.[20] According to Collins, Eckerd was a genius blessed with monumental personal energy and a genetic gift for market insight and shrewd deal making. With that gift, he acquired his way from two little stores in Wilmington, Delaware, to a drugstore empire of over a thousand stores spread across the southeastern United States. By the late 1970s, Eckerd's revenues equaled those of Walgreens, and it looked like Eckerd might triumph as the great company in the industry. But then Jack Eckerd left to pursue his passion for politics, running for senator and joining the Ford administration in Washington, D.C. Without his guiding genius, Eckerd's company began a long decline until it eventually was acquired by J. C. Penney.

Such an outcome is not preordained, however. While Eckerd may have wilted without its founder, plenty of helpers have become leaders. The point is rather that, in the presence of a powerful person, a future leader or even visionary may need to act the part of helper to get the desired results. That does not mean helping is the only thing that people in the helping role are capable of doing. Yes, René Vietto never won a Tour de France, but he is the one who is remembered today as King René.

Although we don't yet know for certain, it's possible that Tim Cook, chief operating officer of Apple and Jobs's helper, may someday become Apple's outright leader. Cook took over as acting chief executive the day after Steve Jobs announced his medical leave of absence from Apple. And those who know Tim feel he was up to the job. Here is what *Time* magazine had to say: "Jobs is . . . a leader synonymous with his company's brand—and its success. But . . . the man stepping into Jobs' New Balance sneakers, chief operating officer Tim Cook is viewed as a brainy and capable leader who has long helped steer Apple's ship behind the scenes."[21]

Part of Tim Cook's own genius may well be that he has been able to be a leader while staying comfortable in the role of helper. This means he has indeed provided an enormous amount of help, kept out of the limelight, and gotten along with his boss extremely well. He has also shown that he can switch between the helper and the leader roles and is comfortable in both, depending on what his organization's needs are. He had already stepped into the chief executive officer's post during an earlier leave of absence by Jobs.

There are also others like Tim Cook. Nadir Mohamed took over as chief executive of Rogers Communications after the death of its founder, Ted Rogers. Though it had been led by a highly controlling founder, the company did not have to look on the outside for a successor. The succession happened only when there was no other way: Mohamed took the top job after Ted Rogers had passed away. But so far it appears that the business is managing quite well under the next generation of leadership.

We can learn a lot from individuals who worked for powerful people and were leaders in their own right. Here are three people to whom we will return in the coming pages:

» Frank Stanton, the right-hand man of CBS Chairman Bill Paley, started out in the research department. In 1945, by then a vice president and general manager, Stanton had a memorable meeting with the chairman. "By the way, Frank, I want to you to run the company," Paley said during a walk after dinner. Paley went on to explain that he wanted to be free from the day-to-day problems of running CBS. Stanton reorganized CBS and proved himself as a highly capable administrator and innovator. He excelled as an ardent defender of free speech when called before the House Commerce Committee over CBS's reporting of the war in Vietnam. And he did all of this while "managing the Chairman" and fighting such battles as one over the color of CBS's Manhattan headquarters, which Paley wanted to be pink.[22] After leaving CBS, Stanton went on to become chairman and chief operating officer of the American Red Cross.

» Colin Powell served as secretary of state in the George W. Bush administration and was chairman of the Joint Chiefs of Staff during the Gulf War.[23] While Powell has certainly been a powerful person in his own right, a review of his curriculum vitae reveals that much of his success and ascent can be traced to his effective and highly principled engagement of other powerful people. As a soldier, he knew to keep his superiors happy (and off his back) and then go and get done what really mattered. Colin Powell combined the sensitivity and charm of a charismatic politician with the bearing and crisp efficiency of a soldier. It was therefore no accident that one of Powell's key tasks during the Gulf War was to interface with the temperamental personality of General Norman Schwarzkopf.

» Georgi Konstantinovich Zhukov remains the most respected and decorated hero in the history of Russia and the Soviet Union. During the Great Patriotic War, as World War II is known in Russia, Marshal Zhukov distinguished himself as the responsible commander in the defense of Moscow. However, even more critical was his ability to achieve victory while answering to his supreme commander, one of the world's most feared and ruthless tyrants, Joseph Stalin. In Zhukov's biography,[24] Otto Preston Chaney describes how Zhukov spent much of his time in the Kremlin with Stalin, arguing, debating, and developing Stalin's strategic war plans as his supreme deputy commander in chief.[25] To survive and succeed, Zhukov needed to be much more than a competent military leader, though competence was certainly required. Selfless ambition, independence, and political skill emerge as the personal attributes behind Zhukov's remarkable feats of victory, survival, and rehabilitation. Eventually, he earned a post as minister of defense.

ARE BOARD MEMBERS HELPERS, TOO?

Experts in corporate governance will take immediate offense at the notion that members of a board of directors might be classified as "helpers." After all, in the prevailing governance view, the board's central purpose is *control* and acting as a watchdog on behalf of shareholders. A more enlightened view adds to the role of the board the responsibility to provide the counsel and coaching every chief executive needs. But even with that, legal experts insist that "the board's most important job is to make sure that the corporation has the right chief executive officer."[26]

However, if you are on the board of a larger-than-life chief executive, you may find that your CEO sees the world differently. Few controlling stakeholders believe it is the board's job to hire and fire him or her. Most, if not all, of them will see it the other way around.

Caroline Van Hasselt reports a story that reflects such an attitude on the part of Ted Rogers. He became involved in a spat with his longtime chairman, Garfield Emerson, who had replaced Rogers's stepfather as board chair after his death. At 6:00 P.M. on March 9, 2006, in his office, Rogers, then seventy-three years old, demanded that the much-respected chairman Emerson resign. None of that had been discussed with the board. It was done without any sort of warning or heads-up. Rogers, the CEO, simply handed Emerson a letter requesting his resignation from the Rogers Communications board for "personal reasons." Emerson, then sixty-five, had been the independent chairman of Rogers for thirteen years and company director for seventeen years; he had helped guide the founder and the company through some of its most challenging corporate deals and financial periods. Van Hasselt goes on to say that in a publicly traded company, the CEO can't just oust the chair of the board or a director. Only the shareholders can elect and remove directors. But "the only shareholder at Rogers who mattered was Rogers." He controlled the votes—the vast majority of them anyway. The name on the building was his. The owner/operator called the shots. He had earned the right to do as he saw fit.[27]

Aspiring directors must remember that while widely held corporations are the majority in the United States and the United Kingdom, both countries have a considerable number of corporations with a controlling shareholder. And firms that are controlled by very few shareholders remain quite common, if not predominant, in other industrialized countries, such as Germany, Japan, and Canada.[28] Scholars have now picked up on the fact that public companies that are either controlled or at least influenced by individual founders or members of the founder's family are a significant phenomenon. And they point out that these circumstances make director service much more challenging and that the regular governance paradigm does not apply.[29] In other words, influence rather than raw power becomes the name of the game.

Board Members Can Also Be "Trophies"

In addition to being helpers and kindred spirits, board members can be trophies or people who make life interesting. Conrad Black's board of high-profile celebrities included former secretary of state Henry Kissinger, former Defense Policy Board chairman Richard Pearle, four-term Illinois governor James Thompson, and retired U.S. ambassadors Richard Burt and Raymond Seitz. After acquiring the *Daily Telegraph*, Black added former NATO secretary general Lord Carrington, Sir Evelyn de Rothschild, British Airways chairman Lord

King of Wartnaby, financier Sir James Goldsmith, and the chairman of Jardine Matheson Holdings, Henry Keswick. His international advisory board included Fiat chairman Giovanni Agnelli, former president of Israel Chaim Herzog, and Margaret Thatcher. Warren Buffett declined an offer to join the advisory board.[30] According to Black's biographer, Black put together his own high-level invitation-only think tank. The fact that Black struggled with the role of his directors as "governors" became more than clear when the board formed a special committee to investigate the allegations of impropriety. Black later described Richard Breeden, the former Securities and Exchange Commission chairman who headed up the committee, as "a governance terrorist."[31]

> *Even if you hold an elevated position, like that of a board member, larger-than-life powerful people may still perceive you as a helper. Keep your emotions in check, and resist the temptation to lay down the law. Instead, make a calm assessment whether smart influence will be the better way to get your point across and arrive at the solution that is best for everyone.*

Given their fame and outside accomplishments, board members are usually afforded greater courtesy than executive helpers. In a way, they have some attributes of customers—a group of people that often brings out an amazing display of emotional and social intelligence, sensitivity, and humility in powerful people. However, they usually do not have any intimate knowledge of the business—a fact that makes them inferior to the powerful person, at least in the context of his or her company, and provides the powerful person with a good reason to overrule them.

Helpers as Leaders

When a founder takes a company public after a long history of being private, it's highly likely that he or she will not be able to let go of the helper paradigm. The founder will continue to expect to lead and to expect the helpers to help the founder accomplish his or her goals. But given the founder's high level of identification with and attachment to the company, personal and company goals can be in perfect alignment. If you want to have influence, this insight is a good place to start.

I therefore disagree with leadership scholar Jean Lipman-Blumen, who, in her book *The Allure of Toxic Leaders,* concluded that in the face of domineering leaders, "boards of directors commonly turn from shepherds into sheep" and "slip from their role as overseers of organizational leaders into postures of acquiescent and adulating followers."[32] Dismissing the boards of powerful people as weak and compliant in a wholesale fashion misses the point. The power of a controlling shareholder to make changes on the board is real. And as governance scholars are now discovering, you simply cannot approach the directorship in a controlled company (legal or de facto) the same way you approach it in a widely held company.

The point is not to pass judgment on "weak" directors and simply call for stronger ones. Rather, it is to illustrate the mind-set of a powerful business owner or chief executive officer as a starting point for effectively engaging with him or her.

Finally, many high-profile governance controversies show that powerful people cannot, in the end, make *all* their own rules. But they certainly can and will make some rules. Effective directors will keep that fact in mind. Armchair commentators should do the same.

Professional Service Providers: Helpers from the Outside

Professional service providers and other advisers are "outside helpers," who, much like senior executives and board members, are there to help implement the vision, plans, and aspirations of the powerful leader. Some of them, however, may be more of a necessary evil. This is especially true of public-company auditors. Professor Jean Lipman-Blumen's judgment is damning yet again. She points out that the roles of oversight and certifying bodies, including accountants, demand that they exercise their critical faculties as they review the CEO's plans and action. Yet, in her judgment, all too often, accountants, responsible for certifying the validity of corporate leaders' financial statements, "succumb to pressures that transform them into followers, rather than upholders of the public trust."[33]

Her prime exhibit, of course, is Enron's external auditors from Arthur Andersen. There can be no question that, following the demise of Arthur Andersen, the independence standard for auditors has become a generally accepted and followed practice. However, the shift in governance norms regarding external advisers is less intuitive when it comes to other advisers. For example, powerful chief executives will expect nothing less from their legal counsel than to be fully in their corner. As Harvard professor Detlev Vagts puts it, they will think their relationship with corporate general counsel is "as similar to the feeling one would have for a family doctor or solicitor."[34]

The fact is, however, that in the context of a public company, legal counsel, like other advisers, are more and more expected to be acting for the corporation, rather than for management. This development in governance rules has created a paradigm conflict not dissimilar to how a powerful owner perceives board members. Auditors, lawyers, compensation consultants, and sometimes financial advisers technically work for the board and have a legal obligation to act with independence from management and in the best interest of the corporation (as defined by the board). Of course, that view does not mesh well with a legal or de facto owner who is steeped in a philosophy of *l'entreprise c'est moi.*

From the perspective of powerful people, the first and foremost expectation will still be for any professional adviser (except possibly auditors) to be acting as *their* helpers. You will therefore do well to understand first whether your client is really looking for advice or simply help in implementing his or her plans. A lecture that attempts to set the leader straight about your role and allegiances will not be the best departure point for a strong relationship. All of this has to be balanced by a healthy dose of independence. The right calibration of these competing concepts will help you build your influence over time and serve your client well as a result.

> *When you serve as a professional service provider and adviser, your role may simply be to get things done, rather than provide high-level advice. Therefore, start with a humble assessment of what is expected from you.*

Super Helpers

One class of advisers may truly be more than helpers: advisers with the status of equals. A prime example would be Bill Gates turning for advice to Warren Buffett and accepting him as a guide and confidante.[35] Indeed, board members or management consultants who are larger than life in their own right, as Peter Drucker was, may be able to play a unique role: they don't just give excellent advice, they also carry tremendous credibility or are extremely skilled at giving impactful advice. But even they cannot completely rely on superior status, especially if they are professional consultants and not owners. As Rupert Murdoch would say, "At the end of the day their power is rented—they don't own it."[36]

What to do when . . .

. . . you are called to make the big presentation

You have been asked to make a presentation in the presence of a powerful person. This could be your first update at a board meeting, a proposal at management meeting, a business overview during a visit to the local subsidiary, or a sales pitch for an internal project or to an external client.

As a first rule, preparation is the key. Gather as much intelligence as possible to understand what is expected. In particular, you must find out whether there is information this person typically wants to know, such as purpose/mission, key strategies, people, numbers, or risks. Consider sending the presentation ahead of time; this will help you focus on the key issues ("You have seen the presentation; is there anything you want me to focus on?").

Manage your time; even if there are a lot of questions, you are still responsible for the time budget. Therefore, you must remain flexible. Don't think you have to read your entire presentation or cover everything you have prepared. You may have to make up time if you get sidetracked or bring the discussion back to the key point. A summary of key points (three is always a good number) allows you to skip to what really matters. Detail in an appendix shows preparation; you can go there if necessary.

If things go well, make sure you ask for what you came for, such as budget approval, go-ahead, or a purchase order. Quit while you are ahead. Don't oversell! If things fall apart because your preparation is shaky, consider conceding that "this needs more work," and try to get out. Don't let powerful audience members work themselves into a rage if you can avoid it. However, if you are on solid ground, show some spirit, and get into the debate. No matter what, retain your composure. Being able to take some flak shows resilience, which a powerful listener might well appreciate.

Master the Art of First Impressions

> **Thankfully he [Big John] took an instant liking to me or I would have been out on the street.**
>
> —TED ROGERS, FOUNDER AND CEO, ROGERS COMMUNICATIONS

During my time as human resources director, I was looking for a research and development manager. A search consultant had found a candidate with all the right qualifications. However, he was working for a competitor, so he set up a clandestine meeting at an airport hotel. I made the flight from Toronto to Boston in great anticipation. I walked into the hotel lobby, where the candidate was already waiting for me. The meeting was supposed to be held in a suite on an upper floor, and we made our way to the elevator. Halfway there, I noticed that the candidate was trailing me. He was walking a bit slower, and I had to wait for him. I realized right then and there that he was the wrong person for the job and that I would be wasting the next hour or so in a polite interview, waiting for my return flight. A slow-walking person would simply not fit into my company's corporate culture, which was built on intensity and an overwhelming sense of urgency. Therefore, I would not dare present him as a candidate. It's possible the company missed a very talented research manager, but I simply could not get over my first intuitive reaction to the person I had just met.

First Impressions Matter a Great Deal

Of course, job interviews are about a lot more than how someone walks in the door. The right skills matter a great deal. But the concept of "the right fit" has become a much more pronounced requirement as companies are trying to build a cohesive culture, however elusive that concept may be. And that's where first impressions have become an even more critical concept. A young Ted Rogers, for example, used his insight into powerful people when he had his first appointment with a powerful person in his life, the controversial John "Big John" Bassett, who is considered one of the architects of Canadian television. In his memoirs, Rogers remembered that Big John was an entrepreneur, and that entrepreneurs decide quickly whether or not they like people. Of his encounter with Big John, Rogers recalls, "Thankfully he took an instant liking to me or I would have been out on the street."[1]

When thinking about making a good first impression with a powerful person, you have to think beyond the traditional interview setting in an office, even though that may be part of it. First, you must remember that powerful people have a constant preoccupation with how they can further their business; when a powerful person runs into people, he or she tends to think of them in terms of how they can be potential helpers to achieving the powerful person's goals. So will those who work with persons in power, because a person who is the right fit is a valuable commodity. For example, a manager who was in charge of the corporate driving service once called me very excitedly to tell me he had run into a very friendly and courteous cab driver and felt this person would be a good addition to the team.

In addition, even if you are part of a formal hiring process, you should be ready for the fact that many powerful people want to get a feel for prospective employees in a variety of settings. Therefore, senior executives, prospective board members, and professional service providers will often have a "casual" meeting at the powerful person's residence or another off-site location, which will in many cases involve spouses. While the setting may be casual, you must be sure to approach such occasions with great care, as they have many pitfalls. Conversely, however, given the fact that powerful people are intuitive and like to make on-the-spot decisions (because they can), the law of first impressions also applies with greater opportunity. The first part of making a good impression (or at least avoiding a bad one) would be to show up on time. If you are not sure about distance or traffic patterns, it is always a good idea to locate a nearby coffee shop or other spot where you can arrive with much time to spare, wait as long as necessary, and then miraculously arrive at the appointed time—because you don't want to be early either!

> *Powerful people make decisions quickly. Therefore, make a conscious effort to make a good first impression.*

It's About Them

Making a good first impression is not a matter of chance, but something for which we can prepare. As an underlying base, you have to know what you are doing (in your chosen field), and you have to display impeccable social graces. These requirements will be discussed in more detail with regard to Rule 4. Never try to fake competence, and be clear on what you know and what you don't know.

Beyond that, a key secret for making a good first impression is to remember that it is all about them. This insight is not always intuitive, as you may rightfully think the interview is about you—and some will be. But don't assume that, ever.

A masterful description of how to handle a job interview is delivered by Ferdinand Piëch's account of his first meeting with Ignacio Lopez, who was then considered the master of automotive purchasing:

> From the get-go Lopez was completely on my wavelength. He was incredibly intense in his expression, very quick to pick up the ball and play it back. He wasn't a product developer but he had a technical understanding from product design to production.[2]

Note that Piëch likes his counterpart's intensity; no one is walking slowly here! Piëch goes on to observe how Lopez engages members of Volkswagen's supervisory board, all of whom had quite varied backgrounds. They included chairman Klaus Liessen, a distinguished business executive; trade union leaders Franz Steinkühler and Klaus Volkert (members of the board by virtue of German law on *Mitbestimmung* or co-governance); and political heavyweight Gerhard Schröder, who later became chancellor of the Federal Republic of Germany. When joining Lopez in the meetings, Piëch observed that Lopez was able to relate to the industrialist, the union bosses, and the politician with equal ease. He looked for common experiences and explored personal backgrounds and roots. Thus, he discovered that the chancellor once was a fine-china dealer and that one of the union leaders had apprenticed as a blacksmith; with the other, he found a common approach to workers' issues. All of this made a big impression: "Every conversation lasted for two hours and there was only positive feedback. I personally was impressed with his manner to relate to the diverse areas with interest that was wide awake and not artificial in any way."[3]

Two observations are important here. First, Lopez did not impress by spewing out purchasing theory and best practice. Instead, he focused on his counterparts and *related to them*. In the circumstances, not only did Lopez come across well himself, he also made his host, Ferdinand Piëch, look good in that he allowed him to introduce an impressive and engaging person to his board. Second, Piëch notes that Lopez moved with intensity but was "not artificial in any way." Maybe Lopez was indeed genuine, maybe he was accomplished, but most likely he was both. Taking an interest in people is something we can practice until it becomes second nature.

Incidentally, Lopez and Piëch did not talk about compensation. "Money was not an issue anyway," noted Piëch.[4] The old adage probably applies that if you ask for the price, you probably cannot afford it. And even if you are not in quite as lofty a pay bracket, it will pay to have the hiring manager be excited about the contribution you can make before discussing dollars and cents.

Taking a genuine interest in the powerful person from the first moment, relating to that person's ambitions, interests, and way of thinking, is an art. You may be a natural at it, but you will likely do better with preparation. Reading the person's biography, learning about his or her enterprise, and thinking of some intelligent questions would be the minimum. But even if you are not interviewing with a larger-than-life person, you'll want to prepare. I once interviewed a finance manager from Europe who had intelligent questions about the company's publicly available financial and strategy documents. I was impressed right away. During the interview, I checked the chief financial officer's schedule, because I felt he had to meet this guy right away. That's the reaction you want to evoke!

Relating well from the outset sends an all-important signal: "I know that it is all about you (and/or your organization), and I am making the best use of the privilege of meeting you." When Piëch finally asks Lopez about his life's priorities, Lopez mentions three: "Homeland, family, and success."[5] Crisp, simple, and yet profound. Maybe the powerful person will be inspired to ask follow-up questions. But maybe he or she will not be. That must be OK, too.

> It's never about you, even in the job interview. Ask questions that show your genuine interest. Keep answers simple (yet profound), and observe whether the powerful person wants more information.

In my experience, accomplished consultants and senior sales executives master the art of the (reverse) interview the best. They know they are selling themselves *and* their service. They are masters at concentrating on their counterparts/customers, because it is part of the art of the sale. Prospective board members are often at a disadvantage. They perceive themselves as (and often are) powerful people in their own right. Therefore, they are more eager to share their own experiences and expect intelligent questions about themselves. This propensity can frequently result in the powerful person tagging such people with the label of "talking too much" or being arrogant. The simple fact, of course, is that we all more easily detect our own flaws in other people.

Likability Helps

Younger people have a tremendous opportunity to make a great first impression. The reason is that powerful people, especially those who are older, can see themselves in ambitious, well-mannered younger workers or managers. And there is enough distance that the thought of competition does not even enter the picture. In that circumstance, sharing things in common is a great plus.

For example, Frank Stronach took to Fred Jaekel, who was born to German émigrés in Argentina and had trained as a tool and die maker. According to Wayne Lilley, Jaekel's determined push for the introduction of new technology made Stronach see "something of himself as a young man," which allowed Jaekel to get away with things others did not. While Jaekel often went too far, leading to several firings, he was hired back just the same.[6]

As a great example of favorable first impressions, Ted Rogers described his first meeting with his eventual successor, Nadir Mohamed, which occurred on a Sunday morning at Ted Rogers's home. Rogers liked Mohamed right away. He learned that Mohamed had been born in Tanzania and that his family had come to Canada from India. (There obviously was no human resource manager present, who would have voiced concerns over the exploration of personal and family roots in a job interview.) Rogers also appreciated the entrepreneurial role models in his life, included grandparents who had run a lumber business. A further common experience was boarding school. So Rogers summed the meeting up as follows: "Entrepreneurs, as I have said, tend to be emotional and relationship-oriented people, we make decisions quickly and take to people (or not) quickly, too. *I liked Nadir right from the start and wanted him to take over from Charlie* [Charlie Hoffman, president of Rogers Wireless]."[7]

The connection between Ted Rogers and Nadir Mohamed was immediate. Like Rogers, Mohamed had an entrepreneurial family background and had been to boarding school. That similarity provided the foundation for "liking." It confirms Robert Cialdini's classic insight on the psychology of influence and persuasion, that we like people who are similar to us and prefer to say yes to the requests of someone we know and like.[8] But similarity does not mean sameness. With commonalities as a departure point, Mohamed's Indian/African background provided a welcome contrast to Ted Rogers's own Anglo-Canadian roots, which, incidentally, he traced back to the Norman Conquest of England by William the Conqueror in 1066. Because Ted Rogers valued diversity as part of what makes Canada special, presumably the same applied to his company.

I believe the Rogers/Mohamed connection has broad application. I would therefore venture to modify Cialdini's dictum such that, when it comes to powerful people, liking is based on similarity *and* a dash of personality.

To round out the Nadir Mohamed illustration, we should add that later Ted Rogers invited Mohamed's wife, Shabin, to attend the Rogers board meeting and noted, "Both Nadir and Shabin are wonderful people and that's important in a family company like Rogers."[9] Senior executives don't just have to fit into the company culture; they have to fit into "the family."

> *Being liked and likable always helps. Try to discover common background and interests to increase likability. However, don't be afraid to display a dash of true personality—without going over the top, of course.*

Again, the odds of likability are better with preparation. Don't just try to hit the right buzzwords of professional experience. Think about something that is interesting based on the research about your counterpart. It could be a hobby, unique trip, or other experience. Make sure you check the reaction, and drop it if you don't get any.

Manage Your Appearance

When you are preparing for an interview, it goes without saying that your appearance has to be carefully managed. Clean, neat, and appropriate dress and a clean and appropriate vehicle are the basics. Again, none of this can be artificial, and you must feel at ease with the image you are projecting. Adopting over time a style similar to what the powerful person is modeling is usually a smart move. We saw in an earlier anecdote how Lady Thatcher, in the middle of a cabinet meeting, ordered her chancellor to get a haircut. Considering that the Iron Lady was immaculately dressed and coiffed at all times, we can realize that her public reprimand, embarrassing as it might have been, was not completely unforeseeable and could in fact have been avoided.

There are some cautions. If the boss likes a high-end style, you should make sure that your adaptation is smart yet appropriate to your pay grade. Most likely, the same tailor will not be in your budget anyway. It is not about sameness but about appropriateness. Conversely, even if the boss is super casual for a weekend at the cottage, you should still adopt a professional minimum standard for your own dress. If you must, proper Bermuda shorts would be better than cut-off jeans.

The dress code and vehicle readiness must be maintained at all times. Because, back to our interview scenario, the boss may just decide to show you the production plant or the office after the Sunday-morning interview at the residence and decide (quite intentionally) to hop into your car for the ride! You absolutely do not want the embarrassment of empty coffee cups, candy wrappers, and other junk lying around. The first impression you worked so hard to create would evaporate immediately.

Be Ready for the Chance Encounter

When you are not working directly for a powerful person, meeting such a person for the first time can happen in a variety of circumstances. You may just run into influential people, may attend a meeting with them, or may get introduced at a company function or similar occasion. That interaction can have significant consequences—for better or for worse. Being prepared and making a great first impression are must-have survival skills.

The insight that powerful people are people of action should govern the most casual contact, because there really is no such thing as "casual." Many powerful people are known for taking a firsthand look that goes way beyond the traditional management by walking around. In fact, most of them are chronic insomniacs, and there is just no telling when and where they will show up.

Ferdinand Piëch has been known to appear unannounced on a factory workshop floor in the middle of the night, look over an engineer's shoulder, and make "suggestions" or corrections.[10] In Michael Wolff's biography of Rupert Murdoch, Piers Morgan, then editor of *News of the World*, explains how Murdoch would "scare the daylights out of you by drifting in like a ghost" and getting involved in the details of his newsroom.[11] Bill Marriott Jr. loves to visit his company's hotels and inspect kitchens.[12] To be fair, he also gives autographs to staff. And we are told that Mickey Drexler, the former CEO of Gap who took J. Crew public and is a self-admitted "control freak," loves nothing more than to walk into every one of his stores and quiz associates about what they are hearing and seeing on the sales floor.[13] People at CBS were wary of any direct contact with Bill Paley: "If you had any contact with Mr. Paley at all, you were in some jeopardy."[14]

As head of an army corps in Germany, General Colin Powell subscribed to a similar philosophy, pointing out that the smell of fresh paint during a planned visit reveals an insecure commander, whereas unannounced inspections will reveal true combat readiness.[15] You should therefore have an idea what expectations there may be for your office, desk, or work space. In some settings, a messy desk may indicate creativity; in others, it may be thought of as disorganized. But especially when you are dealing with a business owner, you should know how he or she perceives such issues and conduct yourself accordingly.

Your preparation for surprise interaction must include being ready for "casual" conversation in a nonwork setting. You may run into the big boss anywhere from the elevator to the parking lot to the food line-up at the company barbeque. The chief may even strike up a conversation in the bathroom! My own (and not only) experience of this kind was a discussion with a renowned expert on international maritime law in Geneva whose seminar I was attending. The first thing you can do to prepare for surprise visits is to find out whether there is a "usual question" from this person and to have a fresh answer ready. In more general terms, you must be ready to explain what you are doing at the moment; how it fits into the big picture of your department, the customer, and the company; and what you are doing to make things better. Having a brief speech on how to grow the business is a must for managers. It gives the opportunity to demonstrate enthusiasm and creativity. Of course, criticism of the immediate boss has to be avoided. As always, calibration is everything.

Sometimes the surprise interaction can (or should) be anticipated. For example, a person may be called upon to make a presentation or host a plant tour. In this instance, far-reaching conclusions are even more likely. For example, when Sergio Marchionne, the Italian-Canadian CEO of Fiat, who brought that company back from near ruin, took on the challenge of saving Chrysler, he acted on the day he took the reins. Business reporters Mike Ramsey and Sara Gay Forden describe Marchionne as an "intense workaholic" who sleeps three to four hours a night. In addition to running Fiat and Chrysler, he juggled the additional jobs of chairman of farm equipment maker Case New Holland, vice chairman of the Zurich-based bank UBS, and chairman of Geneva-based goods inspection company GSG. Bloomberg News reporters uncovered that soon after the takeover, Marchionne had installed a new set of twenty-three managers with an average age of just under forty-five. Some were promoted several pay grades, and all of them had been identified during Marchionne's due-diligence visits to Chrysler's headquarters in Auburn Hills, Michigan.[16] These managers had surely made the most of their opportunity to make a good first impression!

> *Even if you do not work directly with the powerful person, always be ready for surprise interaction. It presents great risk and opportunity. Coach the people who work with you accordingly, and practice if necessary.*

If you rely on your team to carry part of the burden, the message is clear. You have to get your people ready for the (surprise) interaction and practice if necessary. But you must remember Ferdinand Piëch: it cannot be artificial in any way. Like a good actor, you must fully identify with your role to the point that it becomes natural and looks easy.

Beware of Confined Spaces

As a special point on practical survival skills and first impressions, you cannot underestimate the challenge imposed by confined spaces. A first example is the ride on the company airplane. While evoking the notion of glamour and luxury perpetuated by reality TV shows such as Donald Trump's "The Apprentice," this experience is probably one of the most overrated. Yes, there may be the allure of comfortable leather seats, fine dining, and hassle-free check-in. But it leads to lengthy confinement with the powerful person in a very small space. And that provides plenty of opportunity for the powerful person to find out that you are not nearly as smart as he or she thought you were (or as you made yourself out to be). Sergio Marchionne likes to drink and play cards with executives on the Fiat plane,[17] and one would be well advised to play smart. Ted Rogers's plane had the nickname

Quiz Air because of the endless and intense questioning that would inevitably ensue when one was sitting close to the boss. Therefore, choosing the farthest seat away is usually a good strategy.

Alas, it may not always work. Caroline Van Hasselt reports how on one flight on Ted Rogers's corporate jet, two senior executive were late and raced up the ramp, almost pushing each other out of the way and bumping in the door. The reason for the mad rush was to occupy the seat farthest away from Rogers. As veterans, they knew that if they ended up sitting beside the founder, they would be spending the entire flight in intense conversation and be peppered with endless questions. According to former Rogers cable executive John H. Tory, "you don't get frequent flyer points" for flying on Quiz Air; "you get aspirin."[18]

> *Flights on corporate aircraft are not a perk, but hard work. Stay alert, and take your signals from the boss: if the boss is all business, you should be, too!*

If veteran high-ranking staff members are fighting over seat assignments on the corporate jet, it is certainly worthwhile for the rest of us to be aware of the potential social traps that lie ahead, especially during one's maiden voyage.

Instead of settling into your onboard club chairs, ready to relax, you must keep your antennae focused and observe how more experienced travelers handle the situation. One preparation would be to bring plenty of work along, so that you are seen to be using your "down time" productively. One veteran corporate traveler told me the story of a rookie on the corporate plane who brought along a novel as reading material, as if he expected to be able to catch up on his pleasure reading while on board with the top boss—not a recommended strategy! Instead, watch for opportunities: if you are working for the powerful person directly, this may be a good time to knock some agenda items off the list. As we will discuss later, you must seize every opportunity when the powerful person's mood is favorable (and as long as the flight isn't so long that he or she might have too much time to think about it and might end up changing his or her mind).

Some executives have resorted to suddenly discovering "urgent business" that prevented them from joining the ride on the corporate jet and "forced" them to take a commercial flight to the same destination. Or there could be merit in trying to have other people invited on board to dilute the impact. In any event, the worst thing is to seek out the joint plane ride as some sort of a special perk or demonstration to colleagues of just how close you are to the boss. Again, if it is your first flight, watch the veterans. There is always the chance that this flight on the corporate jet may be your last!

The perils and stress of prolonged time with a powerful person in a confined space are not limited to airplane rides. The command center of Desert Storm was a prime example. The place was a cramped bunker, the size of a tennis court, forty feet beneath the concrete fortress of the Ministry of Defense and Aviation in Riyadh, Saudi Arabia. And as Rick Atkinson informs us, even for seasoned and battle-hardened soldiers, the time they spent in Norman Schwarzkopf's basement was as stressful as many an encounter with the enemy.[19] Maybe Atkinson is exaggerating, but one thing remains true: the stresses of spending time with a powerful person in a confined space simply cannot be underestimated.

It may not always be an aircraft or a bunker, but an office or a boardroom can become pretty confining, too! This is especially valid if you are in such an environment for the first time, so be on high alert. If someone brings in coffee and doughnuts, don't be the first to the tray. If your water glass is empty, fill those of other people first. Use the opportunity to make a good impression with little things.

What to do when . . .

. . . you have been invited to a job interview with a powerful person

You have been through a round of job interviews, and you have been invited to the final interview with the powerful person. You may or may not be working for this person, but given the importance of the hiring decision, his or her approval is needed to bring you on board.

Be sure to take this interview seriously; even if everyone else liked you, the powerful person can easily reverse the decision. Once you are there, keep your answers to the point, because powerful people don't have time for long explanations. Therefore, watch carefully whether the person wants more information before you go on too long about anything.

Have your questions ready. Don't ask about salary, benefits, perks, or other things that concern you. These are questions for human resources or the search consultant. Instead, ask about the powerful person, the organization, and how you can make a contribution.

Make the discussion about your counterpart and his or her company. Refer to what you noticed during other interviews, when visiting the premises, during your research, and so on. Refer to things you heard about the person and/or the company; this is an opportunity to offer some free intelligence to the powerful person. Finally, have a great answer to the question "Why do you want to work here?"

RULE 4

Know What You Are Doing

A person can only perform from strength.

—PETER DRUCKER, WRITER AND CONSULTANT
KNOW AS THE FATHER OF MODERN MANAGEMENT

Powerful people like to make decisions. Often these decisions are made spontaneously from the gut, and this propensity can work greatly in your favor if you make a strong first impression. But the reverse is equally true. Powerful people will be just as quick to pass judgment on your suitability for the job once you have started to work for them and will not be afraid to make a change. They will not endure an employee, service provider, or even board member who is deemed not to be a fit.

While Donald Trump's trademark line, "You're fired!" is probably the most famous verbal expression of this concept, the revolving door is a theme in the biography of almost every larger-than-life figure. It has been reported that Bill Paley often fired people without warning and that Ted Rogers had "an awful lot of people going through his revolving door in twenty years."[1] Business reporter Thomas Watson tells us that while Frank Stronach does not perceive himself to be anything like television's famous axman Donald Trump, he would not hesitate to make changes nonetheless when a new hire "was not a fit." The simple reason was that "the longer you keep them, the more harm they do."[2] However, it would be wrong to assume that all powerful people enjoy hiring and firing. They need good helpers. They just have a propensity to act when they see a problem and an aversion to compromise.

Even if your boss is not as quick to hire and fire, you are not inherently in the clear. In many organizations, there is now a much greater emphasis on methodical performance management. A human resource review conducted by an independent corporate department may be designed to uncover weaknesses, or a downsizing may involve an intense review of skills and capabilities. When the review comes, you want to be found to be the absolute right person for the job. And that requires competence first and foremost.

Of course, only an idiot—or an imposter—would be intentionally incompetent. But unintentional incompetence can, as we will see, occur in many contexts: professional, social, or even leisure. Finally, we need to be keenly aware that the ability to work with the powerful person is a competence in and of itself. Hence, of course, this book.

Powerful People Have High Expectations for Professional Competence

Powerful people are incredibly demanding. That is why, contrary to what some might believe, they have extremely competent people working for them. Tim Cook, who works for Steve Jobs, is a highly competent chief operating officer who streamlined a maze of manufacturing and distribution operations.[3] Frank Stanton, who worked for Bill Paley as CBS's president, was a highly respected central figure in the development of television broadcasting in the United States. And when Ferdinand Piëch was looking for a cost-cutting warrior, he went to none other than Ignacio Lopez, who—despite much controversy—has left an imprint on the best practices in global purchasing that lasts to this day. All of these people were and are highly capable, and none of them fit the stereotype of a yes-man.

But high expectations are not the exclusive domain of larger-than-life people. A difficult competitive environment, financial constraints, or corporate performance targets can all lead to demanding bosses; in those situations, leaders simply do not have another choice.

BEWARE OF STRETCH ASSIGNMENTS
THAT ARE BEYOND REACH

With their impulsive style and their belief that anything can be achieved if only one puts one's mind to it, powerful people are quick to add new responsibilities or give someone they like a shot at a new job. The same can happen when a restructuring effort leads to absorption of departments or people who leave are not replaced.

That change, along with the powerful person's willingness to try new things, can lead to tremendous opportunities once such leaders have "discovered" (or even just noticed) someone with talent and ability. Powerful people also have a general disdain of bureaucracy, so they are prone to issue "battlefield promotions" and thrust unconventional assignments on people, even if that means circumventing or ignoring existing staffing processes.

When you are on the receiving end of such spontaneous "career development," you must control your natural eagerness to please. Acceptance of the next big challenge is different from blind enthusiasm: the former leads to personal growth, whereas the latter leads to failure. Therefore, you must withstand the tendency to immediately say yes (assuming for a moment that the powerful person even gives you that option!). There is, of course, the circumstance where you get the job you always wanted and have been waiting for. Quite often, however, a new assignment may take you outside your strengths and skills. That can be lethal if the job comes with high expectations, and it would be naive to point out your deficiencies (or "areas for development") and ask for leniency in the performance expectations. In other cases, you may not have the resources to do the job, and the powerful person and/or restructured organization may be expecting more than the usual miracle. A few cases in point follow.

One of the people who took on a bigger (or at least different) than expected challenge in Frank Stronach's Magna empire was Brian Tobin. Tobin was certainly no lightweight in Canadian politics, and the brash Newfoundlander was a natural in the role of federal fisheries minister in Jean Chrétien's Liberal cabinet. In 1995, Tobin made international headlines when he took on the European Union in the so-called Turbot War, charging Canada's European allies with overfishing in the North Atlantic. The war escalated when Tobin ordered the arrest of the Spanish trawler *Estai* outside the declared Canadian Exclusive Economic Zone and dramatically displayed its illegal trawl net in a news conference conducted from a barge on the East River outside the United Nations headquarters in New York. The episode earned Tobin the nom de guerre of Captain Canada, and Newfoundland's favorite son handily won the election to become the province's premier in 1996.

After retiring from politics in early 2002, Tobin joined the boards of several Canadian corporations, and in March 2004, he took on the post of chief executive officer of MI Developments (MID). At that time, MID owned much of Magna's vast real estate holdings and had a controlling equity stake in Magna Entertainment Corporation (MEC), the horse-racing company. Tobin's first task on the job became the implementation of Frank Stronach's (and his board's, of course) idea to privatize MEC and fold it into MID. We are told by Wayne Lilley that when Tobin went on the road to sell the plan to investors, he ran into a rather aggressive group of hedge fund managers in New York, led by one David Einhorn.[4] Einhorn and his partners at Greenlight Capital told Tobin that they would have none of the plan. The privatization deal did not go through, and soon after, in August 2004, Tobin resigned. This was only months after he had taken his first post as a business executive.

After the departure, Tobin and Stronach expressed their continued respect for each other.[5] But the business press concluded there had been other reasons for Tobin's early exit. Commentators point to a lack of autonomy and the fact that the project to be implemented was just too controversial.[6] Thus, the Toronto *Globe and Mail*'s Derek DeCloet comments that Brian Tobin must have "discovered that Tories in question period are a bunch of sweethearts compared to angry hedge fund managers."[7] Whether or not Stronach's plan was salable in the first place is not the point. Brian Tobin, capable and battle hardened as he was, had no experience in the horse-racing industry, in dealing with hedge fund managers, or in working for an all-powerful entrepreneur, even though one might observe that Tobin's former boss, Jean Chrétien, the tough-minded Canadian prime minister from Shawinigan, Quebec, was not an easy taskmaster either. In that regard, Wayne Lilley is probably right that Tobin had no appreciation for the kind of strings that were attached to his position as CEO.[8]

Be that as it may, we do know one thing for sure: despite Tobin's lack of experience with the task at hand, Frank Stronach did not hesitate to give Captain Canada a try, and the job just proved to be too much or at least not a fit. And when trouble came, a change was inevitable.

Tobin's experience was much different from that of Robert Gruber. Gruber was Frank Stronach's well-educated, highly skilled, and indefatigable finance director in Europe. He had been the man on the ground to oversee the impressive growth and development of Magna's Austro-European automotive ventures. As we have seen, he understood his boss well when it came to looking for a suitable head-quarters building. Stronach soon had big ideas for Magna Europe and developed plans for setting up a luxury airline, a casino-racetrack, and a theme park.[9] Wayne Lilley tells the story of how Stronach tried to persuade Gruber to take over the running and development of the nonautomotive business activities, seeing a clear benefit in Gruber's credentials and reputation.[10] Gruber, however, held firm to his belief that his expertise was in automotive and that he did not want to make a switch to other ventures. He eventually left Magna to join Porsche's Austrian operations. Thus, knowing that his professional competence was in the automotive industry, Gruber did not allow himself to be taken off track, even by a very convincing Frank Stronach.

Tobin's and Gruber's experiences have application and relevance well beyond the realm of larger-than-life bosses. In fact, it can serve as a confirmation of the Peter Principle, so called after its discoverer, Dr. Laurence J. Peter. The Peter Principle says people will continue to receive promotions based on competent performance until they eventually end up in positions where they are no longer competent. You can, of course, say this is the organization's problem and not yours. But such a view would be very shortsighted. First of all, a decisive powerful person may easily defy the

> *There is nothing wrong with accepting a big challenge, but do not engage in blind bravado.*

Peter Principle and move you out just as quickly as he or she moved you in. Second, as stated earlier, as companies are pushed to become more efficient, they will review performance more closely and assess whether they have the right people in their key positions. Or in case of a mandated downsizing, they will conduct a thorough review rather than cut staff based on seniority or other objective criteria. Or the company may bring in a new executive who wants to assess the situation from scratch. In an instance like this, you cannot simply point out that you did the company a favor by taking the job in the first place.

ASK FOR HELP AT THE OUTSET

Of course, I am not saying you should never accept a new challenge that is outside your comfort zone. On the contrary, there is a great opportunity here to stretch and discover new strengths and interests. The point is that getting tapped on the shoulder for a big challenge is not always the result of a thorough assessment of your abilities. It may simply be out of necessity, an experiment, or a willingness to see what you can do. Before getting too starry-eyed and ego-inflated ("I must be really good, since the powerful person asked me to do this"), you will benefit from a realistic evaluation of whether or not the job can be done and whether you can do it. If the promotion takes you outside your proven area of strength and expertise, you may need proper orientation, training, or support. Bear in mind that these things are much easier to ask for (or negotiate) at the outset of the assignment. That's when the need to get you going will give you a more open-minded response. Also, asking for training and/or resources is much more elegant and in the best interest of the company than asking for a big raise—and it can be equally valuable in the long run. If you instead are so eager to be a hero that you wait to ask for help until roadblocks have turned up, suspicion will arise that you are merely looking for excuses.

CONSIDER TAKING THE LESSER JOB

As we have seen, a competence reality check is appropriate and necessary when you are tapped for a new assignment within your current organization. It is also indispensable when you are taking a new job that involves switching industries or moving to a different sector, as Brian Tobin did. In such instances, you should give serious thought to initially considering a lesser, more manageable position in order to gain traction. Learning a new industry, a new company culture, and a new job while working with a new strong-willed person—all under intense expectations to perform from day one—can be too much even for the very best. Of course, that step back may go against your ego and ambition. It also may not look so great on your résumé. But I have seen people make that choice. They accepted the advice to agree to a less exposed position as in their best interest; they took a task in their natural area of strength, which allowed them to show success from the get-go and build a track record; and they built a strong base for professional growth step by step.

This lesson applies, I believe, in an even more pronounced way to professional service providers. There is always the desire and temptation to sell additional services. Often this propensity may dovetail nicely with the powerful client's quest for a silver bullet for the latest problem or idea. However, these assignments can easily fail because of a lack of competence or unrealistic expectations. Or you may have to add other people from your firm who do not mesh as well with the client. Therefore, before eagerly pushing ahead with increasing the scope of your services, remember that more is at stake than just losing the opportunity to acquire additional work. The fact is also that some powerful people can change their mind quickly about people they work with, and you can lose your hard-earned credibility quickly and suddenly. Therefore, a failed assignment, even or especially if it was ill conceived to begin with, can change the powerful person's opinion on the suitability of the professional service provider for any (or all) other assignments. Staying within the area of your core competence, with a clear definition of what you as professional service provider do and do not do, will therefore be the better way to go the vast majority of the time. As a side effect, turning away work will increase your credibility with regard to matters that are within your proven expertise.

> *Taking a smaller assignment within your natural area of strength requires humility but may be more effective in the long run than simply gunning for the biggest possible job at any given point in time.*

The Camera Is Always Rolling

In his book *Executive Warfare*, David D'Alessandro points out that the first thing people are told when they go into politics is, "Get used to the scrutiny." He goes on to say that this applies just as well to top management: "You are being judged every minute, and small things can tip the balance in your favor or against it."[11] I could not agree more when it comes to interacting with powerful people at any level. They will observe every interaction with equal intensity and make every behavior subject to immediate evaluation. They will draw conclusions from the smallest of incidents, not just because they are perfectionists, but also because, in the final analysis, you as their helper are a reflection on them. As one former chief executive officer turned corporate director once counseled me: "Dirk, the camera is always rolling."

This scrutiny applies to professional and social interactions with equal rigor. You therefore need professional and social competence. Accordingly, condescension to a waiter in a restaurant can be just as deadly as treating the host/hostess at a function poorly, showing up with an over- or underdone party gift, drinking too much at a company event (or anywhere else for that matter), failing to send a thank-you note, or not escorting the powerful person visiting from headquarters to the waiting limousine (insisting to drive them to the airport personally is much better still, of course). In the case of offering a ride, in addition to courtesy, your gesture sends an important message: "I value my time with you and want to maximize the opportunity to learn from you."

> Be genuine and show your personality, but be sure to know, understand, and respect the unseen and unwritten boundaries.

This lesson is particularly important for junior people who enter the executive world. Careers can end because of something as trivial as chewing gum in a meeting; this goes back to the management of interaction in confined spaces. At the same time, I have seen young managers make great impressions because they had the right mix of politeness and confidence. They knew when to talk and when to shut up, and the powerful person was confident he or she could send them places and they would be good ambassadors.

Therefore, social graces and respect in all interactions, whether with the powerful person or with others in their presence, are an absolute must. Even if the occasion calls for being tough (with others in the leader's presence) and showing that you have what it takes, you can rarely go wrong with respect and firmness. Showing off how loudly you can shout won't impress anyone.

OBSERVE: HOW DOES THE POWERFUL PERSON TREAT OTHER POWERFUL PEOPLE?

If you want to truly understand how the powerful person wants and expects to be treated, it is best to observe how this person treats others whom he or she considers powerful and worthy of respect. You will find that often powerful people are skilled at showing impeccable professional courtesy. They know all about personal attention, finding out likes and dislikes, asking for advice before going ahead with a course of action, and perfectly calibrating their interactions. What an opportunity to learn!

THERE IS NO SUCH THING AS "PRIVATE" INTERACTION

You must also remember that there is simply no such thing as a "private" interaction with an intense boss, because (let's say it again) the camera is always rolling. If, for example, you provide the boss with information on people or situations, you must factor in the strong likelihood that he or she will want to act on that information immediately. There is no such thing as "for your information only"; the powerful person is much more likely to pick up the phone right there, state that he or she has heard about a problem, and then demand answers. The consequences for your relationship with others can be devastating Even if the surroundings suggest confidentiality and relaxation, you must keep up your guard and, as always, think before you speak.

The concept of managing your conduct or social competence extends beyond your behavior in the direct presence of the powerful person. Other missteps can reflect poorly on you and, by extension, on the powerful person's image. David D'Alessandro, then chairman and chief executive officer of John Hancock Financial Services, tells a story that illustrates the point well. One day he went into a little store in small-town Vermont. He wanted to pay for his purchases, and near the box of maple sugar candies by the cash register, there was a board with photocopies of people's driver's licenses and their checks that had been returned for insufficient funds. While taking a closer look, he recognized one of his own employees, whose $40 check had bounced. Says D'Alessandro, "He wasn't a criminal obviously. But every time I saw that guy after that—or glanced at his name on a list of possible promotions—I thought, how responsible can he be?"[12] Personally, I do not think the amazing thing is that D'Alessandro doubted the man's character from that moment on; rather, the amazing thing is that he allowed him to keep his job!

Refrain from Gossip

A final social competence is to refrain from gossip or other undue negative talk about the powerful person. Yes, you will need the therapy of speaking to someone about the inexhaustible supply of unbelievable stories and get a chance to vent your frustrations. But you must be careful not to do so in the moment and with just anyone who is willing to lend an ear. There are two key reasons why caution is called for: First, there may be people who want to gain favor with the powerful person and go as far as making you believe you can entrust them with your deepest secrets. Second, there are others who may be genuinely listening to you at the moment but may carelessly talk later on or may feel they have to use the information when they get into a situation that puts them under pressure and they need to deflect it.

But even when you speak with your most trusted confidant, it will be wise to use respectful language at all times, so that your direct quotes meet a minimum standard of decency and propriety. In other words, you can never go wrong by being respectful of the powerful person, whether that person is present or not. A wise counselor will be very able to read between the lines.

One additional and very practical reason for such discretion is that it never makes sense to burn bridges with a powerful person. Frank Stronach, for example, has found that many people return to work for him after leaving, voluntarily or involuntarily. There are stories of people who were fired four times over their career[13] or fired and rehired in the same year.[14] In fact, former employees are a target group for the recruiting strategies of many human resource managers.

The reason is that former employees know the company, know what is expected, and may have acquired new skills at the expense of a new employer. So when the recruiting manager asks around about you, you do not want him or her to run into a disgruntled former boss or other person with whom you had an unnecessary falling out. Thus, in the previously mentioned case of Brian Tobin, both men mentioned their mutual respect; the fact that the assignment did not work out was not reason to let go of their basic appreciation for their respective track records and accomplishments.

Be very careful to whom you talk about the boss and how. Showing respect is always right. Remember that electronic communication can easily be forwarded to the wrong person, by accident or intentionally.

What goes without saying is that the rule against incriminating gossip applies even more to electronic communication. Given the abundance of storage media and back-up requirements, e-mail can never really be erased and can be easily forwarded, accidentally or intentionally, with catastrophic consequences. Likewise, social or professional networking sites can leave an indelible imprint. Therefore, we must be aware of the added dimension of social competence and etiquette in a digital age.

Even Leisure Requires Competence

Powerful people are competitive, a trait that easily spills over into their "leisure" time. For Bill Paley, golf was a "pursuit," and Frank Stronach displays his energetic daring whether he is skiing moguls or attacking the net on the tennis court.[15] It would therefore be unwise to join someone like a Frank Stronach on a ski trip without knowing how to ski—and ski well. Certainly, you had better know how to drive a car when you work for Ferdinand Piëch. As an extreme car enthusiast, Piëch has been known to take his executives on grueling test drives. Therefore, if a financial person is interested in managing money only, we are told, Piëch believes the person should be working for a bank, not a world-class car company.[16]

"Leisure" is really a misnomer when you are dealing with people to whom competitiveness is second nature. A few years back, I listened to Jack Welch speak at the World Economic Forum in New York. Welch told us, his audience, about a time when he was playing golf with some of his executives. During the game, he noticed one of them letting a golf ball slide onto the course through a hole in his pants pocket lining. There was no question for Jack: the guy had to go. Someone who cheats at a golf game, he reasoned, will surely cheat in business. Therefore, if you have to cheat to keep up, stay away!

It follows from this insight that company functions such as golf tournaments, Christmas parties, summer barbecues, and retreats of any kind are not just fun activities—at least not when the powerful person is present. We can learn this lesson in Technicolor from one of Oprah Winfrey's staff Christmas parties, as described by one of her former producers. A highlight of the party was an elaborate exchange of Christmas gifts. One of the new junior producers did not believe that this could possibly be an overly serious affair. This naïveté caused a veteran executive producer to make the point quite vividly. She explained to the newcomer that the year before, she had given Winfrey an antique tea set, and that she had hand-stamped the tissue wrapping paper with little cups and saucers. The junior producer commented that Winfrey could not possibly have noticed. In response, the veteran picked up the phone: "Oprah, I'm here in the office with all of the producers. . . . We're just curious, but do you remember the tea service I gave you last year?" The response came back: "The one with the hand stamped tissue paper?"[17]

> Everything can turn into a competition and a potential performance evaluation. If you are not good at it, learn if you must, or don't do it. However, don't get carried away. While the powerful person may be competitive, you should keep your drive to win in check.

This story makes the point clearly. First of all, with powerful people, no detail is too small to be noticed, especially if the circumstance is near and dear to the person's hearts, be it Christmas gifts or cars. Second, what may seem like a casual affair to the uninitiated can in fact be very serious business to the powerful person, because it is safe to assume that otherwise, he or she wouldn't be doing it. Finally, anything we do can quickly become a performance evaluation or, as in the case of Jack Welch's golf game, reveal character flaws. Of course you can have fun at work, and not every boss is as discerning as Jack Welch or Oprah Winfrey. But company "team-building activities" do serve a company purpose, and they are not vacation times.

LEISURE CAN WORK IN YOUR FAVOR

By contrast, the mastery of a powerful person's leisure competency can have unexpected benefits. In fact, we are told that his skill at cards paved the way for Jimmy Cayne at Bear Stearns. As *Fortune*'s William Cohan tells the story,[18] young Jimmy Cayne's lackluster job interview at the brokerage took a sudden turn for the better when, by chance, the conversation turned to bridge. The game was the favorite pastime of Ace Greenberg, Cayne's eventual boss and predecessor. Cayne, who had won a national bridge championship and was on his way to going professional, made an immediate connection with Greenberg. And Cayne's first major brokerage account was with Laurence Tisch, the self-made billionaire who would come to own CBS, who also was a bridge aficionado.

This point does require a word of caution. Being a ferocious competitor in all instances would be just as wrong as being incapable or a cheat. David D'Alessandro once witnessed a mixed-doubles tennis game where the chief executive's wife and another executive's wife played against two senior managers. The two women were decent tennis players, but the men were much stronger, and the "friendly game" turned fiercely competitive. One of the managers was using his best serve on the chief executive's wife, which she was unable to return. During one serve, the ball bounced and hit her eye. D'Alessandro recounts that he was at the CEO's table for dinner that night. The executive came to apologize to the wife, who was wearing more than her usual amount of makeup. She was quite good about it. She laughed and said, "Oh, don't worry about it." The CEO only said to him, "I hear you have quite the serve." D'Alessandro says that the rest of the group at the table knew what that meant. That meant the executive's life at the company was over.[19]

Therefore, versatility, adaptability, and a sense for the situation and its context remain vital. As I have said before, every action and reaction has to be calibrated just right in a way that appears natural and unrehearsed. Indeed, after a time, it will be natural, because practice does make perfect.

Interacting with Powerful People Is a Competence in and of Itself

This is a book about effectively working with powerful people and therefore is as a whole about the "powerful-people competence." But the point should still be stated expressly that it is indeed a specific competence; it must be identified as such, so that it can be developed with intention and purpose. Some people just don't get that working for a powerful person is different.

The point is illustrated well by a story told by Michael Wolff about a senior Fox News executive who attended a meeting with Rupert Murdoch.[20] The main agenda item was boosting advertising sales at the local Fox stations. A hands-on Murdoch proposed one of his tried-and-true methods from Australia, which was to let go of the salesperson who had earned least that month. The news executive was quite incredulous and might have thought Murdoch couldn't possibly be serious. Unwisely, he failed to control his reaction adequately. Wolff reports that Murdoch rebuked him with a "Wipe that smirk off your face!" and that the executive lost his job after the meeting.

> Use every opportunity to observe and learn. It is a lot less costly to learn from the mistakes of others than from your own!

Working for an intense powerful person is different and requires special skills. Full control over one's facial expressions is one of them, because any intentional or unintentional reaction will be picked up with radar-like sensitivity. And much will be read into it: An employee who smirks at a serious suggestion when the bottom is falling out of the sales budget obviously does not understand the seriousness of the situation. That can be very harmful, especially if the person has a leadership position. Thus, the problem is not the smirk itself, but the much broader attitude it appears to reflect. Again, this is not a matter of being stone-faced at all times. It is a matter of acting intentionally and appropriately with the right calibration for the situation and what you are trying to accomplish. To say it again, smirking when a powerful or any boss is making a point about revitalizing sales, especially at a time of crisis, is an amateurish mistake if there has ever been one.

In complete contrast to the Fox executive stands Rupert Murdoch's key executive Gary Ginsberg. Wolff writes, "Ginsberg is everybody's point man."[21] Everybody confers with Ginsberg about what the chief is thinking and trying to achieve. "Everybody tends to have just their piece of the story—Ginsberg pieces together the pieces."[22] Thus, Ginsberg's ability to relate to and work with the boss is a source of company-wide influence.

Another person who clearly recognized that dealing with a brilliant, energetic, and at times volatile powerful person is a distinct and highly necessary skill was then-U.S. defense secretary Dick Cheney during Operations Desert Shield and Desert Storm. While he had his concerns, Cheney clearly recognized General Schwarzkopf's qualities and, as a good politician, was attuned to the fact that the American people loved a general with Schwarzkopf's panache. But to make sure that not too much china was broken, he assigned a capable deputy commander in General Calvin Waller to work with the commander in chief (also known as "CINC") on the ground in Saudi Arabia. And he had an equally capable liaison in Washington in the person of Colin Powell, chairman of the Joint Chiefs. Cheney called it "managing the Schwarzkopf account,"[23] a very apt expression of what was going on. Cheney also recognized an equally important fact: not everyone is equally capable of managing a high-profile account.

Adding the powerful-person competence to your repertoire can indeed become a source of great professional development and advancement. In particular, this is the case when subject-matter experts lack the skill to relate well. For example, a financial or legal expert may be stuck in technical jargon and have difficulty relating his or her expertise to the practical business problem at hand. In this instance, the boss will easily have doubts whether the technical expert really grasps the big picture. That's where an interface will be required, and that's where you can—competently—gain exposure to whole new fields of endeavor.

What to do when . . .

. . . the powerful person gets you in a friendly chat after a long day

You find yourself with your powerful boss at the end of a long day. You may have traveled overnight and gone straight to the office. You spent a grueling day in business meetings, negotiations, and presentations. Now you are sitting down to "relax" after dinner.

Don't be shocked if the boss is still all business and now asks you for your thoughts and ideas. This is not the time to let down your guard and share whatever is on your mind. Resist the temptation to think out loud. Stay sharp and make sure any "ideas" you have are solid. Remember that any negative comments on people or plans may lead to immediate follow-up. Most of all, be aware that even now, you may still be judged and evaluated.

Save Energy for When It Counts

I envy people who thrive on three or four hours of sleep at night. They have so much more time to work, learn, and play.

—BILL GATES, FOUNDER AND CHAIRMAN, MICROSOFT

Powerful people have boundless energy. They love what they do, and it energizes them. They do not need much sleep. And while they do not expect more from others than they expect from themselves, their expectations of themselves just happen to be sky-high. It seems only fitting, therefore, that among Frank Stronach's many, many business projects is an energy drink appropriately named Frank.

With that tremendous energy comes an unbridled passion for what they do. And the single-minded focus on the goal and the task at hand rarely leaves room for making people around them feel calm and appreciated. When one task is accomplished, powerful people likely are already on to the next, leaving you in constant catch-up mode. If things do not go their way or they are dissatisfied, their temper takes over, causing fear and trepidation. General Schwarzkopf is not the only one who is capable of volcanic explosions:[1] Similar temper outbursts have been reported about Ted Rogers[2] and Steve Jobs.[3] And the frosty and enigmatic silence, which has been said to be Ferdinand Piëch's trademark,[4] can have an equal if not more unsettling effect.

In other words, with powerful people, the tension is constant.

By no means, of course, do larger-than-life bosses have a corner on stressful workplaces. High pressure is a constant in many performance-driven occupations: a salesperson may have the pressure of the weekly sales budget, lawyers may have to log a grueling amount of billable hours, tax advisers have to sustain tax season, and working through a merger or similar transaction means long hours for everyone involved. The pressure can increase further during a time of crisis, from a financial meltdown to an environmental disaster. The most compassionate bosses will likely become difficult when their stress level goes off the charts.

You Need Physical Energy: Keeping Up Takes Stamina

Thus, the fifth rule of effectively working with powerful people simply relates to the ability to keep up with them. You have got to have the energy.

Keeping up requires physical stamina. Marathon meetings, a huge amount of follow-up work, calls in the middle of the night, jet lag, motivational surprise visits to the night shift, late-night dinners with early-morning follow-ups—working for a powerful person, especially in the larger-than-life category, takes a toll. There is always a crisis somewhere and always one more fire to fight. As Ted Rogers's biographer Caroline Van Hasselt put it: "Only the strong survive in Ted Rogers' world."[5]

AN ENERGETIC DISPOSITION HELPS

It therefore will come as no surprise that people who have successfully worked for high-profile powerful bosses have a tremendous amount of energy themselves. We are told that as a bachelor, Apple's Tim Cook is known as a workaholic who often fires off e-mails in the wee hours of the morning—and a workout fanatic.[6] He also is an admirer of Lance Armstrong.

Sally Bedell Smith gives an account of the workaholism of CBS's Frank Stanton. Stanton's idea of relaxation was arriving in the office on a Sunday wearing a smart casual outfit. He often slept no more than five hours a night. His workday continued late in the evening, when he would read the *New York Times* and watch the late news before going to bed at 1:00 A.M. As soon as he woke up, he would tune in to the six o'clock morning news.[7]

Energy is also one of the characteristics that Otto Preston Chaney identifies in our Red Army hero Marshal Zhukov. When it came to organizing the defenses of Moscow, whose weaknesses were making the supreme commander nervous and angry, the marshal approached his task with vigor and long hours, so much so that some of his subordinates literally collapsed on their feet.[8]

It will come as no surprise, therefore, that an energetic disposition will help when you are working with powerful people. But not everyone is blessed with an unlimited supply of vigor. You therefore have to manage your energy level carefully and avoid wasting it wherever you can.

THE BASICS MATTER

Regardless of the deluge of health and fitness literature (which almost rivals the volumes written on leadership), the "big three" fundamental principles of stress-resilient living have not changed: eat healthy, exercise regularly, and get a good night's sleep. Of course, following a healthy living regimen is easier said than done. When long hours at work start to consume your life, diet, exercise, and sleep are often the first victims. Add jet lag to the mix, and you have a potent mix for energy drainage. But there are very practical things you can do. Ride an exercise bike while watching the news, plan your meals, make sure you have healthy foods around, and replace your sugary soda with water. The point is to make it easy; an expensive health club membership doesn't do anything if you don't have time to go there. All of this is just plain good practice and should not be dismissed just because of its simplicity.

Also, you should periodically review how you are doing in the basic three. A personal trainer or a spouse can be key people for adding accountability, and you may even want to think about a wellness coach to get you started.

DON'T IGNORE PHYSICAL LIMITATIONS

No matter how intense the expectations, there are physical limitations that you simply cannot ignore. Driving while overtired would be one example of what not to try. Another one is the expectation to work in the boss's time zone. I have been in many global meetings where meeting organizers had simply given no thought to a twelve-hour time difference and having people on the other side of the world work straight through the night. If that's you, you can simply start by raising some awareness. There may also be an opportunity to alternate off-hour meeting times, especially when it is simply a matter of educating people who are unaware.

When working with towering individuals, however, the demands of the job can become strenuous in ways that are truly out of the ordinary. In that sense, an altogether human challenge of physically keeping up with the boss was encountered by Margaret Thatcher's defense and foreign-policy adviser, Charles Powell. The story is told by Claire Berlinski.[9] In the last days of the Cold War, the British prime minister visited the Soviet Union for a meeting with General Secretary Mikhail Gorbachev. The session in the Kremlin, which lasted thirteen hours, became a turning point in the resolution of the East-West conflict. The only people present were Thatcher, Gorbachev, the Russian foreign minister, Powell, and two interpreters. The discussion covered the Soviet and Cuban presence in Africa and the whole question of intermediate- and short-range missiles in Europe. At the end of the meeting, Powell was in a total state of exhaustion, and his bladder was about to burst. Finally, he excused himself to look for the bathroom but could not figure out how to get out of the room. Gorbachev was amused; Powell recalls the episode as "one of the most embarrassing moments of his life."[10] The Soviet leader finally pushed a button, a door slid open, and Powell was able to escape. Powell later explained that Prime Minister Thatcher did not need to use the bathroom. Not even once. "The Iron Bladder held out for the whole thirteen hours."

> *You need physical energy; don't waste any! Follow basic rules for healthy living: eat well, exercise, and get some sleep.*

This extreme situation illustrates the insight that there are physical limitations we should not ignore even if we may feel embarrassed.

My own experience of having to go to the restroom occurred when serving as assistant to the presiding judge during an appeals court session. When the proceedings dragged on, my bladder made it hard to pay attention. There was no end in sight, and I debated with myself what to do. I finally decided it was time to go. The presiding judge, the attorneys, the parties, and the spectators were equally astonished. I also had to endure some "humor" after. But had I made a different decision, the embarrassment could have only been bigger, and I would have missed even more of what was going on. The lesson clearly is this: Some physical limitations just cannot be overcome. And we should not wait until it is too late!

A GREAT TEAM MULTIPLIES ENERGY

If you are in any kind of leadership or management position, by far the most effective way to conserve energy is to have great people working for you. If you have the right people, you can delegate a huge amount of work and be certain they will take responsibility for it because they will know the stakes. Also, with the right people, you can rely on them to engage the powerful person directly, rather than having to filter every issue. That frees up your time and provides them with valuable experience. It would be utterly wrong to think you personally must handle every issue that involves the boss. Of course, you do not want to abandon your boss either.

> *Teach your team to represent you well and interact effectively with the powerful person.*

For example, if you are facing a budget meeting with the boss or the finance chief, you may think about letting some of your people present their areas. Help them prepare key points, pinpoint how their work fits into the overall strategy of the organization, and anticipate questions. Then let them do the talking. Jump in only if required. Afterward, review what worked well and what they and you could have done differently.

Overall, there can be no question that investing the time, discipline, and energy required to assemble a great team, coaching them in how to effectively interface with the powerful person in your life, and working hard to keep them motivated and on board pays huge dividends. We will return to some of this later. For now, remember the key insight: a team of great people, each of whom can handle the temperamental boss, is *the* multiplier of energy.

Be Ready for Conflict: It Takes Emotional Energy

In addition to the demanding nature and zest for ever more activities, projects, and initiatives exhibited by hard-charging personalities, their willingness (and, in some cases, eagerness) to engage in conflict is a huge energy drain for those helping them. Engaging a powerful person requires the emotional energy to persevere through conflict. Powerful people are not afraid of conflict and even thrive on it. They can make every issue into a drama, enjoy the thrill of fighting things through, and become defiant when challenged.

In addition, there is a proliferation of internal conflict that has been brought on by the emergence of the flat global organization. Absent a clear hierarchy, competing departments represent different stakeholders and priorities, and conflict arises between a centralized headquarters and local views. People have to get things done without owning all the resources while often running into powerful interests. Moving ahead in such an environment requires energy and an emotional readiness for conflict.

JUST WATCH ME

Pierre Elliott Trudeau, the Canadian prime minister known equally for his charisma and controversial policies, once provided a very public demonstration of defiance by a strong character. In the dark days of the crisis unleashed by the separatist/terrorist Front de Libération du Québec (FLQ), which resorted to brutal violence in an effort to achieve their province's independence from the dominion, the prime minister had posted armed guards around Parliament and suspended civil liberties. In a lengthy exchange, prickly reporters challenged the prime minister on the steps of Parliament Hill and asked how far he would go with his emergency measures. "Just watch me," was the answer of a belligerent Trudeau, a phrase that became famous in Canadian politics and could be called the preferred motto of any powerful person when challenged.

CHOOSE YOUR BATTLES WISELY

Preserving energy during conflict requires a calculated assessment of whether the battle is worth it. In other words, you must choose your battles wisely. The question of whether the issue is really the bridge on which we want to die, or whether it is even a flag we want to carry into battle, needs to be answered first. Engaging in a power struggle with an agitated powerful person is rarely a good idea. Therefore, you must develop a habit of not sweating the small stuff; let him or her be right most of the time, and conserve your energy for when it really counts. That decision will require some honest reflection. There are people who will develop a habit of avoiding *all* battles and never challenging *any* decision. That, of course, cannot be the tactic to adopt if you want to be truly helpful. But you simply do not want to engage in lost causes that are not worth it.

Staying with the military analogy, we can get a good example for what not to do from Colin Powell's experience. As military experts will tell us, the only thing worse than picking the wrong fight is walking into a minefield. There are situations that can only lead to an explosion and leave you without any possible defense. Powell learned that lesson the hard way when he worked for Major General John Hudachek at Fort Carson.[11] The general was a tough overseer of his subordinates on the base, and Powell soon learned that the wives "reported" to Mrs. Hudachek. Powell credited her with a deep commitment to the welfare of the soldiers under her husband's command, as well as to their families, but felt that her leadership style of various committees was overbearing.

Against the advice of the general's chief of staff, Powell broached the issue with the boss. He told him that while Mrs. Hudachek had wonderful ideas and intentions, he felt she needed to find a way to pursue her interests "with a little more participation by the other wives."[12] When Powell returned home that night, his wife greeted him with an incredulous, "What did you do?" She had been invited over for a cup of tea with Mrs. Hudachek, who then expressed her displeasure. At the next evaluation period, Powell received a less than glowing report, which would have stalled his career, had it not been for the intervention of some higher-ups who had taken notice of him earlier.

From this follows an important lesson: Criticizing the boss's spouse, even if your words be ever so gentle, is not a bridge on which you want to die, nor a flag you want to carry into battle, it is simply a minefield. The signpost reads, "Just don't go there." If criticizing the boss's spouse is unwise, the same goes for the reverse. Complaining to the boss's spouse in search of empathy can backfire just as easily. At a minimum, you should not automatically assume that the spouse will lend a sympathetic ear. In other words, proceed only with the greatest of caution.

> *Few bridges are worth dying on; choose your battles wisely.*

GET READY FOR MANAGEMENT BY CONFLICT

When working in an organization dominated by driven and competitive people, conflict is not limited to your interaction with the boss. Since many powerful people thrive on conflict, they not only tolerate it among their subordinates, but may actually encourage it.

This management technique can, of course, simply be healthy competition among various business groups for the best sales or profits results, quality metrics, safety record, cost/expense reduction, or other key achievement areas. The winning techniques and best practices can then be publicized and implemented throughout the organization, and success stories celebrated. This kind of competition can provide a stimulus to bring out the best in people. Who wouldn't want to be the salesperson of the year, receive a nice award on stage, and earn bragging rights? At the same time, high spenders and poor performers can be shamed into improvement and/or a more judicious use of company resources.

But some bosses will go further. Ferdinand Piëch's biographer Rita Stiens quotes the Volkswagen chief as saying he loves to have two brands run against each other because "they will get a lot faster as a result." She goes on to point out that Piëch's love for competition extends to having two teams within the company running against each other. Creative competition becomes part of a leadership style.[13] Working in such an environment of permanent competition requires significant energy.

Beyond shaking things up through competition, powerful people may also intentionally create conflict. This practice can take several forms. First, there can be a tendency to encourage members of different parts of the organization to point out flaws in one another. This will give insight into areas for improvement and the power to decide who is right. Then, there can be competition for resources, which can lead to ever bolder promises of success and, in return, pressure to deliver what has been promised. And finally, I have even heard of the extreme practice of hiring two competitors for the same job and waiting to see who succeeds. While one can easily take issue with such an approach, some hard-driving bosses will not see anything wrong with such management techniques. They love to compete, thrive on conflict, and will sincerely believe that a challenge will bring out the best in people and weed out those who can't take the heat. If put in that position themselves, they would certainly be up for it.

As noted earlier, the point here is not to judge but to deal effectively with the reality of the situation. One of those realities is that, given a competitive leader's tendency toward management by conflict, working for that type of person requires high levels of awareness and sensitivity to your surroundings. To use a military term, a certain combat readiness is needed. By combat readiness, I do not mean or advocate using creative conflict as a tool for tripping up or sniping at competitors at every possible opportunity. While you may be able to score a few points this way, it will also create an environment where people will be waiting to get back at you. Dysfunctional conflict is not in the interest of the organization, and it is not in your interest either.

As some of your colleagues will embrace and seek to exploit the conflict and competition, you cannot afford to be naive. Therefore, if the senior sales manager is seeking to score points with anecdotes of poor product quality letting competitors in the door and harming sales, you must have good data ready to defend your overall quality record. If the finance manager is complaining that salespeople are giving away margins, you must have your analysis of market pricing ready. You must know what is going on, and you must have your facts ready. A few anecdotes of your own will help, too.

You also need an early-warning system to alert you when trouble is coming. This way, you will be better prepared to respond quickly and decisively to the inevitable ambushes. Confidently and

> *Know your facts, and have an early-warning system in place. Be vigilant, confident, and, when needed, feisty.*

calmly pointing out the facts is a highly effective defense. This confidence puts competitors on notice that you are ready for a fight, if that's what they are looking for. They must know that you will not allow them to score points at your expense or deflect from their own problems by rechanneling the boss's wrath against you. All of this means you have to be vigilant, organized, confident, and, when needed, feisty.

Resilience to Stress

Emotional energy further requires a great deal of resilience to stress, because in a competitive, high-strung environment, the drama is constant, and there is always the crisis of the day. Numerous experts have pointed to scientific evidence of a strong link between stress and illness.[14] In its extreme form, overwhelming stress can lead to a breakdown of protective mechanisms in the body and affect it where it is the weakest, leading to serious health issues.[15] As an antidote, the experts recommend acknowledging the phenomenon, sharing one's experiences with professionals, and periodically seeking a safe zone to harness "the healing power of taking breaks."[16]

While this advice certainly makes sense, it has to be applied with caution. Yes, you should be very aware of the fact that you are working in a high-intensity zone, especially if you are among executives who work with a larger-than-life person full-time. A regular physical exam should be the rule. However, to ask for professional counseling still carries a significant stigma, even though a conversation with a psychologist has now become part of most "executive physicals." I will personally confess that I never confided in the psychologists made available by the executive medical providers and have taken great license in filling out their questionnaires. In turn, they have told me (after the fact) that they never expected me to tell the truth in the first place. Also, some of them just haven't been there and don't quite understand the realities, pressures, and constraints. However, a physician who has been part of a corporate environment can more easily relate, and a family doctor who is clearly on your side can be exceedingly helpful. I would therefore also recognize the value of relationships with experienced people who can relate to what we do, have a level head and common sense, and are prepared to support us over the distance.

Intentionally creating safe zones, such as family, also will help. This of course means that socializing with the powerful person (and his or her family) for the purpose of "relaxation" is counterproductive. Yes, it can be useful for building the relationship, but it cannot be considered downtime. It is work.

And you must periodically review the need for a break. A holiday interrupted by daily phone calls and a deluge of e-mail messages does not rejuvenate; more likely, it will increase frustration and resentment of family members who have to compete constantly for attention. Even if it is just a twenty-minute call, depending on the issue and the person who is calling, it may preoccupy you for much longer. Choosing a vacation spot without telephone and Internet access is an option that may not always be feasible but deserves serious consideration. Leaving behind a capable and empowered colleague (a favor you should then return) will provide a first defense against inevitable emergencies. But it will not be easy. Most powerful people do not perceive work as work, and it will not be intuitive to them why someone would want to be out of touch for more than a few hours.

This need for a break may at some point mean more than a holiday; it may require leaving the employ of the powerful person for a time. The examples of people in this book show that quite a few of them have left their jobs with powerful bosses for a while and returned to

> *Have a safe recovery zone, and take true breaks. Take advice from others as to when it is time to do so.*

work for them later on, sometimes in very different capacities. On occasion, the "sabbatical" may even increase the powerful person's appreciation for the work that has been done.

Count the Cost

Finally, especially when working with a larger-than-life person, the reality of conflict and the need for constant attention and energy should warrant serious reflection before deciding to take any job in his or her orbit. It is your responsibility to yourself and your family to count the costs and make an informed decision.

Here are two hypothetical situations where energy should be a significant factor in your decision: First, you may be recruited away from a position where you are doing well. Of course, there is the allure of career advancement, more money, and the charm factor. Also, recruiters can play a big role, as they are usually very skilled at facilitating change. But especially if the job change involves relocation and changes for your family, you should take a long, hard look before moving ahead and determine what you are getting yourself into. Second, there may be people who decide to become involved with a powerful person late in their careers—as a member of a board of directors, for example. Before taking on such an assignment, you have to realize that sitting on a powerful person's board is hardly a comfortable postretirement job. It is full of action and activity, and it may require the energy to make it through times of sustained conflict. Also, as a prospective board member, keep in mind that the powerful person's concept of governance could potentially follow a different model than what might be expected, especially if his or her level of power is greater than what you're accustomed to.

> *Deciding not to work for or with a powerful person is not a sign of weakness but of wisdom.*

Therefore, not taking the position is unrelated to weakness; rather, it is a conscious decision of what you do and do not want to put up with at any particular stage in life, where personal needs, family, and ambition must all be factored. The same goes for a resignation. The decision to depart a position or company does not need to be fueled by spite, frustration, or the desire to make a point. It may just come as a result of the mature insight that you either cannot sustain the necessary level of energy to do the job right or simply would rather direct your energy elsewhere.

What to do when . . .

. . . you are asked to cut to the chase

You are in the middle of a brilliant presentation on your favorite project. You are presenting a detailed background analysis and a mass of supporting data. The powerful person in the room gets impatient and finally interrupts you brusquely: "Cut to the chase, and tell me what it will take."

There can be no hesitation now. You must have three crisp and compelling points ready, such as "We need Christine Jones to lead the project; we need an investment of $5 million; and we need your full support to remove resistance from people who don't like change." It will be good to have similar answers to ambush questions like "What will it take to double the business?" "What will it take to crack the Smith account?" or "What will it take to bring the product to market now?"

Of course, you cannot make this up on the spot. Think about the top five questions a powerful person might have, and get your answers ready. Thinking through these questions may also inspire you to take action right away, regardless of whether someone else is asking!

Practice Humility

Humility is a good quality, but it can be overdone.

—CONRAD BLACK, HISTORIAN, COLUMNIST,
AND ERSTWHILE MEDIA TYCOON

There is room for only one ego. While one may speculate whether ego begets power, or vice versa, or both,
the cold, hard psychological assessment from the previously referenced experts at Stanford and UC Berkeley
is that powerful individuals have "a highly favorable self-concept
and as a consequence are not easily impressed by the less powerful."[1] In other words, it is all about them.

It also is important to remember that power comes in many
shades and colors. You can be dealing with a head of state; the
president of a multibillion-dollar corporation; the owner of a small
business; the head of a small, local subsidiary; or a customs official.
In each context, the leader's power may appear grand, no matter
who he or she is.

While those in charge are always on the lookout for capable
people, their basic stance is one of skepticism and "show me." Some
very practical conclusions follow from the insight that powerful
people are at the center of attention.

Learn to Roll with the Punches

If powerful people have a penchant for volcanic temperaments that will fluster even strong personalities, you had better be able to take a punch. That's a requirement, especially for executive helpers who are in close contact with larger-than-life people day in and day out. Anything else would be like becoming a boxer and expecting to make it through a twelve-round match without taking a hit. A thick skin, mental preparedness, and a strong center of balance are required equipment, together with a good dose of humility.

Colin Watson, who was one of Ted Rogers's key lieutenants and, as operational head for cable TV, endured much of Rogers's wrath, took a philosophical perspective. He explained that you had to learn to live with Rogers and that you had to assume he did not mean any harm by his overbearing behavior. Caroline Van Hasselt quotes him as saying, "We used to laugh that if Rogers wasn't yelling at you, you didn't matter anymore. I am being a bit facetious. It is kind of his way of caring. He is just very intense, and that's the way he manages. You don't let it get to you. If you did you'd go crazy. I suppose a lot of people did let it get to them, now that I think about it."[2]

Watson's advice is sound. You can't let it get to you. If being shouted at confirms that you or what you do matters, it should not interfere with your ego.

We should note, by the way, that packing a punch is by no means an exclusive domain for men. That was the experience of U.S. Defense Secretary Caspar Weinberger in an encounter with Prime Minister Margaret Thatcher. The episode developed from a strategic defense purchasing decision made by the Pentagon. The Americans had procured a multibillion-dollar military cellular-phone system from the French, even though the British had a competing product. In *My American Journey*, Colin Powell, who accompanied Secretary Weinberger when he went to see Thatcher to explain the situation, gives this account:

> The prime minister, perfectly coiffed, came in wearing a suit that managed to look both feminine and businesslike. Cap Weinberger started easing his way into his unpleasant task. He had barely opened his mouth when the prime minister cut him off. "My dear

Cap, I want you to know how very, very distressed I am by this shabby business . . . nothing you can say will convince me that there wasn't dirty work at the crossroads. We've been cheated. Do you hear me? Cheated. And don't try to tell me otherwise."[3]

Powell recounts that Weinberger remained stoic as Thatcher continued her mantra about dirty work and being cheated. When she stopped long enough to catch her breath, Weinberger started explaining the U.S. decision, but the prime minister cut him off at his knees. When he tried again, she kept going on about dirty work at the crossroads, like a schoolteacher lecturing a student. Powell calls it a fascinating performance. Weinberger's wilted head had just received a swing of Thatcher's famous verbal handbag!

Of course, there are limits to everything. But more often than not, your real job will be protecting others who are not quite as able to take the hit. In the meantime, you must suppress the urge to explain yourself, set the record straight, or, worse, try to be right. None of that is

> *If you are secure enough, you can handle a little belittling.*

very effective and may easily incite more anger. Remember Margaret Thatcher: "Nothing you can say will convince me." If you are at that stage, hunker down, let the storm pass, and move on.

Don't Seek Any Glory for Yourself

The second mark of humility is that we do not seek any glory for ourselves. Pastor Rick Warren's bestseller *The Purpose Driven Life* starts with the memorable sentence "It's not about you."[4] And certainly, when you are working with a powerful person, it is most likely about them, not you. In the same way that powerful people will be extremely quick to notice and react to socially inappropriate behavior, they will quickly react to behavior that appears conspicuous in any way. Wayne Lilley lets Fred Jaekel tell the story of presenting to the board the results of his Magna unit (Cosma). Jaekel recounts that he was bragging about having brought in $725 million in profits instead of the planned $500 million. Jaekel recalls that after the meeting, "Frank [Stronach] got upset about that . . . because I was outshining the rest of the groups."[5] The lesson is clear: bragging and gloating can only backfire.

In a similar vein, you should always leave the limelight to the larger-than-life boss. Two examples offer excellent illustrations. According to *Fortune* magazine reporter Adam Lashinsky, Tim Cook, who has filled in for Steve Jobs as chief executive, is an excellent example of humility.[6] "Come on, replace Steve? No. He is irreplaceable," *Fortune* quotes Cook as saying. "That's something people have to get over. I see Steve there with gray hair in his 70s, long after I'm retired." Cook is obviously very comfortable with his role, and he has his ego firmly in hand. That's possibly yet another reason, in addition to his smarts and capability, why Jobs felt comfortable when Cook filled in for him a second time.

Another executive who understood well that you want to leave the publicity to the boss is Dennis Mills at Magna. When Hurricane Katrina struck New Orleans in August 2005, Frank Stronach and the Magna group of companies stepped in to provide shelter for evacuees at Magna Entertainment Corp.'s training center in Palm Meadows, Florida. The Stronach team, whose efforts were skillfully and tirelessly directed by Mills, even went on to build an experimental model farming community in Simmesport, Louisiana. The project, initially named Magnaville and then dubbed Canadaville, was publicized and warmly received across the United States. This was especially so because it was viewed in contrast to the slow-moving bureaucracy and the infamous "FEMA trailers" in the aftermath of the catastrophe. Canadaville resulted in tremendous goodwill for Magna, Canada, and, of course, Frank Stronach. Wayne Lilley notes that much of the credit was given to Frank Stronach, and Dennis Mills would do the same.[7] While Lilley seems to be critical of that approach, I do not agree at all with his criticism. First of all, the project would simply not have happened without Frank Stronach, his generosity, and his desire to help people devastated by a catastrophe. And Mills knew very well that Stronach did not want to see Mills's name in the paper. Magna and its chairman received some excellent publicity, and the people of New Orleans received some badly need help. They felt good, Stronach felt good, and Mills probably felt good as well: win-win-win.

As one senior executive with applicable experience told me, "The press coverage of the powerful person as compared to your own should be at a ratio of ten-to-one." That's good advice. Marshal Zhukov knew that lesson well. His biographer notes, "Zhukov emerged as the *spasitel* (savior) of Moscow, but he wisely and tactfully attributed his success to the guidance of Stalin and the unconquerable fighting qualities of his men."[8] Similarly, an *Izvestiya* newspaper editorial in praise of Zhukov says he "carried out Stalin's plans for the repulsion of the Germans." It therefore may come as no surprise that in his bestselling book *The 48 Laws of Power*, Robert Greene even identifies avoidance of the limelight as the very first law of power: "Never outshine the master."[9]

Incidentally, I have found that not seeking a higher profile is in no way detrimental to getting the attention of—and making friends with—some great people. I have been at meetings where I left the limelight to the person in charge and added little or nothing to the conversation. Some of the very perceptive (and equally powerful) counterparts in attendance read the situation well. They realized that a low profile did not equate to having nothing to say; instead, they understood that this was not the time and place for me to voice my opinion. In fact, some went out of their way to follow up with me at a later date to have a personal conversation and get my take on the issue that had been discussed.

> *Remember, it's all about them. Don't brag or outshine the master.*

Be a Team Player

Humility may be harder to practice when the power differential is smaller. It is one thing to be put in your place by a prime minister or the founder of a large company; it is quite another to deal with a colleague or member of a project team who is obnoxious and feeling quite superior. But even in such situations, humility is a great policy. Waiting for the right moment to make your point and keeping focused on moving issues forward will distinguish you from attention seekers and enhance your reputation as a team player.

Develop a Big Sense of Humor

Powerful people can carry things to extremes that leave us speechless. But even then, you must keep your composure and, if possible, see the humor of the situation. As a widely reported story about Conrad Black indicates, one person who just couldn't believe what was happening was the features editor of the *Telegraph*, Eleanor Mills. As Richard Siklos tells the story,[10] one day in 1998, Eleanor Mills was recommended on short notice as a last-minute fill-in at a dinner party for which the Blacks suddenly required an additional woman to balance out the guest list. Mills, who was at the newspaper, went home and changed into evening wardrobe before making her way to the Blacks' residence. When she arrived, Conrad Black thanked her for coming, and she began sipping a glass of wine. About twenty minutes later, Black came up and informed her that there had been an embarrassing mix-up and that they didn't need another woman after all. He asked Mills to finish her drink and run along; his wife, Barbara, would assist her in getting a taxi. Finally, a housekeeper led her through the kitchen (where the chef was frying scallops) to the trade entrance. Mills did not want to wait there but left in a hurry. The next day, she was summoned to the chairman's office, where an assistant handed her a basket of bath soaps with a note from Conrad and Barbara, thanking her "for being a good sport."

The whole episode left Mills extremely upset, and of course she was treated very poorly. But I believe Mills failed to understand that she was a helper and her help was no longer needed at the moment. There is no point to objecting to the lack of social grace; someone like Conrad Black will not understand the problem. We have to assume that for him, hosting the perfect dinner party was the overriding concern. He would have thought that everyone understood that. And as Peter Oborne points out when reporting the same story in the *Spectator*, this episode is counterbalanced by many episodes of generosity and kindness.[11] Therefore, I believe that if you do complain in a situation like this, you will likely be perceived as being the one with the big ego. So unless your personal line is crossed (we will get to that), the way to proceed is with humility, a sense of humor, and a commitment to being "a good sport."

The reality is that most people will be aware of the powerful person's reputation for this sort of behavior, so it will reflect on him or her, rather than on you. In addition, the better you can adroitly maneuver such episodes (even if they border on the bizarre), the more you gain credibility and become, like Gary Ginsberg for Rupert Murdoch, the sought-after expert in how to relate to the all-powerful boss. Psychologist Bruce Peltier, who offers some insightful and highly practical advice in his book *The Psychology of Executive Coaching*, would call it "taking the existential stance" when he recommends that we should "welcome and appreciate the absurd."[12] We should indeed.

> *The more bizarre the episode you navigate, the more you become an expert on relating to the powerful person.*

But even when dealing with less obvious snubs from less powerful people, it will be good to relax. The fact simply is that many people can be insensitive and self-centered (you and me included), and a perceived snub really wasn't intended as such. In such situations, it never pays to read too much into things. Even if the discourteous behavior was intentional, keeping your composure and grace will provide a powerful contrast that will not go unnoticed. The conclusion is therefore that humility is a quality that can scarcely be overdone.

Master the Art of Confession

It is never good if the boss hears bad news from someone else. The same goes for a client. If other people become the bearer of your bad news, you are deprived of the opportunity to put it into context. Further, you may cause the boss to question whether you would have ever told him or her (if the word had not come via another source) and, worse, whether you are hiding other things: "I wonder what else he/she hasn't told me?"

Therefore, in some instances, humility has to be proactive. A beautiful illustration is provided by the example of a man who is regarded by many as the master of power and politics at his time: Otto von Bismarck, known as Germany's Iron Chancellor. Bismarck epitomizes the mastery of influencing powerful people by eventually being the one to lead his boss, the king of Prussia and later Germany's Emperor William I, rather than being led by him.

The episode told by his authoritative biographer Erich Eyck, however, shows that humility was needed for Bismarck to cover some of his earlier missteps. During his early years as prime minister of Prussia, the precursor of the German *Reich*, Bismarck needed to win members of the liberal opposition for his cabinet. When talking to one of the liberals, Bismarck compared his boss, King William, to "a horse that shied at every new object and became restive and unmanageable if one tried force, but would get accustomed little by little."[13]

While this quip shows Bismarck's attitude well, it was not kept a secret, and Bismarck knew that he had a problem and his slip would eventually find its way back to King William. At the time, the king was away from the capital of Berlin and, unfortunately for Bismarck, was in the company of the queen and their daughter and son-in-law, the Grand Duchess and Grand Duke of Baden, none of whom were friends of Bismarck. The king was about to make his way back from Baden to Berlin. To win the king back, Bismarck did not wait to have his boss come back to the office (so to speak), but met him at the last train station before Berlin, the town of Jüterborg. He knew his apology had to be made promptly, in person, and with humility. Thus, he survived the episode and eventually attained a position in which he would dominate the affairs of the *Reich* and would come to "lead the orchestra whose music was heard through twenty-eight years by Prussia, by Germany, nay, by the whole of Europe."[14]

In her book *Managing Up*, Rosanne Badowski, "the woman who works side by side with the legendary Jack Welch,"[15] gives straightforward advice for the "art of confession" that confirms this principle. She counsels that giving full disclosure and admitting mistakes before the boss hears about them from someone else both go a long way in building trust. Her rule of thumb is to admit mistakes by the end of the business day—at the latest.[16] In addition, as we have seen, proactive confession preempts attempts by others who, in the spirit of creative conflict, may try to communicate our mistakes to the boss in order to score a few points.

When admitting mistakes, you must also withstand the temptation to try to minimize their severity. The boss must know that you take your mistakes seriously. First of all, when bosses know that you take your problems seriously and are worried about mistakes, they know they don't have to. Second, if the powerful person comes to the conclusion that the mistake might not have been earth shattering after all, it allows him or her to show some kindness if so inclined. Don't take that opportunity away from your boss and don't be presumptuous. Finally, a mistake may even have a silver lining. On one occasion, in a sensitive negotiation, I electronically forwarded a proposal to the other side by accident (in the age of electronic communication, such mistakes have become a much bigger concern). As a result, we received a reaction that allowed us to find out the other side's thinking, which turned out to be quite helpful. However, it had still been my mistake, and it was not my place to see the "silver lining." The boss graciously did, knowing I was mortified by the mistake.

> *Admit mistakes promptly and without minimizing them.*

Don't Consider Yourself to Be Above a Menial Task

A final application of the humility rule is that you should not feel above doing a task you might consider menial. An example of such a task might be some of the assignments that were handed out by General Norman Schwarzkopf. We are told that he once ordered a major to stand in the bathroom line at the end of a fifteen-hour flight to Riyadh in order to hold the spot for the commander, and that he had a colonel on his hands and knees on the floor of the plane in order to press his uniform.[17] It would be easy to dismiss such assignments as humiliating, and I would not blame a major or colonel for doing so. However, if such assignments occur only on the odd occasion and do not become part of your regular job description, you can show strength of character and confidence in who you are by simply getting the work done. In my early legal career, I had a similar bathroom assignment. The founding partner of the law firm had to be taken to the men's room because of an infirmity. As I was the rookie in the firm, the task fell to me. I survived the experience, and I could not say that it in any way stalled my career. The opposite is probably the case.

In addition to being a good exercise in practical humility, some "menial assignments" present real opportunities. My personal favorite is taking minutes in meetings. This is hardly a task that generates widespread enthusiasm. But especially for a junior person, it provides a reason for being in the meeting and will get you exposure that may otherwise be above your pay grade. It is also an excellent opportunity to start the helper relationship by getting something done and getting it done well. In the case of minutes, you can show your ability to grasp complex issues, crisply formulate the key points, and put them into the proper context. You can also show that you understand what is going on and can deal with sensitive information if necessary. The larger point is this: If the powerful person hands you an assignment, he or she obviously feels that it is important. The fact that it is important to this person should be a good enough reason for you to do it, and do it well. As a general rule, you will have much more to gain than you stand to lose.

> *Some seemingly low-level tasks present significant opportunity.*

What to do when . . .

. . . the powerful person humiliates you in public

You have just presented your strategy at the national sales meeting. The entire sales force is assembled, as well as board members and managers from other parts of the organization. You have clearly pointed out the economic challenges, the aggressive stance of the competition, and your conclusion that meeting the sales budget will take a lot of blood, sweat, and tears. The CEO is displeased. He wanted a more rousing, upbeat message to rally the troops. He comes to the podium, apologizes for the defeatist talk you have just given, and delivers his own optimistic outlook.

Of course, you will be a bit shaken, but you must remember that powerful people will not worry about your feelings when something much more important is at stake: the success of the company. You must also remember that what you do now will be watched by the rank and file and the powerful person. Getting into a public battle over the economic outlook will not lead anywhere. Inserting some humor may diffuse the situation—something like "Thanks for setting us straight, boss."

No matter what you do, you should see and use the incident as an opportunity to show that you are resilient and not easily flustered. Everyone will respect your ability to take some brutal criticism and carry on (relatively) unfazed.

RULE 7

Show Appreciation

**The deepest craving in human nature is
the craving to be appreciated.**

—DALE CARNEGIE, *HOW TO WIN FRIENDS AND INFLUENCE PEOPLE*[1]

The communications manager at a financial services firm faced a thorny challenge. One of the firm's senior partners had appeared in a newspaper article on the financial crisis, and some elements of the piece, while certainly not devastating, were less than flattering. The partner was outraged, as she felt that with her long and distinguished track record in the community, including some high-profile awards, she had deserved nothing short of unconditional praise. She demanded that the communications manager prepare a pointed letter to the editor that would set the record straight. The communications manager felt that, given the raft of negative press for the financial community, the article was actually rather benign and that complaining would do more harm than good. At best, a letter to the editor would make the partner appear petty and thin-skinned; at worst, it could provoke anger and a more pointed response. The communications manager did, however, realize that given his junior standing in a firm of high-powered partners, the demand for a well-crafted letter was to be taken seriously. It would not simply go away if he pointed out the fact that lack of flattery was a prerogative of a free press and that today's newspaper is tomorrow's fish wrap.

Know Your Customer

Every salesperson knows that the most important part of managing an account is to know the customer. Therefore, if you work with a powerful person, the first thing you must do is get to know him or her, not only as a type of person, but exactly who that person is. None of that will strike anyone as new news, but it is a point you must understand well. In his bestselling book *Social Intelligence*, Daniel Goleman refers to the know-your-customer rule as "empathetic accuracy" and contends that it is an essential expertise. Goleman says it distinguishes "the most tactful advisors, the most diplomatic officials, the most electable politicians, the most productive salespersons, the most successful teachers, and the most insightful therapists."[2] Knowing what the boss was like, how he thought, and how he felt was an essential aspect of Frank Stanton's success in working with Bill Paley at CBS. Jeffery Pfeffer comments that "Stanton and Paley had little in common. Paley was mercurial and often fired people without warning. To survive long at CBS, Stanton needed both to understand Paley and know how to manage him."[3] Therefore, even though they were different people, Stanton "knew his customer."

ENGAGE IN KEEN OBSERVATION

This sensitivity to and understanding of the person in charge requires keen observation, and *every* interaction should be used for that purpose. If you are in the presence of a senior leader, you should never tune out because the issue at hand does not involve you. Instead, you must observe what is going on, notice how the leader reacts, and as much as possible ask yourself the question "why?" And because high-profile characters live in a different world, you must free yourself from your assumptions about what might be "normal." Instead, you must as far as possible immerse yourself in their perspective. That perspective takes into account a wide range of considerations, including their goals, interests, preferences, needs, bothers, and even fears. All of these things are potentially quite different from yours. Over time, you will see patterns and will be able to predict how they might react to certain situations and ideas from their logic and view of the world. Of course, sometimes the only prediction will be that the powerful person is unpredictable, but even that is valuable insight!

When I took a group of foreign-subsidiary managers through a "perspective taking exercise" (i.e., an exploration of how a certain problem presents itself from the perspective of various stakeholders), they realized they had to dig much deeper when trying to understand the chief executive's viewpoint. They assumed that the boss was focused on making the enterprise profitable, which he certainly was. But he also had to balance short-term results and long-term prospects, manage tensions among stakeholders (such as owners, customers, and employees), think about sustainability and corporate culture, and chart a long-term sustainable competitive advantage for the firm. Exploring the details and complexity went a long way toward helping the managers understand and appreciate some of the decisions that had been made.

UNDERSTAND POWERFUL PEOPLE AND THEIR PURPOSE

Building a productive relationship with a powerful person requires a genuine appreciation for who the person is and what he or she is trying to do, even if you do not always like (agree with) the person's style and methods. Otherwise, it would be schizophrenic if you were trying to "help" that person—even in the broadest possible meaning of helping—but in some way were starting to work against him or her (an endeavor that is almost certainly bound to fail and will definitely have negative consequences).

The first thing you must understand about powerful people in order to appreciate them is their purpose. Especially if you are dealing with businesspeople, you must understand that purpose cannot be purely expressed in financial terms. In particular, you have to understand that many powerful people are not "spreadsheet executives" who are driven by an emotionally detached concept of shareholder value. The fact that they may be at the helm of a publicly traded corporation changes little.

PepsiCo's CEO Indra Nooyi is a high-profile example of a leader who is looking beyond cost management and earnings growth. She introduced a corporate directive of "Performance with Purpose"[4] and has steered the product offerings of the snack food and soft-drink giant toward more healthful and sustainable choices. The $14 billion acquisition of Quaker Oats, which she initiated earlier in her career, is a high-profile expression of a strategy with a purpose.

When turning around Volkswagen, Ferdinand Piëch wanted much more than just to save an ailing automaker and return it to profitability. Instead, his mission was saving the German auto industry as a whole and preventing Asian rivals from dominating the world of the automobile.[5] As we will see, that purpose had some real implications. In particular, saving the company simply by outsourcing to cheaper locales was not the be-all and end-all solution; although it might have saved Volkswagen, it would not have saved the German car-making industry. Incidentally, we find a similar attitude in many Chinese business leaders. In addition to seeking profits, they have a bigger mission rooted in putting their country first and the strong desire to make it a success on the world stage.[6] Centuries of domination by foreign powers have left an imprint and that leads to motivations that go beyond the logic of the spreadsheet.

Failure to understand and relate to a powerful person's purpose cost a large cosmetics company a lucrative deal with Oprah Winfrey. As Winfrey tells the story, the company proposed a cosmetics line for women of color.[7] The deal would have included eighty thousand employees nationwide and shelf space in every major department store. In the middle of a meeting, Winfrey asked, "Why would I do that?" The response from the corporate executives focused on revenue potential and her personal enrichment. She then asked, "And what would be the other reason?" After they scrambled to improvise the concept of "creating a cosmetic line with a purpose"—with no clear idea of what that purpose might be—Winfrey turned down the offer.

A lack of empathy for and consideration of a powerful business-woman's purpose had killed the deal. In particular, the cosmetics executives failed to understand that, as the complete owner of her enterprise, Winfrey was not answering to shareholders and, with all of her success, was well past getting starry-eyed by the promise of national reach and more money. The assumption that Winfrey would automatically relate to a cosmetics line for women of color without further thought or reason was too superficial at best and an insult at worst. Of course, Winfrey's trademark intuition must have immediately told her that her counterparts were winging it anyway.

APPRECIATE WHAT THEY DO

When it comes to relating to powerful people, we must remain realistic and have sympathy at the same time. As we have seen, waiting for a domineering powerful person to subjugate his or her ego and turn into a caring and modest leader will likely be a futile endeavor. So is taking it upon yourself to change them into someone they simply are not or, if we are in the image management business, trying to portray them as such. Steve Jobs, Rupert Murdoch, Ferdinand Piëch, Frank Stronach, Norman Schwarzkopf, Margaret Thatcher, and their peers will never be "nice people" (nor will they profess to be) and will always be challenging taskmasters. Thus, when Xerox's Ursula Burns is described as a "classic New Yorker" who is known for "being very frank,"[8] we can probably guess by now what that might look like in practice.

The point is, however, that we can respect and even admire them while remaining realistic as to who they are. Therefore, with larger-than-life characters, you can appreciate that with their brilliance, energy, and charisma, they make an extraordinary contribution to our world and pursue worthwhile endeavors with unmatched vigor. In addition, working for and with them can offer unique experiences and learning opportunities. And it is not something you have to do for your entire life. In other words, you make a rational calculation of the trade-off, and you decide that it is worthwhile to put in the required effort and grow thick skin. The reality may simply be that you need the job for now. If you cannot come to that conclusion, you run the danger of becoming quite miserable. There may also be instances where the person you have been working with changes and causes you to lose the admiration that was there in the early days. But even then, you will want to make a gracious exit and remember everything you have learned, the opportunity you have been given, and the great things that have been achieved.

> *You must develop an accurate understanding of, and basic appreciation for, the powerful person and what he or she is trying to accomplish. Better still, you have to like the person, even if you do not always agree with or approve of the person's actions.*

Again, I believe Colin Powell's attitude is exemplary. He recounts his transoceanic shouting matches with Norman Schwarzkopf that were filled with barracks profanity. He also acknowledges that Schwarzkopf's subordinates took plenty of heat. But Powell says he and

Schwarzkopf developed a mutual respect for each other that eventually grew into a deepening affection. And he considered Schwarzkopf to be the right man in the right place.[9]

Therefore, when working closely with a powerful person, you need at least a measure of "sympathetic" empathy in addition to accurate empathy. Or as one former executive who worked closely with a powerful person featured in this book put it to me: "You basically have to like the man."

Working for Powerful Individuals Is Different

The importance of an empathetic relationship when working for a powerful individual is highlighted by two very different chief executive officers who headed up the automotive part of Frank Stronach's Magna. One of them is American auto executive John Doddridge. Doddridge joined Magna in May 1993, leaving a successful career at Dana Corporation. As a highly competent and professional manager with a large-company background, he was expected to take a more structured approach to running a rapidly growing Magna. The hope was that he would help the company mature from an entrepreneurial, risk-taking company into a more professionally managed operation.[10] According to Wayne Lilley's account, the plan seemed to be working when Frank Stronach announced he was moving permanently to Europe. While he was not "retiring," at least it appeared that he was stepping back from mainstream management. Once in Europe, however, Stronach was buoyed by the abundant opportunities and started to draw on Magna's North American profits to get things going—without, of course, asking John Doddridge for permission. "A company can't have two CEOs,"[11] was Doddridge's comment after resigning from his new post less than two years into the job. "It wasn't working and I didn't want to be there as a figurehead."[12]

Doddridge was quickly replaced by Frank Stronach's (now former) son-in-law, Don Walker. The thirty-eight-year-old Walker had built a track record in the Magna organization after having worked for seven years at General Motors in engineering and manufacturing positions, including involvement in the launch of new vehicles. He shared his father-in-law's views on the power of investment in technology, a rapid European expansion, and a can-do culture. He ran Magna's day-to-day business in North America and met with his father-in-law/chairman when he was in Canada to discuss his long-term strategy. Far from being a figurehead, Don Walker nonetheless understood that his position was not like any other chief executive officer's job. His competence as an auto executive *and* his effective working relationship with the still-dominant chairman led to growth and prosperity for Magna. Walker also stepped aside with ease to hand the chief executive job to his (then) wife Belinda Stronach in 2001 and went on to become chief executive officer of Intier, a Magna spin-off, only to return as Magna's co-CEO in 2005. Accurate and sympathetic empathy made Walker a successful and lasting fixture in Frank Stronach's empire.

LISTEN AND REFLECT UNDERSTANDING

As a practical point, it is critical not just to have the understanding of the powerful person but also to reflect that understanding back to that person. Powerful people must know that you know what they are trying to achieve. They must know that you understand them. This will prove especially effective if you can organize, articulate, and present their thoughts more clearly than they have been able to do up to this point.

This is a point of general application. It has been said that being understood is one of the greatest human needs. That is why even murderers whose culpability could have never been in doubt are entitled to representation in court. The point of representation is not (just) to try to get them off the hook, but to explain to others, on their behalf, what led to the crime. It is what defense attorney turned novelist Ferdinand von Schirach has called "a pleading for human dignity."[13] That is also why effective, win-win-oriented negotiators place such a premium on listening and understanding.

Ultimately, this means that when dealing with intense bosses, you must learn to listen well. Like anything else when dealing with extreme characters, you may have to go to extreme lengths to do it.

For example, if someone like Frank Stronach loves to explain his theory of "fair enterprise," you must listen even if you have heard it many times. That is certainly what David Einhorn, a hedge fund manager and powerful person in his own right, did when he met Frank Stronach for the first time.[14] Without question, Einhorn took the famous felt-tip marker illustration depicting the enterprise model as a memento of the meeting. There could be nothing worse, in a situation like that, than rolling your eyes or showing impatience or even boredom. Instead, if you listen with all antennae focused, you show respect and, as a bonus, may end up learning something new. The story usually has a way of evolving with greater nuance over time, and you can use the opportunity to let the powerful person know (again) that you understand his or her perspective. Since you are a captive audience, you might as well use the time productively.

Psychologists and negotiation experts call this process active listening. It consists of asking clarifying questions, paraphrasing what has been said, and acknowledging emotions. It is an essential skill when dealing with powerful people. They are so full of ideas and thoughts that they need to get them out of their system before they may be able to take anything in.

Robert Mnookin, the director of the Harvard Negotiation Research Project, therefore stresses that you must let people say their piece and, if necessary, blow off steam if you want to get their attention when it is your turn to speak. You must show them that you have listened and that you have understood.[15]

That's especially true if what you're being asked to pay attention to is the discussion of a problem, in which case you must acknowledge it. Salespeople who deal with angry customers understand this point especially well. Proper and genuine acknowledgment of the customer's frustration is the only way to move toward resolution and keep the customer coming back. If you are dealing with a senior financial manager who is upset that your numbers are behind, don't launch into a justification right away. Acknowledge that, yes, the numbers are behind. Once the manager knows you have understood the problem, you can get into the reasons why and the turnaround plan. As explained in the art of confession (see Rule 6), it does not pay to minimize mistakes. Be matter-of-fact, and almost put yourself into the position of having taken over your project from someone else; most people are better at pointing out others' mistakes.

Properly reflecting understanding back can be extremely powerful in a cross-cultural business environment. A common source of conflict is the fact that rules, policies, and business practices emanating from headquarters do not work when they are brought down to the local business environment. For example, if a company standardizes a certain model of company cars, it will likely get pushback from local managers in countries where the car you drive defines who you are. But nothing will drive the head-office manager crazier than a local manager who will immediately launch into an argument of why this won't work. If you first explain your understanding of the rules and their reasons, you will become the person who gets it. You show that you are conversant in both cultures. You then can become a credible partner for mediating the conflict—an activity that we will explore in more detail in Rule 12.

> *Careful listening and reflecting your understanding back in a manner that fits the powerful person's learning and communication style is a prerequisite for providing input and counsel of your own.*

LOOK OUT FOR "IMMEDIATE CONCERNS"

When listening to a powerful person, you must resist the urge to follow a set agenda, even though, of course, it is good to have one prepared. The reason is that powerful people often have things on their mind that supersede what you came to discuss. In fact, their world is so full of change and turbulence that any one issue might have become a preoccupation. Those concerns, crises, or unexpected opportunities are real, and they become what matters now. You cannot ignore them. While your role may be to steer the agenda back to its original purpose, you must listen and make an assessment as to whether or not the new issue has taken over completely.

If that is indeed the case, you must preserve your mental flexibility and dump the previously established agenda of the meeting. You may even have to go as far as postponing a meeting with people who have made an extended journey to attend. While that is potentially embarrassing, you have to realize that the meeting would be derailed anyway. Postponing at least provides an opportunity to pick things up another time. And, as we will see, it is your job to manage this change with other people in the most elegant way possible.

Even when dealing with people in the peer category, the concept of the immediate concern is powerful. If people arrive after a harrowing trip, let them tell the story. In one leadership seminar, I noticed that some participants were distracted by a business issue. Rather than exhorting them to concentrate on the topic at hand, I gave the class a thirty-minute break to allow them to set an action plan in motion. In return, I asked for their commitment to the rest of the class. They dealt with their immediate concern, and we were able to move on.

FIGURE OUT THEIR COMMUNICATION STYLE

Effectively reflecting back and communicating your own perspective requires sensitivity to the leader's communication style. Typically, you will have to be precise and to the point. Many powerful people will be suspicious if an issue cannot be explained on one or two pages or better still in three crisp points with a compelling conclusion. They don't have time for chitchat and long explanations; with a larger-than-life business or political leader, a few minutes will be all the time you have! Therefore, preparing talking points is not reserved for presentations to large audiences. It forces you to order your mind for any important conversation.

Peter Drucker made the now-classic distinction between being a "reader" and a "listener," and he maintained that people are rarely both. He told the story of General Dwight Eisenhower, who was a darling of the press as supreme commander of the Allied Forces in Europe and was held in open contempt by the press ten years later as president. The difference was that as supreme commander, Eisenhower had received all questions in writing ahead of time. Accordingly, he made a grave error when he adopted the free-for-all press conferences favored by his "listener" predecessors Franklin D. Roosevelt and Harry Truman. Hearing questions was very different from reading them. In the reverse manner, Lyndon Johnson kept John F. Kennedy's writers on staff even though he was a listener. According to Drucker, President Johnson apparently "never understood one word of what they wrote."[16]

Therefore, one of the first questions should be whether the powerful person in our lives is a reader or a listener and how that person takes in information. Thus, if Frank Stronach loves simple depictions of his fair-enterprise model, it will likely be more effective to present thoughts to him in a clear, compelling, and easily depicted structure as well—which will also help with a notoriously short attention span. If, as the story goes, he does not respond well to PowerPoint presentations and would be averse to the format "even if it had been prepared by Steven Spielberg himself,"[17] then in dealing with such a presence, the medium you choose to deliver your message has the potential to devalue the content you're trying to express. Therefore, give careful consideration as to whether you want to speak, write, or present to the powerful person you are trying to engage. (It also goes again without saying that disciplined thought and order must go into anything you are communicating. While the powerful person has the privilege of thinking out loud, you certainly do not.)

Different styles can also relate to big picture or detail. A senior sales leader may get excited by vivid descriptions of opportunities even in anecdotal format; a financial person may want a spreadsheet with detailed analysis and rates of return. No matter what you do, you must speak the language of your audience.

There are further variations on the theme of effective communication. We can learn one of them from Robin Uler, the chief creative officer of the Marriott hotel chain, who needed to convince the seventy-seven-year-old chairman and chief executive officer that the brand needed sprucing up. *Fortune*'s Marc Gunther tells the story of Uler taking Bill Marriott Jr. to dinner at Prime One Twelve, a high-end steak house in Miami's South Beach.[18] Noisy and crowded, with wood floors, contemporary décor, and a menu to match, the place was hopping despite its high prices. Then they returned to the Marriott restaurant across the street, which was dead. "So do you still want carpets and booths far away from another with no noise?" Uler asked him. In this case, the experience was worth a thousand words.

Ferdinand Piëch used the same technique when he was still at Audi and wanted to build the now-legendary four-wheel-drive Audi Quattro. He had to convince Volkswagen's president, Toni Schmucker —a sales expert and (shockingly) not a car designer—that the high development costs were worthwhile. So he arranged for Schmucker to try driving a front-wheel drive Audi 100 up a grassy slope that his engineers had earlier drenched with water. He then gave the boss a four-wheel-drive car that negotiated the slope easily. The project, so the story goes, was soon approved.[19]

LISTENING MAY REQUIRE SOME WORK

An important variation relates to the fact that sometimes listening may require doing some work. If the powerful person is convinced of a certain approach, it may be advisable to give the plan a try, rather than arguing against it too early, even if you are convinced that the person is wrong. Having tried the approach with a genuine effort shows the powerful person that you have listened. Ideally, you won't have to take that type of active listening too far. For example, you may get away with translating your boss's thoughts into a detailed project plan from which some of the flaws may naturally emerge when you discuss it with him or her. The point is that if you are willing to render some of your own work and effort obsolete in the process of listening, you will add credibility to your argument. Better still, if you build the plan, the boss can demonstrate why it does not work!

The solution to our introductory case at the beginning of this chapter falls into this category. It would be a big mistake for our (junior) communications manager to simply reject the suggestion of writing a letter to the editor. The danger is that the partner feels the communications manager does not understand how important her reputation is. In fact, he should tell her that her reputation is important. He should even go as far as drafting the letter. The letter to the editor would, in fact, show how well he understands the problem. Once they review the brilliant draft letter, the communications manager has a platform for putting forward his view of not sending it. In fact, he would even throw away his own carefully crafted work. That approach requires more effort, but it demonstrates respect, understanding, and a serious approach to the executive's concerns. It gives tremendous credibility to the advice against sending a letter. While you may not always be able to spend that amount of time and effort, you must look at such expenditures as an investment in the relationship that will pay off when similar issues occur in the future.

DON'T GUESS: STICK WITH WHAT YOU KNOW

One trap you cannot afford to fall into when communicating with a powerful person is to give a definitive answer to a question when in fact you are unsure. Saying "I don't know" beats making assertions that are not grounded in actual knowledge. According to Rick Atkinson, this was exactly the advice that Norman Schwarzkopf's deputy Calvin Waller gave to the chief of intelligence during Operation Desert Storm. The intelligence officer, General John Leide, was exhausted from a series of twenty-hour workdays and had repeatedly endured Schwarzkopf's temper. Leide was taking it upon himself to provide the commander with *exact* combat effectiveness reports of Iraqi troops when there was in fact no way to obtain exact numbers. This became evident when Schwarzkopf challenged the reports and their supposed exactness. Deputy Waller, the experienced "manager of the Schwarzkopf account," told Leide, "There will be times when you'll have to tell him, 'Sir, I just don't know.'"[20] Based on Waller's advice, Leide put in place a "common sense" estimation system that combined objective damage assessment of enemy units with subjective estimates. The former were clearly marked with an O, the latter with an X. Incidentally, Schwarzkopf, who liked common sense, came to appreciate the system and took it as an example of "using sound military judgment."[21]

> *If you don't know, say so—or say nothing.*

Stay Close

In addition to listening and communicating well, building a relationship with a powerful person will require staying close to that person. Contact is as important as content. Of course, we are running yet again into a bit of a contradiction, as I have earlier, in Rules 4 and 5, warned against the danger of energy-consuming overexposure and the perils of socializing with the powerful person. As with so many of these principles, there is a tension of competing principles that requires fine-tuning and balance that ultimately can be achieved only through experimentation. Therefore, spending time with the powerful person should be a regular activity and, as we have seen, should be used for keen observation of thoughts and patterns. That exposure will also make it possible to understand issues without too much explanation or any at all, something an impatient powerful person will certainly appreciate.

Staying close will also allow you to keep track of the latest changes, as well as the influence of others, who may be just as skilled at getting to the boss. A second Bismarck story told by Erich Eyck illustrates the point. In 1863, Bismarck had been working hard to diminish Austria's influence as a counterweight to Prussia in Germany. Dissuading King William from accepting an Austrian invitation to attend the Congress of German Princes in Frankfurt held that year was critical to his plan. King William, at this time, was on a spa vacation at Gastein on Austrian territory. On the advice of his ministers, Austrian emperor Francis Joseph decided to pay the king a personal visit and to present his invitation. This seemed to be the most polite way and the one that promised the best chance of success. But Bismarck was with the king at Gastein. He wanted to be near the king as much as possible in order to prevent the monarch from being subjected to influences opposed to his policy. Indeed, Eyck concluded that there could have been no doubt that William would have accepted the invitation if he had been alone and left to his own counsel.[22]

Staying close to his superior at a critical moment was a key part of Bismarck's success in uniting the German Empire with Prussia as its hegemon and himself as chancellor. In today's world, few take the time and leisure to relax for weeks at a spa town, though perhaps a round of golf is the modern equivalent. More likely, they will be traveling around the world. But making the effort to stay in touch is critical to keeping priorities straight and avoiding surprises.

> *You cannot afford to ignore the fact that others may be good influencers, too.*

Staying close to a powerful boss can be difficult if you work in a global company where the boss may be far away and you have become part of a virtual team. Sending a weekly informal update via e-mail, in addition to the required formal reports, may help. Don't put it into an attachment, but make it easy to read and digest on a handheld device. It allows the boss to catch up with you at his or her own pace (maybe during a flight) and simply hit the return button. Especially when there is a language barrier, I have found this form of regular informal updates very effective. However, e-mail and telephone calls are no complete replacement for personal interaction, so it may make sense to catch up with a world traveler on a portion of his or her trip.

Michael Wolff makes the additional point that people who communicate well and hold the powerful person's attention can have significant influence if they are the last one the boss has talked to.[23] There is no question: you cannot afford for the wrong person to be that last person!

What to do when . . .

. . . you are quitting because you have a better job

You have received a great job offer and have decided to move on. However, you are somewhat apprehensive about telling the boss.

Leaving the employ of a powerful person is harder than you may think. Experienced executive search consultants will coach their prospective hires extensively to make sure they go through with the transition. Once you have made up your mind, it will most often be best to stick with your decision even if there is a counteroffer. Prepare a script of talking points and, if necessary, practice. Express your appreciation for what you have learned and the respect you have for the powerful person and his or her company.

Decide carefully whether you want to share where you are going. Some powerful people have been known to place a phone call and convince the new employer to rescind the offer.

Sidestep Power with Diplomacy

It requires political savvy to get things done.

—JEFFREY PFEFFER, THOMAS D. DEE II PROFESSOR
OF ORGANIZATIONAL BEHAVIOR, STANFORD UNIVERSITY

A junior relationship partner at a large law firm had a request from a client to reduce a bill on a sizable account. The client was beside himself because he felt the firm's billing practices were fraudulent. The client threatened to sue, take the matter to the press, and do whatever else might be necessary "to teach the firm a lesson." The partner felt that, while the firm had done nothing wrong, some of the billing rules were not client-friendly. Also she was a bit shaken, since the client had threatened her directly. For a reduction of this size, the partner needed the approval of the senior managing partner, so she called him into a meeting, along with the manager of administration and the two associates who had done most of the work on the file. The junior partner presented her request to reduce the bill, and when the senior partner pushed back, she explained that the client had threatened her. That comment changed the tone of the meeting completely. "I will not give in to threats; this meeting is over," were the last words she heard.

Powerful people will typically say they like to be "direct"—and they certainly are when they are dealing with us, the less powerful. According to her profile in *Fortune*, Indra Nooyi's famous "love letters" include statements like "I have never seen such gross incompetence" or "This is unacceptable" with *unacceptable* underlined three times.[1] The tremendous intuition of these leaders also gives them a sonar-like sensor when someone hesitates with an answer or appears "political" in other ways. Accordingly, some individuals may approach working with powerful people in a candid and straightforward manner. If that's possible with your boss, count your blessings.

Experience and research suggest, however, that in most instances, diplomacy (the art of the indirect) and political savvy do have important roles to play. One research study, for example, started with the bias that politics in organizations arise when power is decentralized. Yet the evidence from the data told a different story. Specifically, the finding was that "the greater the centralization of power in a chief executive, the greater the use of politics within a top management team."[2] Jeffrey Pfeffer quotes Henry Kissinger with a similar insight:

> Before I served as a consultant to Kennedy, I had believed, like most academics, that the process of decision-making was largely intellectual and all one had to do was to walk into the President's office and convince him of the correctness of one's view. This perspective I soon realized is as dangerously immature as it is widely held.[3]

You have to be keenly aware that linear, straightforward communication can easily create resentment, resistance, and a reaction of "Who do you think you are?"—especially when you are trying to introduce unpopular thoughts. In our introductory example, the direct approach failed predictably: The senior partner had to show everyone present that he was unwavering and would not give in to threats, nor should anyone else in the firm. The junior partner's request became a platform to teach that very important lesson to the team.

Figure out whether the powerful people in your life appreciate and react well to straightforward communication. If they do, count your blessings!

Therefore, there usually is a right time, a right place, and a right way of saying or doing things, one that will take into account the idiosyncrasies, preferences, likes, dislikes, moods, circumstances, and, yes, the ego of the powerful person. You should remember that introducing an opposing view may take some time; slowing the powerful person down and buying some time is often the proper immediate goal and preferable to all-out opposition and confrontation.

Avoid Public Conflict

The first practical application of the diplomacy rule is therefore the avoidance of public conflict. It can easily lead to great overreaction and, in extreme cases, provoke dismissal on the spot. That is not to mean you will never stand up to a powerful person. But it means that public confrontation in the middle of a heated outburst is typically not the way to do it. Prime Minister Thatcher is a case in point. One of her advisers noted that, individually or with a few people, Thatcher would listen profoundly. But in a group, where she was determined to get her way, she was inclined not to listen but to hammer her point home. In Blema Steinberg's analysis, for Thatcher, as a dominant personality, the only way to survive in this world was to dominate and control it.[4] Getting in the way of hammer blows is rarely advisable.

People who worked for Bill Paley and Ted Rogers also knew better than to challenge their boss in public. Jeffrey Pfeffer writes that "Stanton understood how important it was not to threaten or challenge Paley in public, and to maintain Paley's feeling of being in control."[5]

Likewise, according to Caroline Van Hasselt, Bob Francis, late chief financial officer for Ted Rogers, would just sit back and listen to his boss's outbursts. He didn't feel he had to respond in kind. His advice on how to handle a blow-up was "Don't react to a situation, but listen. Listen to it.'"[6]

Listen. Again, that's brilliant advice. Not only do you benefit from focusing on the information rather than the noise, it is also very difficult to stay mad at someone who is intently listening. The much better way is to deal with the temper explosion after the meeting and in a one-on-one environment. Thus, Frank Stanton would argue hard with Bill Paley after the meeting and tenaciously hold to his positions. For example, he convinced Paley to issue stock options to top CBS executives after enduring several "changes of the mind" and overcoming the objection that the plan would cut into Paley's own position.[7] As we have seen earlier, even private conflict can be prolonged and will require energy to settle.

One of the most skillful lessons on the wisdom of avoiding public confrontation is delivered by John Tory, a former Rogers executive. The episode would certainly be worthy of a business school case study on the topic. I will start with Ted Rogers's own account in his memoirs, which we will then analyze in some detail. Rogers started by acknowledging that he had a temper and a reputation for shouting and slamming doors. The episode in question occurred in 1999, when Tory, then the president of the cable company, called Rogers out on how often he lost his temper. According to Rogers, Tory said the following:

> You are a dear friend and I have to tell you something . . . . You are an icon in these people's eyes. To be in a meeting with you is an honor and privilege for them, for all of us. But they are not in your so-called "inner circle," so they don't know you the way we do. They admire you and your accomplishments, and rightly so. You have achieved so many great things in your life and when you fly off the handle it lessens you right before them. You simply cannot treat people this way. [8]

At first Rogers thought Tory was exaggerating, and said as much. But his response did not impress Tory. In fact, it infuriated him, and he seized the moment to press the point. After getting up and closing the office door, he told the founder his views about losing one's temper in business: It simply is not good for the boss, the company, and is certainly not good for the person on the other end.[9] Getting into a rage himself (probably because he wasn't really getting anywhere), Tory raised his voice and even swore at the boss, something that was really out of character.

Confront a powerful person in front of others only if you absolutely have to; it could well be your last exchange. Taking conflict off-line into a one-on-one setting is by far the better approach.

Rogers eventually did concede that his lieutenant had made some valid points.

He agreed that he was treating good people unfairly, that he was diminishing himself before them by not controlling his temper, and that he was generating way too much stress and putting his own health at risk. After taking the night to think about the exchange, Rogers returned the next day to thank Tory for raising the issue. In his memoirs, he presented the following conclusion:

> It is not easy for people to change who they are, but [Tory] was right: this behavior was not conducive to running the company well. I have tried to change. I am still hard-driving, but I have succeeded in controlling my temper better. As I said, it is not easy to admit one's failings—to say nothing of publicly disclosing them in a book for the world to see—but there you have the true story about how Ted Rogers slew his legendary temper.[10]

John Tory's intervention was a masterpiece in assertive diplomacy and is well worth reviewing from his perspective:

1. Tory does not take on Rogers during one of his tirades. He speaks to Rogers when they are alone in Rogers's office.
2. He seizes the moment when Rogers brings up the issue of his temper; he obviously has it on his mind. Tory knew intuitively that powerful people can't listen when they are preoccupied by other immediate concerns.
3. Tory appeals to Rogers's status as an icon and his image as a revered business leader; he appeals first to his boss's image and ego. The message is "I am doing this to make you look better." He then introduces the good of the company and people at the receiving end as secondary concerns.
4. He makes it clear that he, John Tory, can take the yelling and so can the inner circle. Therefore, he does not say that *he* can't take it anymore (which would have been a sign of weakness), but that he is intervening on behalf of more junior people who don't know Rogers as well. This inference also allows Rogers to save face. The implication is that Rogers and Tory know that Rogers means well; it is the others who do not.
5. He shows some passion himself when Rogers pushes back, including the dramatic gesture of closing the door as well as raising his voice and swearing, both of which are out of

character. He shows grit and that he is not a pushover. The contrast between raising his voice and his usual calm demeanor increases the effect. A note of caution, however: while showing passion at the right moment can have the desired effect, swearing at the boss rarely accomplishes much and can easily backfire.

6. Tory pushes hard but is not looking for immediate resolution. He gives Rogers time to reflect and come to his own conclusions. The immediate goal is to make the point with empathy ("I know you mean no harm when you yell") and assertiveness ("You have to listen to what I say; this is serious"). However, he does not expect Rogers to capitulate right then and there.

7. John Tory was the right person for giving the feedback. He had a strong relationship with Rogers, he was respected, and his goal was to help Rogers, not tear him down.

The combination of these seven points beats shouting back in front of others anytime.

Ask Questions

Other diplomatic techniques for raising objections must become part of your repertoire as well. A low-key way of making a suggestion or presenting an objection is phrasing it in the form of a question. This technique works especially well for more junior people or outside facilitators. Asking a question avoids responses like "Who do you think you are?" or "That's a really stupid idea." Or at least, it mitigates the risk. Contrary to popular wisdom, some powerful people do believe there is such a thing as a stupid question.

To state the obvious, the more intelligent the question, the better. David D'Alessandro tells the story of how "his bosses suddenly looked at him as if he might be the most valuable person in the room"; this occurred just because he had asked an intelligent question. At the time, John Hancock was considering a joint venture with the Colombian government, and D'Alessandro asked whether the threat of guerilla warfare could pose an undue risk.[11] Question diplomacy, of course, has the additional advantage of allowing powerful persons to figure things out for themselves and see the eventual decision as their idea.

Asking questions is a smart way to make a point and parlay your ideas into their ideas. Making it theirs is the best guarantee of implementation.

A further strategy to employ is to ask questions of others, especially if you know their answers. In preparation for a project meeting with a collection of powerful people, I learned that one of the outside advisers had a particularly good idea. However, it conflicted with the thinking of one of the people who would be present, and we wanted to avoid the impression that the outside adviser was pushing a particular agenda or taking over the meeting. When the time came, I simply asked him a question, which allowed him to make his contribution without being perceived as pushy.

Create the Right Environment for Congenial Interaction

Other variations of the art of indirect suggestion relate to helping the powerful person adopt the right frame of mind when looking at an issue. This can be done in a number of practical ways.

The story of selling a proposal to Bill Paley, told by Sally Bedell Smith, serves as an illustration. Early in his career as CBS president, Frank Stanton concocted a scheme with the head of sales, William Hylan. They were looking to push a plan for an early-morning news and information program that had been proposed by the CBS station manager from New York, Arthur Hayes. Hylan knew that the chairman (Paley) looked down on the stations. He therefore placed the proposal on a coffee table in his apartment on an evening when Paley was joining him for cocktails. Sure enough, "when Paley arrived, he spotted the report on the table in [Hylan's] living room, and asked Hylan what it was. Hylan told him, Paley leapt on the idea, and directed Hayes to implement it. Had Paley received a formal proposal from Hayes, a mere station man, he might well have spurned it."[12]

The additional lesson from this story is that Stanton and Hylan put Paley into the role of a man of action who can make things happen. Had the proposal been made in a formal meeting of CBS management or even of the board, over which he was presiding, Paley could have easily felt that his role was to shoot holes into it and do a bit of grandstanding. Therefore, setting the stage properly can make the difference between enthusiastic support for and all-out opposition to an idea or proposal.

For that, we do not always need a cocktail party. For instance, you can create a circumstance where the powerful person happens upon a proposal that is lying on your desk or being discussed in a meeting at a time where they are "just dropping by." Often a powerful leader will be curious as to what is going on, and you can introduce the issue on the spot, even if "we are not quite ready." This spontaneity will likely appeal to the leader's sense of being the person who can remove bureaucracy and get things done without getting caught up in normal channels. Framing the situation in the right way can transform the powerful person from a "change blocker" into a change agent.

> Generate situations that put the powerful person into the role of a change agent, rather than a change blocker.

Decide Who Communicates

In the context of objection and controversy, sidestepping rather than confronting resistance becomes a critical issue, and thought should be given as to who is charged with approaching the boss. Having a friendly, empathetic messenger can go a long way. If, for example, a board of directors is thinking of opposing the powerful chief executive's plans, the board members may want to send a friendly director ahead. Thus, when Ted Rogers was overruled sixteen-to-one in the decision against entering the wireless business, one board member helped him with a plan to invest privately and have the company take over the venture at a later time.[13]

When you think about approaching a person who may not outrank you but works in a different department, you must realize that such a person can easily be worried about his or her turf and get defensive as a result. I once was told by a technical support manager that he had a tough time interfacing with a production manager. The reason was that people in production perceived the tech support manager as a representative of the sales organization, which had a long history of complaining about product quality in order to explain why sales were down. But once he had convinced

> *Present yourself as a friendly helper when introducing thorny issues.*

the production manager that he was on that manager's side and was looking to help him solve his problems, the conversation changed completely.

Going back to our example of the board of directors versus the chief executive, the friendly messenger can communicate obstacles to the CEO as follows: "I understand what you [the powerful person] are trying to accomplish with this strategic investment. You know we will need board approval or at least need to notify the board. We need to prepare for the board meeting and prepare our answers in case objections are raised [by those who do not understand your vision because they are concerned with lesser things such as spreadsheet return on investment, liability avoidance, governance, etc.]." Now the objections are being presented by a friendly helper who is trying to pave the way. At the very least, the powerful person is now put in a position where he or she can listen to the objections without viewing them as confrontational or the result of insubordination. In the course of working through the arguments against the objections, the chief executive and friendly helper may actually discover that some objections are valid and should be addressed. Again, they can figure out for themselves why the plan won't work. The remaining objections will at least be better understood so that there is no (or less) need for hostility. The powerful person can listen to the arguments and think about them without having to provide an answer right away.

At a minimum, this approach will reduce boardroom confrontation. The example also makes it clear that meetings with powerful people require preparation and an understanding of potentially controversial issues. Having controversy surface as a surprise will almost always lead to a stubborn, defensive posture: "Just watch me."

This strategy of a friendly messenger also underscores that, taken to an extreme, the requirement for independent directors under governance rules can become counterproductive. In many instances, a relationship is needed in order to facilitate constructive communication. Therefore, in the case of controlled public companies, investors should withstand the urge to be too quick to criticize non-independent directors (according to the technical definition), as such directors may be playing a very important role.

Diplomacy Can Be Assertive

At times, there will be issues where you have to push harder in order to be convincing. And there is a place for assertive diplomacy. One way of doing this is to make an issue personal. As in the earlier example of John Tory confronting Ted Rogers about his temper, you can display some passion that shows the powerful person you care about the issue and the organization as much as he or she does. And you can let the powerful person know that you, like him or her, have skin in the game.

One of Norman Schwarzkopf's subordinates—in fact, we are told by Rick Atkinson that he was the general's favorite—teaches that lesson well. Barry McCaffrey was a division commander during Desert Storm and he had much of his boss's flamboyance, fearlessness, and controversial manner. During a briefing, he assured Defense Secretary Dick Cheney that his attack plan on Jalibah, a base in southern Iraq, would be achieved with speed, hard-hitting violence, and minimal U.S. casualties. Cheney was not sold and asked the general what he was worried about. "I am a very cautious person," McCaffrey replied slowly. "I've been wounded in combat three times. My son is in the 82nd Airborne and his life is at stake." He paused, and then leaned toward Cheney with dramatic effect, saying, "But I am not worried about a thing." McCaffrey's speech got everyone's attention and made the point powerfully. Cheney was impressed.[14]

Colin Powell tells us of using a similar tactic on General Schwarzkopf. In one episode dealing with whether the purpose of the war was not only to liberate Kuwait but also to destroy Iraq's offensive capability, Schwarzkopf attacked Powell viciously. He charged him with political expediency while he, Schwarzkopf, was looking out for the lives of his soldiers. Powell, who had prided himself in ignoring Schwarzkopf's attacks, lost it. The suggestion that only the on-the-ground commander cared about American lives infuriated the chairman. With a roar that filled his office, he lashed out: "Wait a minute buddy! Don't you patronize me! Don't pull that on me, that *we* don't care about soldiers." As abruptly as it began, the storm subsided.[15]

McCaffrey's and Powell's performances clearly confirm that there does come a time where some drama and personal conviction will carry the day. Learn from our powerful bosses how it is done well, because many of them are masters of passion and drama. Especially when you are involved in interdepartmental conflict, where one group—say, finance or marketing—has the greater power, there comes a time to assert that everyone is contributing to the organization. In those instances, you can use an insult on their part strategically and as a launching point for some righteous indignation. For example, if someone calls your department noncontributing overhead, you can use it as a launch pad to explain what you do and how hard you work. Don't counter with an insult of your own. In other words, when you are insulted, don't waste the opportunity to hold the moral high ground, but do set the record straight.

However, a word of caution on the Powell episode: Yes, there comes a time when righteous indignation will be called for. And there comes a time when the rule prohibiting public conflict must be suspended. But we must remember that Powell was not just any subordinate. In fact, while an impressive model of confident humility, he was the chairman of the Joint Chiefs of Staff.

Be Ready to Seize the Moment

Diplomacy requires flexibility. We have seen earlier that powerful people can be distracted by an immediate concern, or they can be in a combative mood. In these instances, it will be better to quietly close your file folder with the list of issues to be discussed or to say that your proposal needs more work. Living to fight another day beats a firm no anytime.

The reverse is equally true. If there is an opening for constructive discussion, you must be ready to seize it. Practically speaking, you must have your paperwork and list of issues with you at all times, so you can take advantage of an

> *Be ready to discuss issues when the situation is favorable and postpone when the time is not right.*

unscheduled meeting or telephone call with some extra time. This is where even the dreaded ride on the company plane can turn into an opportunity. But always remember to quit while you are ahead. Once you have made your point and your proposal or idea has been accepted, it is time to shut up and move on.

Keep Focused on Realistic Goals: Take It One Step at a Time

Finally, if you do get into a debate with a powerful person, you have to keep the goal in mind. Working with humility, diplomacy, and (undetected) tenacity, your first goal often is not to change the powerful person's mind. Instead, your goal is to put the person in a position where he or she can listen to you and consider your views. Having the powerful person leave the meeting and start thinking is a better and certainly more realistic goal than trying to have him or her back down with the potential of a loss of face. If you are honest with yourself, how often have you been convinced in a conversation and changed your mind because the other side had the better arguments? And how often did you change your mind after quiet reflection? Again, buying time may be the most reasonable and realistic first goal of diplomacy.

> *Buying time is often a good near-term goal on the way to turning an issue around.*

What to do when . . .

. . . the powerful person appropriates your idea

You have pitched a great idea to the boss, and the next day she comes to the team meeting to present it as hers. You are furious because she does not even mention you.

While there may be people who intentionally steal ideas and don't give credit in order to make themselves look good, powerful people by and large genuinely tend to believe that others' ideas are theirs. They may even lecture you with information you have previously told them. However, making your idea their idea is a critical technique in getting it implemented. Therefore, don't sweat the appropriation. Take it as a compliment. It's par for the course.

You can, however, keep a list. If you are ever accused of not being creative or not being a team player, you may want to be able to mention your original thoughts that were picked up and "further developed" by others. You may also have to use your list if you suspect intentional and malicious idea stealing.

Guard Your Independence

**These things were wrong and needed
to be righted—simple as that.**

—RAYMOND SEITZ, U.S. AMBASSADOR TO THE UNITED KINGDOM
AND A CORPORATE DIRECTOR

E arly on in my career, I was assigned to manage an overseas project for a fearsome general manager of a business
division who had built his power base on the fact that
he "contributed most of the profits to the company." The
project was difficult, and he was pleased when it was completed
to his satisfaction. He summoned another manager and me on a
conference call to let us know that the company would send us on
vacation; his financial person would let us know "how these things
were done." Rejecting his gratitude, he told us, would be a great
offense.

Saying no to a powerful person is difficult. Powerful people can
be all-consuming, and they can cross many lines. Therefore, a last
rule related to building the relationship with powerful people is
guarding your independence. Independence provides the necessary
balance to some of the approaches we have discussed so far—in
particular, humility, diplomacy, and sympathetic empathy. It is a
critical insight that independence is not just required for the sake

of keeping your sanity and avoiding a myriad of troubles, legal and otherwise. Keeping your independence is also very much in the interest of the powerful person and the organization you serve, even if the person with power may not realize this—at the moment or ever.

In the realm of publicly traded corporations, the requirement of independence has become a central theme of post-Enron corporate governance reform. It is largely focused on a technical test of whether or not directors who sit on boards are free from (material) relationships with management. Material relationships can range from consulting contracts to prior employment and family ties. However, I believe strongly that this test has its limitations. Real independence cannot be determined by preset criteria, but rather is a function of how people actually behave. In particular, it is perfectly possible that people in a close working relationship are able to think and act more independently than those who are technically independent. The reason is that, more than anything, independence is an attitude and a mind-set. Therefore, employees, professional service providers, and family members, who by definition would not be independent because of their material relationships with a powerful chief executive, may behave much more independently than outside directors who will pass the formal definition test with ease.

Consequently, my rules of independence will not follow the preceding technical definition. Instead, you should look for "real" independence of thought and action while being committed to the best interests of the powerful person and the organization you serve.

Take Control of Your Finances

Powerful people like to control people. They are often generous but then easily become utterly demanding and all-engulfing. Therefore, depending on a powerful person to sustain your livelihood makes it even more stressful to work for them. It can cause people to anxiously anticipate and worry about that person's whims and fancies. If persons with power are known, as we have seen, to fire people without a second thought, the brutal reality is that every day could be your last—and that should be OK. Working with a powerful person can be an exciting roller coaster, but you should be prepared to step off (or fall off, whichever the case may be) at any time.

Incidentally, even if your organization or department is led by the most compassionate manager imaginable, job loss may be only one "downsizing" away. All it takes is a downturn or the fact that your department is no longer part of the company's core business.

As a result, especially when you are an employee of a powerful person, there is much to be said for managing your finances prudently and living well within —or, better, below—your means. Even a modest amount of financial independence does create a different outlook on the situation and reduces worries by taking the sting out of the worst-case scenario. In contrast, living from paycheck to paycheck with a mountain of debt not only is a sure recipe for sleep-robbing stress but also will cloud your judgment.

> *Living well within or below your means is the most reliable way to keep your financial independence and reduce anxiety related to job loss.*

Employee Agreements Are Not Fireproof

Executives, of course, have the possibility of relying for financial independence on employment agreements with severance clauses. However, putting in place employment agreements can be tricky for a number of reasons. The supremely confident boss may feel that the request for an employment agreement, which by its very nature anticipates dismissal, is really a sign of insecurity on the part of the executive. And as a more junior person, you may simply not have enough leverage to demand it anyway. In other instances, some chief executives will simply institute a policy against such agreements.

If you do end up negotiating severance terms, it will often be a good practice to get a reasonable third party, such as outside legal counsel or a search executive, to act as an intermediary. Of course, these experts would need some skill in dealing with powerful people. But their critical contribution will be to attest to the fact that the contemplated provisions (and, by extension, you) are reasonable and customary.

A key element of an executed employee agreement is, of course, that the employee is compensated after having been dismissed. The requirement to pay people for not being there, especially as a matter of predetermined obligation, can irk many bosses, especially entrepreneurs who have never worked for anyone but themselves. It can therefore lead to behavior that professional managers may classify as irrational. Of course, such an assessment forgets that those in power follow their own rationale. A powerful person who is provoked to anger may allege cause in a termination (most employment agreements include that option) and fight all the way to the Supreme Court just to prove their point. Fighting issues on principle has a long tradition in America. One of the most recent examples is Wal-Mart's $2 million fight against a $7,000 fine handed down by the federal Occupational Safety and Health Administration (OSHA), stemming from the death of a temporary employee in 2008. The employee had been trampled to death in a shoppers' stampede. The federal agency, in response to Wal-Mart's appeal, had devoted 4,725 employee-hours to the case.[1]

Therefore, you have to face the fact that while (solid) employment agreements certainly are good practice, they are not bulletproof insurance, or they may be out of reach. Leading a modest and ideally debt-free lifestyle that does not depend on the ongoing financial rewards of working for a powerful person is a safeguard of financial independence that is within your control. And it is certainly not the prerogative of those with huge compensation packages. I once had a manager working for me who, after years of disciplined saving and prudent investment, had built the financial independence to support his modest lifestyle. As a result, he did his job almost with the commitment of a volunteer, because he felt it was important and he enjoyed it. Thus, I was probably more concerned about keeping him on board than he was about losing his job.

Nothing Is Free, so Beware of Gifts

After warring on the beaches of Troy for nine years, the Greeks (also known as the Danaans) faked their withdrawal, leaving behind their famous Trojan horse. According to Virgil's *Aeneid*, the Trojan priest Laocoön distrusted the apparent good fortune and warned his countrymen with his famous (last) words: "Timeo danaos et dona ferentes" (I fear the Greeks even if they are bearing gifts). Laocoön's priestly fears were fully justified, yet his warning went unheard, and the rest is history (or myth).

Many powerful people are charismatic and generous, and they like to give gifts. In fact, generosity is one of their defining traits. I have seen the jaw-dropping impact when a Boy Scout fund-raiser received ten times the amount he was hoping for; those are great moments when working for powerful people. However, we equally have to be aware of the reality that gifts can create obligations and tie the receiver into real or imagined dependence—not legally, perhaps, but certainly socially and psychologically. In addition, the earlier referenced psychological study on power posits that "powerful people will construe others through a lens of self interest."[2] Therefore we have to reckon that some gifts may simply not be free.

David D'Alessandro's views on this point are quite interesting. On the one hand, he counsels executives to keep their private affairs to themselves and minimize social interaction at work. At the same time, he explains how he went out of his way to attend the funeral of a family member of one of his employees who had passed away in very tragic circumstances. He also used his connections to help his employees' families with medical and legal problems.[3] I am not suggesting for a moment that D'Alessandro did not have a genuine desire to lend a hand when it was needed. In fact, his actions were wonderful and admirable. But he goes on to say that his helping hand built indelible loyalty and created "a chit system [that] beats networking every time."[4] And that's just a fact that cannot be escaped.

It is therefore a good idea to keep your personal life as separate from the powerful person as possible and beware of outstanding "chits." This attitude starts by resisting the temptation to use workplace support for one's personal life. Get your own car, computer, Internet, e-mail, cell phone, etc. It makes life a lot easier in case of separation, and it avoids commingling lives. The same applies to perks such as financial planning, special health benefits, and even child care, which has become a perk of "best employers." Especially if those benefits are not portable (for example, disability insurance), you should think about making your own arrangements early on. You can liken it to this: if it is good practice to have a will and your affairs in order in case you die, it is equally prudent to have preparations made in case you lose your job.

Other gifts to be handled with care include offers to use vacation homes, fancy dinner invitations, corporate jets, and other amenities, not to even speak of loans. Having to borrow money from your boss, at least without compelling reason, sends a terrible message that you are unable to control your finances. Don't do it!

> Gifts easily create subtle or unsubtle obligations.

Of course, some social perks may be part of the job (and should be seen as such). And there will always come a time when help is genuinely offered and can be accepted without strings. But those occasions should be exceptions. "I fear the Greeks even if they are bearing gifts."

Don't Crave Approval

Pleasing a powerful person can be an elusive concept, and nothing could be more foolish and frustrating than to base one's sense of worth and security on his or her approval and affirmation. Yet this emotional dependence is a real phenomenon. I have seen managers (both junior and senior) try to gain approval where it simply was not possible. And instead of realizing that fact, they developed an insecurity and sense of inadequacy that went well beyond critical self-evaluation.

The lesson is that you must have a sense of emotional maturity. While few people will be completely emotionally independent (fully validated from within), you cannot look to the powerful person to meet those needs or try to earn such a person's approval through performance. Psychologists therefore counsel one to look elsewhere for self-esteem and not to confuse powerful leaders with parent figures.[5]

This advice about independence may sound difficult in some cultures. I had discussions with a Chinese manager who, in the Confucian tradition, saw himself as a father to his people, which included helping them with their personal affairs. A German human resource manager struggled with instruction from a U.S. headquarters to thin the subsidiary's ranks based on performance. He felt that managers with greater seniority and larger families should be given consideration. But there can be no question that "unemotional" human resource management, which looks at strategic

> *Do not look to powerful people to fulfill your emotional needs for approval and self-esteem. You will not get it.*

priorities and the desire to retain the best talent, will be the stronger current worldwide. Therefore, you cannot rely on the company to be your family. Yes, they should treat you with respect when it comes time to parting company, but they will make decisions that are the right ones for them. You cannot blame them for that, and you must move on.

Don't Wait for the Promotion

Working for a powerful person, especially those larger than life, can and should be an exciting opportunity for contribution, learning, and development. But as we have seen, you should never feel they owe you anything beyond this week's paycheck, paying the latest bill for professional services, or the director's retainer. They do not owe you affirmation or future employment, and they certainly do not owe you further career progression.

This last point requires special reinforcement. Even people as masterful as Frank Stanton had to learn that lesson the hard way. On the one hand, Stanton guarded his independence in exemplary fashion and refused to socialize with his boss: "I told him [Bill Paley] he could have me any time during business hours but not after. I was determined not to be in the position of Colin and Klauber [Bill Paley's legal advisor and administrative assistant] . . . who longed to be accepted by Bill outside the office."[6] But Stanton let his guard down when he put credence in Bill Paley's promise to make him his successor as chief executive officer of CBS, a promise on which Paley later reneged. According to Bedell Smith, this disappointment brought a tragic end to Frank Stanton's career at CBS:

Paley's betrayal had broken his spirit—at least as far as CBS was concerned. He had learned that in Paley's world, even the president of CBS was a hired hand. He coasted toward retirement, hiding his bitterness from all but a few. "In the evening, Frank would sit in my office and pour out his frustration," recalled one former CBS top man. "He would come out of meetings and his head would be red and splotchy. He would say, 'You wouldn't believe what he did to me today.'"[7]

In this context, it is important to remember that what Stanton experienced as betrayal was not necessarily intended as such. Paley had simply changed his mind, a prerogative that those in power will easily claim. They will do "what's right today." That's what you have to understand and be prepared for.

By admirable contrast, the attitude of emotional independence is exemplified by World War II hero Marshal Zhukov. After the war was over, Zhukov had fallen out of favor and was persecuted by rivals who used incriminating testimony that had been obtained under torture. By that time, his boss had also developed a growing jealousy. As a result, the marshal and commander of all Russian ground forces was sent into the equivalent of the wilderness—the relatively unimportant military district of Odessa. However, he refused to let his spirit be broken. He threw himself totally into his work and told his boss, Joseph Stalin, that "he was ready to serve wherever the Party and government desired."[8] Eventually he was fully rehabilitated.

> Remember that things can change, especially with powerful people. Don't bank on that promotion, even if it has been promised.

Beware of Changing Tides

As a further trigger of being no longer needed, you have to be ready for the fact that changes in the powerful person's circumstances—in particular, greater success—can have an impact on your ongoing employment. For example, you may play a critical role in the early days of a start-up company. You may rightfully claim that the founder could have never succeeded without you. But then the business becomes larger, and it changes; the founder may even want to project a different image, while you remind him or her of the past.

There is a lesson here: Powerful people will have a huge trajectory of development over their personal and professional lives. This will include the occasional reinvention of themselves. Bigger status and reach may allow them to surround themselves with people perceived as having a higher profile or being better able to meet their needs. Whether or not these people are actually in a better position to deliver is not the point. The point is that we cannot afford to be bitter if the powerful person feels he or she has outgrown us. We cannot expect their "loyalty" if we take that to mean an entitlement to lifetime employment. We simply say thank you and good-bye, take what we have learned, and move on to make a contribution where it is valued and appreciated.

You must consider that changing succession plans are by no means the exclusive domain of all powerful leaders. For example, your boss may have the best intentions to promote you, but the authority may rest with a corporate human resource department. You may be the most qualified succession candidate on your boss's team but have competition for the job in other departments for reasons you cannot influence. Or an expected promotion may simply fall victim to a freeze order from the finance department. In sum, there is plenty of reason not to stake your self-worth on the extent of your career progression.

While some of this will certainly be hard to swallow, you must remember that powerful people view the world from their perspective. Therefore, as Donald Trump would say, it's not personal, it's business.

And there may even be extreme cases where powerful individuals place blame on their most loyal associates. That's the story Claire Berlinski tells about Margaret Thatcher. The Iron Lady's popularity was declining at the end of her time in office. Monetary policy and rising inflation were again the problem, and Thatcher blamed her chancellor of the exchequer, Nigel Lawson, who had cabinet responsibility for all financial and economic matters. She claimed that Lawson had been following economic policy in preparation for European monetary union without her knowledge and against her wishes. A member of Thatcher's cabinet pursuing independent monetary policy does, of course, have an odd ring to it. As Claire Berlinski rightly points out, the story does not reflect well on Thatcher.[9] If Lawson was doing this without Thatcher's knowledge, she was not in control; if he was doing this against her wishes, she was not in command. In either case, she was not accepting responsibility. Lawson eventually resigned. The fact that this resignation came as a shock to his boss allows the kind conclusion that there had probably been no malice aforethought.

The Rules May Not Apply to Them, but They Do Apply to You

One of the trademark characteristics of the powerful is the shared feeling among them that they are the enterprise, so they can play by their own rules. Of course, they have the genuine conviction that for them to make the rules is truly what's best for the enterprise and its stakeholders. This is never truer than when they happen to be the owners of the enterprise in question. They are the enterprise, they can make the rules, and often the culture they have is the very reason for success. What may be harder to swallow, however, are powerful people within an organization who think they are indispensable and have been (or should have been) given carte blanche by the boss.

When dealing with this phenomenon, you must remember that the power to make and change the rules is not absolute in the final analysis. That is especially so when powerful people, by way of taking their companies public, become fiduciaries of other people's money, or when they find themselves subject to the power of others within an organization.

The epic tale of Hollinger and Conrad Black is one of the most colorful cases in point. At the time of this writing, Lord Black has been released from prison after serving a third of his sentence and winning a decision from the U.S. Supreme Court to appeal his conviction. Thus, he remains embroiled in the fight of his life.

One of the truly tragic characters in the Conrad Black saga is Peter Atkinson, Hollinger's general counsel. Atkinson has been described as a highly respected man of principle, generous, soft-spoken, and "decent to a fault."[10] His résumé includes stints as director on the boards of the highly respected Canadian Tire Corporation and Toronto Hydro. High-profile lawyers and a former federal justice minister were among the many character witnesses to testify on Atkinson's behalf during his trial as one of Conrad Black's codefendants. Once accused of wrongdoing, Atkinson agreed to fully cooperate with the auditors' investigation into controversial noncompete payments, issued a public apology, and agreed to pay back contested funds. But despite showing genuine remorse, he was convicted as one of Conrad Black's codefendants (but has joined the latest appeal) and has been said to have become a broken man.[11]

Unfortunately, Peter Atkinson is not alone. Volkswagen's high-profile human resource director, Peter Hartz, suffered a similar, and some might say worse, fate. Hartz was a key lieutenant in Ferdinand Piëch's quest to keep Volkswagen jobs in Germany—a feat we will examine in more detail when we explore Rule 10. Based on his outstanding accomplishments, he caught the attention of German Chancellor Gerhard Schröder, who made him his close and influential adviser on labor and welfare reform. Hartz helped the chancellor develop and push through a bold restructuring of the German labor market and job agencies, which became the so-called Hartz reforms. The German welfare benefit Hartz IV is named after the fourth stage of his reforms.

In 2005, however, Hartz offered his resignation and confessed to charges of kickbacks to Volkswagen managers and condoning bribes to gain the cooperation of union leaders who served as members of the Volkswagen board, a position afforded to them by way of Germany's laws on labor codetermination (*Mitbestimmung*). The union board members' votes in favor of management's initiatives were necessary in order to implement Hartz's plans. Hartz confessed to the charges and was sentenced to a prison term of two years (but was set free on probation) and to pay a fine.

Atkinson and Hartz are respectable people with otherwise sterling reputations. One could hardly charge that they became embroiled in allegations of wrongdoing because they were seeking personal gain or were rogue operators. Rather, we can assume that in their desire to get things done and make things work, they lost perspective. We cannot speculate on all the motives and issues that were involved. But one thing we know for sure: maintaining an attitude of independent and objective judgment would have gone a long way toward preventing personal disaster that was much worse than losing their jobs would have been. So keep in mind that, no matter what happens, we always remain fully responsible for our own actions.

Decide Ahead of Time

As a matter of essential practice, you need to establish *ahead of time* what you will and will not do, what you will and will not support, what you will and will not let pass. You cannot leave these decisions to the moment of pressure; they need to be made with a clear head, and you must stick to them regardless of the situation. Those decisions or personal rules must include never breaking the law; they could also include never laughing at a disrespectful joke or always registering

> *You cannot leave decisions of right and wrong to the pressure of the moment.*

your disapproval of blatant disrespect or unfairness, even if it is done in a one-on-one setting at a later time. Such and similar matters are well worth thinking through.

None of this means you automatically have to resign when you see something you don't like, and you certainly should never quit in a huff. In fact, more than once, I have observed managers retract a spontaneous resignation, especially when they realized it would cost them their severance pay. Yes, doing the right thing may cost you, but it should not cost more than it has to.

What it does mean is that, in certain instances, you take a stand with respect and clarity and are perfectly willing to accept the consequences. To do this, you need a trusted friend or family member who will, if necessary, hold you accountable and help you keep perspective in order to stay on the straight and narrow. In a way, you must give that trusted person greater power than you give the leadership you serve under and must voluntarily "seek their approval" for critical actions in the realm of right and wrong. I strongly believe that this mechanism of accountability is crucial.

Incidentally, that's how my case with the powerful division manager ended. When the extracurricular vacation was offered, I said nothing. The situation was completely new and unexpected, I had never faced anything like this before, and at least I had the spontaneous good sense not to cheerfully accept. I then mentioned the offer to my wife, who said, "Absolutely not." That left me no

> *A trusted accountability partner, whom you afford more power than you afford the powerful person, can become an essential ally in keeping your independence.*

choice but to decline, because I would rather have been fired by the company than by my wife. It is true that the conversation with the manager was a bit awkward. Later, he fell out of favor, and his business practices were reviewed. As a result, other people lost their jobs. Quite a few of them were decent individuals who had been talked into doing the wrong thing.

The Danger of Personality Fusion

On September 13, 1912, the day of Emperor Meiji's funeral, Japanese General Nogi Maresuke, the hero of the Russo-Japanese war, and his wife, Shizuko, closed the door to their second-floor living room and prepared to end their lives. He had removed his uniform and was clad in white undergarments; she wore black funeral attire. They bowed to portraits of Meiji and of their two sons killed in the war. While the funeral bells tolled, they proceeded to commit ritual suicide. Mrs. Nogi acted first with General Nogi assisting, plunging a dagger into her neck; and then he disemboweled himself with a sword. The departed hero of the Russo-Japanese War left behind ten private notes and a single death poem.[12] General Nogi committed ritual suicide on the day of his Emperor's funeral in accordance with the samurai practice of *junshi*, which requires following one's lord in death.

While there are no known cases of *junshi* since General Nogi, the problem of overidentification with a powerful person remains real. David D'Alessandro points out that "far worse than failing to understand the rules in a good culture or failing to be rewarded in a bad culture is being co-opted by a really bad one."[13] The corruption of good people in the cultlike culture of Jeff Skilling's Enron has been documented by Bethany McLean and Peter Elkind in *The Smartest Guys in the Room: The Amazing Rise and Scandalous Fall of Enron.*

But even if we set aside the extreme case of working for a corrupt person, we always need to keep some mental distance from powerful influences so we can remain ourselves. A case in point may be Beate Baumann, introduced earlier in Rule 2. Baumann is the office manager and closest adviser of German Chancellor Angela Merkel. In 2009, Chancellor Merkel had held the number one spot on *Forbes*'s list of the world's 100 most powerful women for four consecutive years. *Der Spiegel* commentator Ralf Neukirch notes that Baumann has completely dedicated her life to the successful career of another and to a single task: how can Angela Merkel remain chancellor? Neukirch notes, "Baumann identifies herself completely with this task. During the conversation she sometimes says 'I,' when she means Merkel. She then corrects herself quickly: 'I, Merkel.' It appears like presumption, but it could be the opposite: the abandonment of the own self, in order to completely serve another self."[14] To be fair, Neukirch describes Baumann as "not obsessed" but as someone who is enjoying the political game, so we should assume that all is well. But the story should serve as a reminder that even in the present day, the danger of *junshi*-like loyalty remains.

Yes, you must adapt and fit into the culture where you work; otherwise, you will be, as Jim Collins says, "ejected like a virus."[15] But it cannot mean that you stop being your own person. The price is simply too high.

What to do when . . .

. . . the powerful person makes an inappropriate comment in your presence

You are in a meeting with coworkers and possibly people from outside the company. The situation can range from a formal meeting to a job interview with an outside candidate to a casual sit-down at the summer barbecue. The powerful person makes a comment that is inappropriate. The target could be you, some other person present, or someone not present. For example, in an employment interview, the powerful person may refer to the candidate's age or religious background.

Of course, your reaction involves a very personal decision about what you are willing and able to tolerate and what you are willing and able to risk. Here are some guidelines to think about: On the one hand, it cannot be your job to reform the powerful person; such people are who they are and will likely not change. On the other hand, you will be enabling and perpetuating the behavior if you nod in agreement, laugh at off-color jokes, or do nothing.

Possible ways to signal disagreement are simply not laughing at a bad joke (that would actually be doing something), giving a look of disapproval, or mentioning that the comment was inappropriate. If you are really bothered, consider returning to the issue in private. No matter what you do, don't allow your reaction to be driven by the emotion of the moment. Anticipate scenarios and decide your reaction beforehand, based on a rational assessment of the overall situation.

Get Results

**I like pushing things to the edge. That's often
where you find high performance.**

—BILL GATES, FOUNDER AND CHAIRMAN, MICROSOFT

I n October 1993, Peter Hartz made a huge career decision. The son of working-class parents (his father was a steelworker and his mother helped out in her sister's laundry business), Hartz had finished university in night school and earned an excellent reputation as a human resource executive in the steel industry. While it took some convincing, Hartz decided to accept the new job of "works director" (head of personnel) for Volkswagen in Wolfsburg, Germany. His new boss was Ferdinand Piëch, the master of the power game. Volkswagen was in deep trouble. The carmaker was bleeding red ink, the factories in Germany were selling cars below cost, and an employment analysis had shown they also had more than thirty-one thousand redundant workers, representing 30 percent of the total workforce. Piëch demanded a drastic increase in productivity, freeing up funds for innovation and crisis management, and an improvement in competitiveness. However, moving production abroad and abandoning high German labor costs were not an option. Hartz had his work cut out for him.

What Have You Done for *Me*?

Peter Hartz had experience in downsizing and turnaround. The steel industry on the Saar River had suffered a long history of decline, and Hartz had shown his competence. While that experience was crucial for the assignment awaiting him, it did not mean he could rest on his laurels in any way. The moment you walk in the door when working for a powerful person, your credentials and past accomplishments mean nothing. The only question is "What have you done for *me*?" You therefore must throw yourself into the new task. You must also be careful not to keep referring to your previous employer. Powerful people are focused on their enterprise. You are not in Kansas anymore!

When taking a new job with a powerful person, you may have an immediate priority as Peter Hartz did. However, there may be cases where your priorities are not quite as clear. You may be taking over a new department or team, and there may be many things that can and must be fixed or done better. In these situations, it will typically be best to identify an issue that allows for short-term demonstration of a tangible accomplishment. You must build some track record and credibility right away. You should leave the multiyear big-budget transformation projects for a bit later and plan them carefully with key milestones. Because if the powerful boss (or powerful colleagues) loses patience, you may not be around to complete them.

> *Once you have walked in the door, forget your prior accomplishments and credentials. As soon as possible, build a track record that provides a compelling answer to the only question a powerful person will ask: "What have you done for* me?"

The other challenge when starting to work for a powerful person is that there will often be a barrage of assignments, wants, and ideas. Some will actually matter, and others won't. You must discern the difference, because you cannot afford to spend your time and energy on an idea that is here today and gone tomorrow. You must work on what matters. It will therefore be a good idea to spend some time talking to other people in the organization. This will give you a sense of priorities, and to learn which "favorite projects" have been kicking around for some time.

The Challenge of Accomplishing the Impossible

When doing your job for powerful people in the larger-than-life category, you have to get used to the idea that unreasonable expectations are the norm. These people want what they want. Failure just isn't an option. As we have seen, Ferdinand Piëch did not just want to turn around Volkswagen; he wanted to save expensive German jobs at the same time. That expectation of success, while tremendously stressful, can inspire some truly remarkable accomplishments.

Our look at those who have worked successfully for powerful people shows there are three qualities that will greatly increase the odds of achieving the impossible. These are meticulous development of detailed plans, the resourcefulness to improvise, and sheer tenacity.

PLAN FOR SUCCESS

The Volkswagen turnaround called for a bold plan that required radically new thinking. As Piëch writes in his memoirs, the Hartz plan courageously dared to "put aside the notion of laborious trench warfare with the trade unions but called for simply overrunning the usual well known positions."[1] In an unbelievable four weeks, Hartz negotiated a new agreement with the labor unions that introduced a four-day workweek and redistributed the remaining work among the existing German employees, thus saving twenty thousand jobs. This was accomplished in a company where employees were used to free vacations in company-owned resorts and an eight-minute break every hour. And while introducing a four-day workweek may seem plausible in concept, it took over one hundred shift models to accomplish this feat, as plant and machinery had to operate on an ongoing basis.[2] In other words, the grand idea required an incredible amount of detailed work to fashion it into a workable concept that could be implemented. In addition, once all was said and done, workers' income had been reduced by 14 to 16 percent, and executive income had been reduced by 20 percent. It is true that Volkswagen did move a portion of its production abroad, but the company was able to keep one hundred thousand workers in Germany. The grand plans and relentless drive of Piëch, coupled with Hartz's persistent focus on detailed planning, laid the foundation for a revival at the carmaker. Subsequently,

Volkswagen went on to challenge Toyota's leadership on the world scene and swallowed archrival Porsche. The Piëch/Hartz feat has since become the subject of legend and management case studies.

As mentioned in the previous chapter, Hartz got into trouble by using illegal means to obtain union cooperation. We can only speculate whether or not his plan would have come together without that. However, even when called on the witness stand in 2008, Piëch restated his admiration for Hartz and the fact that he had negotiated a plan in just four weeks.[3] Powerful people just love quick results—and are even willing to give credit for them!

Another person with an impressive track record of achieving the impossible while working for a larger-than-life boss is Apple's operations chief (and occasional interim chief executive) Tim Cook. *Fortune* magazine credits Cook with introducing logistical discipline to Apple that brought the company up to par with Dell, which had built an outstanding reputation for computer-manufacturing efficiency. This was no mean feat in and of itself. Beyond that, however, Cook manages to consistently orchestrate a seamless rollout of new products. Although he is rarely in the limelight, Tim Cook's contribution to Apple's success cannot be underestimated. In essence, he enables Apple to achieve something that few companies do. Adam Lachinksy puts it like this: On the one hand, Apple can charge a premium for its exciting products that stem from Jobs's entrepreneurial nature and creative talents. At the same time, the company can keep costs down because Cook's operational savvy enables it to run as if it were a steady-pace business. The result of doing both is massive profit generation.[4]

Planning was also essential to Norman Schwarzkopf's overwhelming blitzkrieg victory in Operation Desert Storm, which has been hailed as nothing short of historic. That war was won in less than a hundred hours and was accomplished with minimum casualties (150) while enemy losses exceeded 100,000 soldiers. To find a precedent, commentators had to reach back to the Battle of Agincourt in 1415, during which English archers killed thousands of Frenchmen (though actual estimates vary wildly) at a cost of only a few of their own countrymen.

To accomplish this feat, overwhelming American military might had to be projected to a faraway place in very little time. Thus, the management experts at McKinsey tell us that the gulf campaign became the largest, fastest, farthest, most elaborate, and most successful military deployment in history.[5] It was a unique enterprise in that the logistical infrastructure to support the war had to be built from scratch, while simultaneously receiving and supporting the forces and their equipment. The man who orchestrated this highly complex supply effort was Lieutenant General William "Gus" Pagonis. His meticulous planning and execution helped make his boss Schwarzkopf the hero he became in the aftermath of Desert Storm.

IT TAKES PLANNING *AND* RESOURCEFULNESS

When you are confronted with the expectation to accomplish the impossible, the solution is not always obvious, or you may run into unexpected difficulties. But when working for a demanding powerful person, you cannot simply point out that you have run into a roadblock.

In that vein, it turns out that Lieutenant General Pagonis was not just a meticulous planner and logistics expert; he was resourceful as well. Norman Schwarzkopf himself tells the story of how, during the troop buildup in the Gulf, the coalition troops needed an inordinate amount of tents to provide shelter from the heat of the Saudi desert. There was no way that the U.S. Army could supply nearly enough. Ordering tents to be made was not an option either, because they were needed *now*. That's when the resourceful master of massive logistics uncovered that the Saudi kingdom had huge numbers of tents in storage. They were used for the hajj, the annual pilgrimage to Mecca. During the hajj, hundreds of thousands of Muslims would come to Saudi Arabia from all over the world to worship; and they would set up on the outskirts of the city in tents. Since the tents were not needed for worshippers at the time of his troop deployment, Pagonis used them to build a huge tent city for hundreds of thousands of troops.[6] For the central briefing areas, which required much larger tents, Pagonis imported ready-to-use shelters from Germany. The Germans were the masters of making large tents for beer festivals (called *fest* tents) and had an ample supply. Thus, Pagonis exploited an unlikely commonality of Islamic worship and German beer drinking, both requiring massive amounts of tents, to get what was needed. That's creativity and resourcefulness in action.

Of course, you cannot come up with all of these ideas yourself. You have to get your team together and generate ideas and options to get the job done. While it may be risky to voice ideas in the presence of

> *Enjoy the challenge of accomplishing the impossible.*

impatient and judgmental leaders, you will benefit greatly from encouraging your team to come up with ideas and thoughts even if they are unconventional at first blush. You cannot afford to miss this opportunity. If you don't have a team, you have to think about who might want to help. I have always found it amazing how many people are willing to help if you ask them.

YOU HAVE TO BE TENACIOUS

Finally, getting the impossible done will require dogged determination and tenacity. I had the privilege to work with a great salesman who simply would not take no for an answer. Even when the order had been given to a competitor, he would rework the deal, submit new proposals, and simply keep going. He was often able to turn the situation around and salvage a lost cause. That tenacity was a tremendous asset. His exceedingly demanding boss would know that nothing had been left untried. Therefore, when others in the company had to endure the wrath of dissatisfaction when business was lost, this sales manager never did. His boss knew that everything humanly (and superhumanly) possible had been done. The salesman's tenacity led both to great results and to a gracious reaction from the boss when the impossible was truly impossible.

Take "Small" Assignments Seriously

A couple of years ago, I attended an academic conference in Toronto that featured a high-profile speaker from the United States. It was the first warm and sunny day of spring—something we crave after a long Canadian winter. The university's senior administration was in full attendance to honor the speaker. Otherwise, however, the lecture hall was sparsely populated. American intellectual horsepower was no match for the first rays of sunshine in the Great White North. The situation was embarrassing, to say the least. Bringing out a celebrated speaker in front of an empty auditorium is painful. Causing the senior administration such embarrassment is truly something I would not wish on my worst enemy.

This episode highlights that the job we are doing for a powerful person is not always a mega project. You are not always saving the country's most venerable brand or organizing the biggest troop buildup in history. But small assignments can be just as tricky and seemingly out of our control. Yet the powerful person will expect the impossible nonetheless. You simply don't want to have such a person speak in front of an empty lecture hall.

Knowing how difficult and vexing these things can be, I therefore have every admiration for Colin Powell. The retired chairman of the Joint Chiefs tells the story of Major General Henry E. "The Gunfighter" Emerson at Camp Casey in South Korea. The Gunfighter's favorite tool for promoting racial tolerance was the 1970 film *Brian's Song*, a movie about the friendship between a black pro football player and his white teammate. The general would ask his staff to run the movie over and over again in the (large) post theater, with a discussion held following each showing. When he heard that the head of the Pentagon's equal opportunity program was coming to Korea, Emerson was excited and wanted him to witness the troops watching *Brian's Song*. Then Colonel Powell drew the assignment. The problem was that most of his men were either in field exercises or had seen the movie many times. Powell therefore proceeded to show the movie in a small service club theater. That's when he got a frantic phone call from Emerson's chief of staff: the general and his visitor were attending the last part of the movie, expecting it to be shown in a *full* post theater. Powell knew that the impossible had to be done. He ordered every warm body in the area to attend—whether asleep, awake, drunk, or sober. Even a handcuffed soldier who had been arrested by military police was diverted to the screening.[7] An empty theater just wasn't an option, and Powell did what it took. Of course, you cannot dragoon students into a lecture hall on a sunny day, but my question is whether free ice cream or Frappuccinos would have done the trick.

Manage the Micromanager

There may be bosses who are just interested in results; however, more often they will micromanage and will have specific, if not idiosyncratic, ideas on how the job should be done. Powerful people can be high up at thirty thousand feet one moment and take a deep dive into the issues on the ground in the next. Therefore, it is in the best interest of those working beneath them to find ways to effectively make them part of the day-to-day work routine.

According to Caroline Van Hasselt, Ron Harmen—a former United Artists–Columbia Cablevision regional manager who worked for Rogers after Rogers had acquired UA–Columbia—was clearly exasperated with Ted Rogers's micromanagement. The manager commented that working together successfully with the founder would have required Ted Rogers to stay out of the business for the most part, acting more like a board member and not getting involved in day-to-day operations with daily phone calls: "That was too much. You couldn't plan your future because you didn't have any idea what Ted was going to come up with the next morning. It really wears on you, especially when you are not accustomed to it. Ted ran it with an iron fist."[8]

> *When the powerful person is a micromanager, keep him or her informed—but not too deeply. Otherwise, get ready for an overabundance of ideas and "help."*

While micromanagement can easily be exasperating, you must remember again that it is very much part of the psyche of many powerful people. It is a brutal fact or constraint that you simply have to accept. Powerful people love their business with all its aspects; perceive that they can improve everything; and, very important, might be quite concerned how your work affects their image. Managing the micromanager requires energy, skill, and a willingness to do so.

WHEN IN DOUBT, COMMUNICATE

The first key to managing the micromanager is good communication. Frank Stanton knew that well. Sally Bedell Smith writes that his first rule for dealing with CBS Chairman Paley was to keep him informed. But Stanton did not offer up too many details either. When the boss was away, Stanton kept notes on issues he thought would interest Paley. He would then send the chief a series of memos that covered the status of various projects, information about the industry, and tidbits about executives and board members. He waited for

Paley to ask for more details if he wanted them. Most important, however, Stanton kept Paley's trust by giving him straight answers.[9]

The Stanton approach is sound and practical. Like many other aspects of working with powerful people, the area of communication requires a carefully balanced approach. Too much communication will invite unwanted "help" or instructions; too little will easily lead to the complaint that you do not keep them up-to-date. At the same time, proactive communication builds trust. Leaving details for follow-up questions respects the boss's time and lets him or her determine how much information he or she wants. While honest communication does not necessarily mean that everything must be reported, you must answer straight questions in a forthright manner. Everything else destroys trust and prevents you from doing your job. Ted Rogers puts it this way with regard to Bob Francis, Rogers's chief financial officer: "[He] was a close, intimate adviser who didn't do anything without my being aware and vice-versa."[10] I cannot emphasize this last point enough. Once powerful people get the feeling that you are conspiring or talking behind their back, you are done.

The rule of "when in doubt, communicate" applies even if communication has to occur at off-hours. Personally, I have never gotten into trouble for "overcommunicating," even if time zone differences meant a late-night call. All of my bosses, clients, and colleagues knew I would not call them unless it was important. Likewise, as a boss, I have never received an off-hours call about a matter I felt was trivial. I always preferred to know whether a crisis was brewing. Colin Powell confirms that lesson in an experience he had when working as military assistant to Secretary of Defense Caspar Weinberger. On September 1, 1983, Powell received a late-night call that a Korean jetliner out of Anchorage en route to Seoul had dropped off the radar screen. He had no further information and had to decide whether to wake up the secretary. He decided to call Weinberger. Far from being upset, the secretary was as composed in the middle of the night as he was at noon at the Pentagon. Rather than reprimanding him for the intrusion, he asked Powell to keep him informed.[11] The fact that

> *In crisis situations, communicate early and immediately, even if you do not (yet) have all the facts.*

the Russians had shot down Korean Air Lines flight 007 did not fully emerge until much later.

Of course, not everything is a crisis of geopolitical proportions. Often it will be more advisable to get enough information to present the whole story. However, at a time of crisis, communicating early, even if incompletely, is the way to go. Powerful people want and need to know what is going on.

DON'T REJECT THE MICROMANAGER

When dealing with micromanagement, you must resist the temptation to reject an overbearing leader's involvement on the basis that the leader is not a subject-matter expert. To begin with, powerful people will simply not accept the rejection, with the predictable consequences. Furthermore, with their renaissance personality, they may be able to make an unexpected contribution. An episode from the dark days of Magna International, told by Wayne Lilley, illustrates the point.

When Magna was on the brink of bankruptcy in 1990, one of the principal lenders, the Bank of Nova Scotia, forced Frank Stronach to bring in forensic accountant David Richardson of Ernst & Young. By that time, Richardson already had a reputation as a capable, experienced, and no-nonsense restructuring expert. In Wayne Lilley's account of the story,[12] Frank Stronach made a brilliant move by rehiring Jim Nicol, the former head of Magna's Decoma division. As a lawyer and graduate of the London School of Economics, Nicol also had experience in restructuring work. Nicol and Richardson came up with an elegant restructuring plan, which redistributed debt between the Magna parent and its operating groups and included a "personal contribution" from Frank Stronach. They also arranged for bridge financing to repay debenture holders who started to become problematic. However, while that took care of the lion's share of the debt, they ended up $60 million short. That's when Frank Stronach entered the scene.

Recognizing that nobody in Canada was likely to make up the difference, Stronach had the idea that U.S. investors, who would not be as familiar as Canadians with Magna's troubles, would respond to an issue of convertible debentures. His instinct proved correct when Magna raised $110 million in the United States with a debt issue that closed a few weeks before the refinancing deadline. The restructuring of Magna was a stunning success, and even Frank Stronach's critics gave him credit for overseeing nothing short of the "the greatest recovery in Canadian business."[13]

This story teaches an important lesson. If you can't keep a powerful leader from meddling, you might as well use his or her ideas, even if unconventional, because some of them might just work and lead to (even) greater success. This is a result I have seen many times. In addition, keeping an open mind toward his or her ideas shows appreciation and respect, and as a result, it builds the relationship.

> *Trying to keep powerful people from helping out will backfire.*

In this example, the boss was making a contribution in an area that was not his primary expertise. The financial people acted as "complementors." We will look at that scenario in more detail under Rule 11, which states, "Cover their weaknesses."

DON'T ABDICATE BECAUSE OF MICROMANAGEMENT

I got a great lesson in perspective when a general manager of a foreign-company subsidiary with a very hierarchical culture complained to me that his people were unable to make decisions. Too often, they asked for his approval or decision on matters they should have been taking care of independently. His subordinates, however, saw the world differently. Their boss was a micromanager who wanted to be involved in the smallest details and got very upset when things went wrong or were not done his way. So what was the solution for the dilemma?

The first thing you must know is that you cannot abdicate decision making or responsibility just because the boss is a micromanager. The boss may actually see you as someone who cannot make decisions. Going ahead on your own, however, can be just as deadly. What I have found to work well in such a situation is the following communication: "Boss, here is the problem/situation. My plan to handle this is as follows. If I am missing something or you want to discuss this in more detail, please let me know. Otherwise, I am going ahead as outlined." This way, you are letting the boss know that you have a plan and allowing him or her to keep micromanaging if that's what he or she wants to do.

Yes, Powerful People Can Make Your Life Easier!

While highly demanding leaders most often make life difficult because you must bring in results *and* make them happy, they can at times make your job easier. This applies, in particular, when dealing with others who do not want to deal with the powerful person. The message to a negotiating counterpart, for example, is simple: "If we cannot get this done, the boss will get personally involved, and neither you nor I want that."

A variation of this tactic was used by Andrew Knight when he was editor of the *London Daily Telegraph*. Incidentally, Knight not only navigated the takeover of the *Telegraph* by Conrad Black, but he later continued his career successfully at Rupert Murdoch's News Corporation, proving in a way that effectively working for powerful people is a generic and transferable skill.

> Chances are, outsiders do not want the powerful person involved, and you can help them avoid the involvement (in return for getting what you want).

But let's get back to the story. The mid-eighties saw some nasty fights between the powerful print unions on London's Fleet Street and some newcomers on the proprietor side, among them Rupert Murdoch and Conrad Black. Murdoch had won a major, and occasionally violent, battle with the print union by exploiting squabbling between unions and using the full force of Margaret Thatcher's new labor laws. In the historic Wapping dispute, he succeeded in switching from offset printing to electronic newspaper composition at a new plant in London's dockyard area known as Wapping. The move reduced the print workforce from 2,000 to 570.[14] While the Wapping dispute was still going on, the *Telegraph*'s Andrew Knight prepared a move from Fleet Street to a new plant on the Isle of Dogs, taking full advantage of Black's and maybe a little bit of Murdoch's reputation. Here is Richard Siklos's commentary on what unfolded:

> Black was happy to remain in Canada for most of this period, which suited Knight, as an element of his scheme to was to portray

Black as a "distant ogre in Canada" who was inaccessible to meet unions. Traditionally the printers had insisted on face-to-face meetings with proprietors when negotiations reached a crucial stage, in effect reducing management to mere puppets. "Conrad played that role brilliantly, and he also played it vis-à-vis the outside community," recalled Knight. "There were all sorts of people in politics and in the rest of Fleet Street all dying to find out who this new, mysterious owner was. And we deliberately cultivated around him an air of mystery."[15]

Therefore, keeping a powerful person away can be a deliberate strategy. Especially when you are negotiating a project with many stakeholders and carefully balanced interests and egos, it will be wise to keep the powerful person at a distance and operate on his or her authority. If necessary, you must provide play-by-play updates so that the boss doesn't feel left out.

Even if the boss is a really nice person, there are quite a few reasons not to bring him or her in. The most obvious one is that not having the decision maker in the room allows you to hedge your bets. If the other side pushes agreement on a point, you can always say, "I will have to take this to the boss." You can either say that the boss's agreement will be difficult to get or that you can see the other side's point and will try to convince the boss. And it doesn't always have to be the boss. You could also refer to the legal or finance department as a party whose approval is required.

But the converse is equally true. There are situations where it is appropriate to bring in the powerful person to let him or her do what only the powerful can do. In one of his most famous performances, one that he enjoyed telling,[16] Ted Rogers found himself in a high-stakes negotiation with the owner of the San Antonio Spurs, Angelo Drossos. Rogers Cable had taken over a long-term multimillion-dollar television contract with the Spurs after its UA–Columbia acquisition, a contract that Rogers Cable simply could not afford. Ted Rogers had withheld the first $1 million installment, and he and Phil Lind (one of Ted Rogers's most trusted executives) were to discuss the matter with Drossos, who had quite a reputation of his own. Rogers and Lind were late for the luncheon meeting, and Drossos, a stickler for punctuality, was getting quite upset. Here is Caroline Van Hasselt's account of what happened next:

Rogers rushed in and grabbed Drossos' hand. He apologized for being late, explaining that he wanted to bring something for their first meeting and that it had been late in arriving. . . . Rogers said, "Angelo, I asked to meet with you because I want to talk about your contract with the previous owner." Drossos visibly stiffened and replied, "Your lunch is cold and you owe me one million dollars." That was Rogers' cue. He said—in a louder than necessary voice— "That's what I want to talk to you about. That's why we are late." The door opened and in walked several armed security guards pushing carts loaded with bags of US$10 bills, totaling $1 million.[17]

Ted Rogers's surprise worked perfectly. The stunt broke the ice, and Drossos's laughter at each bag of money piled on the table signified a transformation in the tone of the meeting to follow, as well as their overall relationship. Drossos, with a smile "as big as Texas," agreed that the deal was not fair and had to be corrected. Rogers ended up getting concessions that amounted to millions of dollars over the life of the agreement and that were used to fund Rogers's foray into the Canadian wireless business, which (as previously discussed) became wildly successful. Ted Rogers, Angelo Drossos, and their respective lieutenants renegotiated the agreement without lawyers. The boss had taken care of business.

DECIDE CAREFULLY WHETHER OR NOT TO BRING IN THE POWERFUL PERSON

You must decide whether or not you want to bring a larger-than-life personality into a situation. The powerful person may want to come in anyway, but then you must decide whether you want to at least advise against it. If so, it is, of course, better to say "Not now" rather than "Not ever." You can simply suggest that the person would have more impact at a later stage, "when it really matters."

If you do decide to bring the powerful person into the situation, you must be aware of the risks. While such people can be crucial to getting things done, they can easily upset a carefully crafted construct with a careless remark or a comment that is perceived as an insult by your counterparts. The potential for volatility comes from the difficulty that those with power have in being scripted or pressed into a mold. Too often, they just like to tell it as it is.

Furthermore, savvy negotiators on the other side can exploit the presence of a powerful person. Previously settled negotiation points can unravel, or something else can undo months of work. Heading off such dangers may require decisive intervention, as illustrated by the following episode recounted by Colin Powell.

In May 1988, President Ronald Reagan traveled to Moscow to ratify the intermediate-range nuclear forces (INF) treaty between the United States and the Soviet Union. During the first one-on-one meeting between Reagan and Gorbachev, the Soviet leader handed the president a draft statement that was to be included in the final communiqué. Reagan read it and liked it. The statement talked about equality of all states, noninterference in internal affairs, and freedom of sociopolitical choice. The language seemed unobjectionable, and it took the perceptiveness of an experienced George Shultz, who was a senior member of the U.S. delegation, to discover the booby trap: an unintended blessing of the Soviets' hold on the Baltic states of Lithuania, Latvia, and Estonia. During the last working session, Gorbachev forcefully put the paper one more time across the table, urging President Reagan's acceptance while a crowd and the media had gathered in the next room to witness the treaty ratification. But Reagan's advisers held firm, and the statement was kept out of the joint communiqué. A smart and bold move by the Russians to push through a seemingly innocuous request in the pressure of the moment had been narrowly avoided.[18]

All of these examples show that even if an assignment is clearly identified, doing your job well when working for a powerful person is not as straightforward as you may want it to be. But getting something done right out of the gate is critical. It builds a track record and, very important, makes you reliable in the powerful person's eyes. That track record and reliability actually provide the very foundation for making your opinions count. In fact, when starting out to work with a powerful leader, you may find that it is a good idea to hold back opinions and good advice on other issues until you have achieved some element of what you were hired to do in the first place.

> *There are things that only powerful people can do, but others may seek to exploit the presence of the powerful for their purposes.*

What to do when . . .

. . . the powerful person gives you a big project that is "impossible" to achieve

The boss gives you a large new responsibility that is impossible. You are to add a new department to your existing portfolio, significantly increase sales, roll out a new product in record time, or spearhead a political campaign against strong opposition.

It is true that, given the right motivation and expectation, great things can be accomplished. But especially when a large project is at stake, you must resist the immediate urge to say yes and commit. You can express excitement over the challenge and your willingness to take it on. But you should hedge your bets and investigate what it will take to get the job done—even assuming superhuman efforts. Get insight from others, brainstorm with your team, and put together a plan that is bold yet realistic. Based on that plan, ask for specific resources (time, money, people, training, support, etc.). With that in mind, your first reaction can be something like "This is an exciting assignment. Let me come back to you with a plan of what it will take to get this done." However, make sure you get back in short order, because if he or she doesn't hear from you, the powerful person will likely assume that you are already getting great things done.

Cover Their Weaknesses

Golfers, like business people, tend to be delusional about their weaknesses.

—MARSHALL GOLDSMITH, AUTHOR AND EXECUTIVE COACH

One Sunday morning, I received a call from a newly promoted chief financial officer who was working on a debt placement with a charismatic business owner. The CFO was exasperated because the business owner had read through the debt marketing document and was dissatisfied. Meanwhile, the company's investment bankers had felt that the document was fine as it was and would certainly lead to a successful placement. The problem was that the owner had built his business with his product and marketing genius. As owner of a successful private company, he did not have regular contact with capital markets and had a general disdain for the financial community; he was a man of the "real economy." Therefore, the fact that the experts had approved the document did not matter much at all. The business owner was dissatisfied, and that was all that mattered.

This scenario shows that working as a *complementor* to a powerful person—filling a necessary position where that person has little or no expertise—can pose a significant challenge. The problem is that powerful people in this situation do not relate to what you do and often don't feel that they have to. If they are willing to leave you alone, which can happen on occasion, there is little to worry about. If, however, as in our example, they do take an interest, especially on a high-profile project, the situation can become much more difficult. You must get your job done and keep a boss who does not understand what you do happy. Handling the situation in our example required the insight that both the owner and the financial market were the audience for the debt marketing document. It would have been futile to convince the owner that things had to be done a certain way for a different audience. Thus, the debt marketing document had to be just as exciting as the launch of a highly anticipated product; it had to be written in a language the owner could understand and appreciate while simultaneously convincing the bankers that the company's debt was a solid investment. Specifically, the CFO had to develop some sales flair, similar to what his boss was accustomed to, so he could do his job the way his boss would do it. That meant a polished image and communication with confidence and impact.

Many Powerful People Have Effective Complementors

While the job of a complementor is challenging, it puts you in a great position of influence if you do it well, because you do something that a person in power cannot do. Deep down, that person will realize that he or she has a deficit and needs help.

The prime example of compensating for a powerful leader's limitations is the pairing of a chief executive officer and a chief operating officer. Probably one of the most notable examples is the combination of technology genius Steve Jobs and his "operations whiz" Tim Cook.[1] There are quite a few other powerful pairings. The turnaround at Xerox, which earned then-CEO Anne Mulcahy the 2008 CEO of the Year Award from *Chief Executive* magazine, was very much a collaboration with her eventual successor, Ursula Burns. As reported in *BusinessWeek*, Mulcahy, a former human resources vice president, entrusted her lieutenant Burns with much of the day-to-day operations while she focused on customer service and Xerox's financial health.[2] The complementary relationship between Bill Paley and his right-hand man Frank Stanton was legendary: "To Paley, Stanton was kind of a corporate Jeeves who took care of the details, cleaned up messes, could be counted on to always do the correct things."[3] And as we are told by Kitty Kelley, in the early days of "The Oprah Winfrey Show," Oprah Winfrey relied heavily on her symbiotic relationship with her executive pro-

> *Be everything the power-ful person is not.*

ducer, Debra DiMaio, to whip her operation into shape. DiMaio took care of the harsher side of business, which included performance management and dealing with people issues, allowing Winfrey to be the gentler personality. As the daughter of a Marine colonel, DiMaio had no problem with the role. On occasion, she even spurred on Winfrey during a commercial break when she seemed less than fully engaged.[4]

MAKE SURE YOUR WORK IS VALUED

While the value of a complementor might be obvious in concept, one aspect is sometimes overlooked. To be able to act and be effective as a complementor requires more than bringing to the table a skill that the powerful person lacks. It requires that the value of the contribution is acknowledged. Otherwise, it will be next to impossible to get the necessary resources to do the job well, especially where there is intense internal competition for talent and finances. In that context, you must realize that it is human to discount what we are lacking and don't know. Powerful people, with their tendency toward favorable self-assessment,[5] will be even more liable to consider what others do as "easy."

To pick up on the example at the beginning of the chapter, a complementary relationship will work well if a visionary chief executive values a chief financial officer who is skilled at keeping pesky investors at bay. It will not work well if the visionary dismisses the CFO as a boring "bean counter."

The problem is not limited to one's relationship with the boss. It is hard to be the operations manager in an environment where sales and marketing are all-powerful because the perception is that they bring in the business and therefore are what keeps the company going. In that case, if salespeople promise too much in terms of product quality, delivery, cost, and customization, the people in operations may be told simply to deal with it. The opposite can, of course, be true where engineering rules and sales is simply told to "sell what we have." And the best people in the company will want to work in the area where there is more appreciation, career progression, and incentive compensation.

Therefore, if you are in the role of a complementor, you have to make sure that your work is valued; if that's not the case, you must think of some creative ways to get there (some thoughts on that in just a moment). Otherwise, you can be assured of resentment and misery.

A good way to move into the position of a valued complementor is to take on work that was previously done by the powerful person. An ideal scenario is that of Frank Stanton and Bill Paley. As we described earlier, Paley asked Stanton to take over as president of CBS because he wanted to be free from the day-to-day management of the enterprise. Paley valued what Stanton was doing, because Paley had done it before and certainly did not want to go back. This kind of opportunity often exists in a rapidly growing start-up company where the founder has been doing every major job. As the company expands, the founder starts to concentrate on his or her core strengths and brings in help, handing off tasks that he or she was not doing well or did not like doing.

> The powerful person must acknowledge his or her lack in certain areas and the value of the complementor. Otherwise, resentment and misery will develop.

A second strategy would be to get the powerful person directly involved in an aspect of your work, so that person can see what is going on. For example, as an underappreciated financial officer, you may want to bring the boss to a contentious investor meeting, so that he or she can experience some of the challenges firsthand and see you handle them. Of course, you have to remember that bringing in the boss creates its own perils (see Rule 10). In a company where engineering is king, a sales manager may want to invite his or her production counterpart to meet with an unhappy customer who needs to be calmed down because of poor product quality. Or a legal department that loves to say no and enforce the rules should join a sales call and share in the burden to close the deal. The concept is, of course, that you get the unappreciative person to walk a mile in your shoes; it will provide a whole new perspective. If the person is reluctant to join you, you may want to ask a friendly counterpart in the investor, customer, or other stakeholder community to issue a compelling "invitation."

A third strategy is to put the value of your contribution into a language your powerful counterpart understands. If the powerful finance manager does not value the contribution of the human resource department and becomes a difficult and overbearing counterpart in budget reviews, you as human resources manager must show your value in a language that a finance expert understands. An audit and benchmarking exercise could yield some hard figures on training and professional development cost per person, reduced recruiting cost through internal talent and leadership development, or reduction in exposure to lawsuits due to improved employment practices. You could also compare the cost of in-house human resources management to outsourced HR (but be prepared to go through with it if it appears to be more favorable). If you are in charge of safety, a "near miss" can make the point, as can a review of average fines handed out by occupational health and safety inspectors. Operations people, of course, can and must develop a whole battery of mission-critical metrics that can be benchmarked and continuously improved. All of this to make the same point: you must promote what you do in a way that is credible and verifiable. And be prepared to give a presentation that has some pizzazz.

Finally, a credible outsider could do a lot of good by complimenting the unappreciated insider. Thus, an audit committee chair of a public company board or the outside auditor could lend a lot of support to the chief financial officer. Salespeople can always get compliments from customers; so can operations people who support customers directly with service and or technical support. A high-profile visitor always provides a good opportunity to generate supportive comments. All of this is to say that you should seriously think about who might serve as a respected third party to lend you credibility, and you shouldn't be shy about asking for a "testimonial." Having others promote you is always more powerful than self-praise.

> *It is up to the complementor to make the relationship work.*

THE APPRECIATED COMPLEMENTOR: A GREAT NICHE

Being an appreciated complementor can be quite gratifying and afford much greater freedoms when you are working with a powerful person. The way Michael Wolff sees it, Roger Ailes's independence as the president of Fox News is at least partly due to the fact that Rupert Murdoch's primary deep-down expertise is in newspapers, not television.[6] Of course, Ailes's tremendous success in building the network, as reported by the *New York Times*,[7] could not possibly hurt.

Working with a powerful person while occupying the same terrain as he or she does can create a much tougher spot. Such was the case with an earlier Enron president, Mick Seidl. Seidl had become Enron's number two man largely on the strength of his friendship with Ken Lay, the company's late chief executive and chairman, and he had much in common with his boss: he was a former academic with a Ph.D. in economics and a former government policy maker. But further similarities started to present a problem, as described in McLean and Elkind's chronicle of the Enron saga. They point out that Seidl shared some of Lay's problematic tendencies. He had a terrible time making decisions that might upset somebody. And he was far more interested in the glamour of being a corporate executive than in the hard work of making a company profitable. "He wanted to be Mr. Outside, but Enron already had a Mr. Outside: Ken Lay himself."[8]

Thus, Mick Seidl was eventually replaced by Rich Kinder, who, as we are told, was in many ways his opposite. Kinder was tough, disciplined, and a deep-down, no-nonsense operator; thus he was "a perfect complement to Ken Lay."[9] The unloved enforcer replaced the kindred-spirit friend. McLean and Elkind describe Kinder as a man who got things done, and they quote one former Enron board member as saying that "it was one of the saddest days for Enron when Rich Kinder left."[10]

At this stage, we have come across something of a contradiction (which, of course, would not be unusual at all in the world of powerful executives): On the one hand, we observed that powerful people like subordinates in whom they can see themselves, as in our example of Ted Rogers and Nadir Mohamed. On the other hand, being different is what gives complementors room to maneuver. Management professor Noel Tichy notes that Ursula Burns "was clearly running the majority of the business" at Xerox while her boss focused on the turnaround.[11]

This conflicting insight offers a couple of takeaway points. First and foremost, Burns, Mohamed, Kinder, and Ailes are highly competent, whereas Seidl was not in his element when he had the job of running the day-to-day affairs of the company as chief operations officer. The other, maybe equally important, point is that Mohamed was much younger than Ted Rogers and took a position that did not put him in competition with the boss. Such distance allows the powerful person to become the mentor of someone he or she likes and wants to see succeed without having to contemplate giving up his or her job before being ready to move on. A look at Ted Rogers's succession may confirm this reasoning: Ted Rogers remained firmly in charge until he fell ill at age seventy-five and could no longer do his job; he obviously was not in a rush to hand over the reins. During his illness, he appointed the company's chairman, Alan Horn, a chartered accountant and a classic complement to himself, as acting chief executive. The board selected Mohamed as the new permanent chief executive officer only after Rogers had succumbed to his illness.[12]

> *If you have set your sights on leadership succession from a complementor position, make sure you showcase how your expertise relates to the strategic future of the organization.*

The lesson here is clear: if you occupy the same spot as a powerful person, you will do well to keep your ambitions in check. While you want to be a candidate for succession planning, you do not want to present yourself as a competitor who has to be put in his or her place.

Complementors on a Board of Directors

Complementing a powerful person becomes especially important and necessary in the context of a board of directors. Finding the right complement to a powerful chief executive, who may also be a major shareholder, is not just an exercise in pulling together a diversity of backgrounds. As U.S. board adviser Beverly Behan puts it, a "balanced" board is not composed of one or two CEOs and a sprinkling of bankers, lawyers, academics, community leaders, and retired politicians. Instead, finding the right complements requires a careful analysis of needs in light of the company's strategic direction and competitive environment. The greatest value will be provided by directors who have already "walked through the fire" on issues that the chief executive is confronting for the first time.[13] The challenge, however, will be to find people who, despite their differing backgrounds, can relate well and whose contribution is appreciated.

In summary, we can safely say that being a complementor to a powerful person can be a very rewarding assignment. Under the best of circumstances, it affords unusual freedom to operate and becomes the basis for a crucial contribution to the success of the organization as well as the powerful individual. It is a great and necessary niche: being everything that the one in power is not.

Succession from a complementor position is difficult. Both Frank Stanton, masterful complementor to Bill Paley, and Richard Kinder, highly effective complementor to Kenneth Lay, wanted their boss's job but were disappointed.[14] However, succeeding as a complementor is not impossible. Ursula Burns accomplished the feat at Xerox, and the business media continue to assert that Tim Cook is a contender for Steve Jobs's position; he has already proven his mettle as Apple's interim chief executive officer during Jobs's absence.

In addition, it may well be that at the time of succession, the company's strategic and competitive realities will demand a successor with a different profile from that of the incumbent. The complementor may thus become the driving genius.

What to do when . . .

. . . you receive an offer to join the board of a powerful person

You have been invited to serve on a prestigious board of directors chaired by a powerful chief executive. You have performed your due diligence on the company and believe its financial and market situation is solid.

Before moving ahead, you should give serious thought to the interpersonal dynamic. A powerful executive, especially a founder, entrepreneur, or major shareholder, will have a strong feeling of ownership. Such a leader may even feel you work for him or her, rather than expect you to exercise oversight over him or her. Also, you must assess your appetite for conflict. Many powerful people thrive on it, and there will be many issues where they just will not back down. This is not a cushy retirement post. This assignment will demand your full energy and attention, especially in a time of crisis and controversy.

RULE 12

Facilitate the Impact of Raw Power

I'll take care of it; now let's move on to something else.

—LIEUTENANT GENERAL CAL WALLER,
VETERAN OF OPERATION DESERT STORM[1]

After joining the ranks of the survivors and acquiring a track record for getting things done, you will have the opportunity to start moving closer to the inner circle. In fact, your ability to interface with powerful people will open up a whole range of career assignments within an organization, especially if it has a number of personalities that are carbon copies of the boss.

Moving closer to power will gain you a much more nuanced understanding of the likes, dislikes, style, and idiosyncrasies of the person in charge. That closeness becomes the foundation for taking on the important task of facilitating the impact that a driven leader has on the organization and other stakeholders. The names given for that activity are not always flattering. They include terms like *cleaning up, fixing, executing*, and even *toxic handling*.[2] Colin Powell talks about the need for a "chaplain." But regardless of the connotations, the fact remains that the raw force of some powerful people, left unchecked, can and will wreak havoc. This phenomenon is by no means limited to larger-than-life people. The owner of a small company, the manager of a far-away subsidiary, or even the "indispensable" head of a department can easily be someone who rules in all his or her glory.

This creates a great, and one could even say strategic, need for facilitation, mediation, and just plain making things work. Most of this will be second nature to those who do the job, but if we categorize and name the diverse aspects of this work, we can be intentional about learning to get better at it and coaching others to do the same.

Make Visionary Pronouncements Operational

Some years ago, I had the opportunity to go to GE's fabled Crotonville campus to meet with GE's (then) chief learning officer, Steve Kerr. When talking about the history of the Crotonville leadership development facility, Kerr explained that he had received the following "instruction" from his boss, Jack Welch: "I want Crotonville to be the common coffee pot of General Electric." Kerr translated this high-level guidance into some very practical points. They included geographical and business diversity of class participants; a strong emphasis on interaction, specifically with Jack Welch in the pit; and a faculty that mixed outsiders (business school professors) with insiders (GE executives).

Kerr had a name for the process of translating the high-level, visionary pronouncements of his boss into actionable specifics: the bull's-eye exercise, so named because it is depicted as a three-ringed target. In the outer ring go the high-level goals and visionary pronouncements, and in the innermost ring is the output of a discussion to make them actionable. That translation into operational clarity fulfills the critical function of connecting vision with the reality on the ground. It gives the troops what they are looking for: the answer to the question "What does that mean to us?"

An example of making a vague, high-level "visionary" pronouncement operational is provided by PepsiCo's chief executive Indra Nooyi. In the mid-1990s, shortly after she joined the company, Pepsi CEO Roger Enrico challenged Nooyi to devise a strategy that could make PepsiCo the "defining corporation of the 21st century."[3] Nooyi went to work by drawing up various scenarios, which included the earlier-mentioned Quaker Oats acquisition and movement toward more healthful foods and drinks; she went on to manage Quaker's successful integration into Pepsi, which, according to *Fortune*'s Betsy Morris, put her on the radar screen for the top job. As we have seen, when she finally took the CEO's job, issuing the corporate directive of "Performance with Purpose" was one of her first actions.[4] To Nooyi, the vague concept had concrete meaning.

No one knows the value and essential importance of a clear mission better than people in the military. Colin Powell rails against the lack of clearly set objectives as one of the big failings of the Vietnam War. He cites the classic wisdom of Carl von Clausewitz, the Prussian general whose first rule was that no sane person would start a war without being clear about what he or she intended to achieve and how he or she intended to achieve it.[5]

An excellent and very practical military example of how to translate high-level and seemingly amorphous objectives into a clear mission is described by General Schwarzkopf in his memoirs. During his 1970s post-Vietnam tour, Schwarzkopf took on a deputy command for General Willard Latham in Alaska. Schwarzkopf describes him as a man who was relentless in his demands, stingy with praise, and extremely harsh when he did not get results. Sounds familiar. But the toughness of the leader was not the brigade's biggest problem. Rather, it was the vagueness of its mission, which was to "defend Alaska." Thus, the various maneuvers would anticipate a Soviet attack on the shores of the Bering Strait or around the U.S. Arctic airbases, or wherever else the Russians might show up. None of that made any sense, given how thinly the troops were spread across the geography.

Thus, in order to make the mission operational, General Latham went about identifying the newly built Alaska pipeline as a high-value strategic target. Consultations with oil company experts revealed that repairing a damaged pipeline could be done with relative ease. However, a strike at the oil fields' complicated manifold systems could be devastating. As a result, defending the pump stations at Prudhoe Bay became a defining mission.[6] The general had translated the political directive of "defending Alaska" into a sensible and concrete mission that turned into practical marching orders for the troops. He had done his job as a leader.

Developing a vision and practical application is not just an exercise for a large corporation. It is useful for small and medium-sized enterprises, as well as groups and teams within organizations. Also, it does not always require a multiday retreat or an army of consultants. Instead, you can do a lot by just listening to the boss, giving his or her pronouncements some thought, getting other input, and keeping it practical by answering the question "What does this really mean to us?"

TRANSLATE POWERFUL PEOPLE FOR OTHERS AND THEMSELVES

Sometimes the job of a facilitator is to provide a straight (or not so straight) translation of what the powerful person said into what he or she meant. But sometimes it is an exercise in figuring out what powerful people might have meant or even helping them to get clarity as to how their high-level visions might play out in the real world. In other words, you translate powerful people for others *and* for themselves.

Translation is a two-way street, however. As an organizational translator, you can help others communicate with the person in charge more clearly and with greater impact. This is because you have learned, practiced, and (hopefully at some point) mastered the art of empathetic listening, and you know how your boss processes information. Taking it down from the lofty concepts of communication style and psychology, effective communication can be just a matter of knowing which buttons to push. Wayne Lilley explains how two Magna veterans under Stronach knew how to get their boss fired up about an idea by explaining that the result would be "the world's first or biggest."[7]

> Translate visionary pronouncements into concrete meaning, plans, and actions. Help others translate their plans and proposals in a way that fits the powerful person's communication style.

Therefore, to get what you need and help others get what they need, you must be sure to make the right appeal. This appeal must relate equally to the powerful person's sustained view of the world and to the priorities of the moment. Priorities and opinions can, of course, change quickly, and you must keep your communication fresh.

Taking Off the Edge

As mentioned earlier, a distinct category of powerful-person facilitation can indeed be best described as cleanup, an activity that *Collins English Dictionary* describes as "the act of making something orderly or presentable." The implication is, of course, that what's being handled is inherently or potentially messy. And there is plenty in that category where powerful people are involved.

Management professors Peter Frost and Sandra Robinson give the example of a middle manager who was instructed by his boss to "tell those idiots out there to get their act together and finish the job by Friday or else they're all doomed."[8] The manager pulled his staff together and put the directive as such: "The boss needs us to complete this task by Friday, so let's put our heads together and see what we need to meet this deadline." One can be certain that the translated directive led to a much more constructive planning session.

This act of diplomatic message relay goes beyond taking the edge off and reducing anxiety among junior staff. It is also needed to manage other helpers who may not be as good at submerging their egos—namely, board members, high-level service providers, or executives with prima donna status. There is usually no value in passing along disrespectful name-calling or insults.

A case in point is told about a real-life translator who worked at 10 Downing Street in London. As the story goes, Margaret Thatcher had been urged by her foreign office, against her better judgment, to receive a notorious Congolese communist. No sooner had the hapless Marxist seated himself in the prime minister's drawing room than she fixed him with an acid glare. She introduced herself with these words: "I *hate* communists." Mortified, the translator stammered and then rendered Thatcher's comments thus: "Prime Minister Thatcher says that she has never been wholly supportive of the ideas of Karl Marx."[9]

> *Soften mean-streak communication, and pass the message along in a way that is constructive yet firm.*

If the translation fails to convey the required urgency or impact, it will be wise to remind the recipients that the message has been conveyed to them using "translated wording." But even then, it may be better to leave what was actually said to the audience's imagination. In the example involving Margaret Thatcher and her Congolese visitor, we are told that her guest was able to guess from her expression where the Iron Lady stood.

THE VALUE OF A CHAPLAIN

It is, of course, very possible that the powerful person lays into people right then and there. Such outbursts can have a devastating effect. That was the message in the courageous intervention of Ted Rogers's top lieutenant John Tory that we analyzed in detail in Rule 8. People who see or, worse, are the target of a temperamental leader's wrath for the first time (or repeatedly) can easily be traumatized, which will affect them and their performance. As we have discussed, it will in most situations be unwise and unproductive to take an enraged boss to task in the heat of the moment, even though we may feel the need to protect our team. Small gestures of support, however, can go a long way.

Charlie Hoffman, the American who was hired by Ted Rogers in 1998 to turn around the wireless division, had much admiration for Alan Horn, the finance chief who eventually became chairman of Rogers Communications after Gar Emerson's departure. "Alan is solid as a rock," Caroline Van Hasselt quotes Hoffman as saying. "He would sometimes support you during Ted's attacks. He'd point out quietly a fact that maybe Ted wasn't aware of. It often didn't help you, but you felt good that there was someone supporting you."[10]

If Charlie Hoffman, who is described as "a veteran of America's cutthroat wireless wars" and a person not afraid of Ted Rogers, appreciated a little help, there is no question that more junior people will be exceedingly grateful for it. If it is not offered in the moment, a little pep talk and some genuine compassion afterward will go a long way, especially if it comes from someone who has been there. It is comforting for people to know that being berated can happen to everyone, including people who are much more senior. In fact, as some veterans of Rogers Communications have remarked, albeit somewhat tongue in cheek, being yelled at shows that one still matters.[11]

Over time, it can be particularly helpful when someone offers to carry the confidence of those affected (and afflicted) by temperament and intensity. This can be either a fatherly senior executive or, even better, a board member, because it is not always a matter of offering advice or solving the problem, but more like being a priest or chaplain. By hearing and keeping secrets well, they allow people to walk away less troubled.

DEFUSE AND DIVERT TENSION

Some friendly support certainly beats piling on. Unfortunately, you have to be aware of the fact that some people may have the rather nasty habit of throwing gasoline on the fire as they attempt to exploit a culture of creative conflict. Others may just stand by, content that they are not the target of the moment.

What is therefore incredibly valuable is someone who actually defuses tension. This can be done by bringing the focus back to the issue at hand, changing the topic altogether, or jumping in to take ownership of a controversial item. Some masterful examples of diverting and defusing are given by Norman Schwarzkopf's deputy commander Calvin Waller. They were chronicled by both Rick Atkinson and Schwarzkopf himself during the tense days in the confined space of the underground war room in Riyadh.[12]

In one instance, if the general would start getting worked up, Waller would quickly interject, "I got it, CINC, I got it. I see what you want. Leave it to me." The fact that Schwarzkopf knew that Waller would "get it"—that is, implicitly know what the commander had in mind—would make that intervention possible. If the barrage continued, Waller would launch into a joke or offer a bit of folklore passed down from his grandmother in Louisiana. The assumption here is that this kind of humor had proven effective before. Or if Schwarzkopf was upset at an ambiguous message and wanted to find the culprit, Waller would pluck the message from his hand and say, "I'll take care of it; now let's move on to something else."

Of course, it helped that Waller had known Schwarzkopf for some time and had his respect. Schwarzkopf himself describes Waller as someone who was not intimidated by him—implying, of course, that others were. We have to give Waller much credit for using his influence for the better of everyone and to advance the cause at hand. He certainly did not play along with creative conflict. Waller played a particularly helpful role when he told a staff member who was terrified of the commander's wrath to bring the problems to him. He would then take them to the chief. This activity of taking over as messenger of bad news adds enormous value. Not only did Waller spare junior people, but, most important, he also ensured that bad news was not suppressed, delayed, or even buried altogether.

While you can divert and ease the pain, to the benefit of everyone involved, you should also carefully observe how people are coping with the full assault. Specifically, you must look for signs that for some reason they incite further fury by rubbing the powerful person the wrong way. For example, I have seen people continue to justify their actions and argue long after the time for reasoning had passed. In other words, when the time had come to shut up and listen, they kept talking. These people need immediate coaching. In some cases, you may even think about moving them out of the way (such as by limiting or eliminating their contact with the powerful person or by reassigning them to a less exposed job). Such a move would allow them to live to come back and fight another day.

> *Defuse tensions by focusing on the issues, rather than on people, and act as a buffer by taking some of the heat (if you can).*

CLEANING UP AFTER BAD NEWS

Cleanup is a particularly valuable and necessary activity when it comes to employment terminations. Any job loss, be it a result of lacking chemistry, poor performance, or part of a corporate downsizing, can be traumatic and the source of lasting resentment. Often people resent less the fact that they lost their jobs and more they way it was done and the way they were treated.

It is therefore imperative to do terminations well, and, with all due respect, using Donald Trump's favorite line of "You're fired!" or sending an e-mail is hardly the way to accomplish that. Fortunately, however, while powerful people are prone to frequent turnover, they often like to leave the actual execution of the task (no pun intended) to others. Thus, we are told that CBS chairman Bill Paley left the uncomfortable task of firing people to Frank Stanton. In fact, when he became disenchanted with an executive, he would give a quiet signal to his capable deputy. Quite the chaplain, Stanton often tried to soften the blow by moving an executive to a less exposed position in the company or giving him or her a reprieve while the person looked for work elsewhere."[13]

A compassionate and orderly separation does not just help those affected; it also protects the image of the powerful person and reduces the risk of lawsuits alleging egregious or high-handed conduct. Incidentally, keeping powerful people away from the actual (formal) termination meeting also prevents the chance of them changing their mind. As we have seen, that would be one of the very practical risks of bringing them in; their presence puts them in position to hear the appeal and issue a reprieve or pardon on the spot. Some may think this is not so bad at all. But if a decisive boss has an emotional response to a termination meeting and reacts to a second thought, he or she can just as easily reverse the firing decision after the fact and leave you to clean up the resulting mess. This is clearly something you don't want.

Conversely, a hatchet man approach on behalf of those who implement the leader's decisions will give rise to resentment and cynicism, both with those who leave and those who stay. Perhaps such a ruthless approach will impress some people. But more likely than not, it won't, and it can only cause further trouble.

The concept of cleaning up after bad news also applies to another series of similar situations: the candidate who did not get the job for reasons that would not be appropriate to spell out in detail; the supplier who did not get the deal, even though he was sure it was in the bag; the manager who thought she had the promotion, only to fall victim to a change of mind or circumstance. The list goes on, and tactful yet firm communication is a task that someone must perform to keep a semblance of order and decorum. Practiced in its advanced form, facilitation will anticipate collisions, get to issues before they bubble up, and defuse tensions before they mushroom into a full-blown crisis.

> *Manage terminations and other bad-news items for the powerful person in a way that leaves relationships intact or at least prevents severe fallout.*

Powerful People Love to Speak Their Mind

A further characteristic of those in power that necessitates cleanup is their tendency to speak their mind. While we have already discussed what to do when you are on the receiving end of your boss's "frank" feedback, candid and uncensored communication with people outside the organization presents its own challenges. For example, the leader may have strong opinions on issues related to trade unions, foreign-trade policy, industry regulation, and similar topics. Especially when such comments reach an audience in a different culture, they can easily raise eyebrows.

Even world leaders are not immune from astonishing conversation pieces. Colin Powell tells the story of how President Ronald Reagan interrupted Soviet leader Mikhail Gorbachev in a jam-packed meeting in the White House Cabinet Room. Gorbachev was impressing the audience with his detailed knowledge of the arms reduction process. Prompted by Reagan, he yielded the floor, and the president proceeded to tell a "story" of an American professor embarking on a flight to the Soviet Union. When being driven to the airport by a student cab driver for his departing flight, the professor asked him about his professional ambitions after school. The student answered, "I don't know, I have not decided yet." At the other end of his trip, in a cab on his way into Moscow, there was another student cab driver. The professor asks the same question. "Don't know," the cab driver answers, "they have not told me yet." "That," Reagan concluded, "is the basic difference between us." [14] As he finished his story, the Americans wanted to disappear under the table.

Having the job to clean up after statements of this nature is truly an unenviable task. Rather than trying to minimize or, worse condone what was said, it is better to ascribe such statement to eccentricity, something that many listeners are prepared to see powerful people as being prone to. In addition, it may be healthy if, from time to time, the powerful person suffers the consequences of his or her behavior in the form of, for example, a letter of complaint. If you insulate powerful individuals too much and too effectively, they will dismiss your warnings, even more than they would anyway. Furthermore, as seen in the complementor rule, if nothing bad ever happens, powerful people may start to dismiss the skill and finesse required to get them out of their self-induced messes.

In the Ronald Reagan episode, Colin Powell took responsibility for his boss's faux pas. He attributed the freewheeling storytelling to a lack of preparation. To avoid reoccurrence, he prepared a well-thought-out set of talking points for the next meeting. These provided focus and eliminated the need for further "stories." Instead, the president was able to combine solid facts with his natural charm and charisma and live up to his reputation of being the Great Communicator.

Some have asked whether the facilitation, absorption, rationalization, apology for, and just plain spin-doctoring of uncivilized behavior is similar to the "enabling" of alcoholics or drug addicts.[15] Especially when it comes to disparagement, it is true that the perpetrators are not the only ones to blame, and there is nothing worse than good people who do nothing. We have discussed some of this in the independence rule, Rule 9. You must preestablish a line that you will not allow to be crossed—not when it comes to yourself, and not when it comes to others. This does not mean you immediately engage in full confrontation. For example, you can say something after the fact like this: "With respect, that statement was inappropriate." At least by doing so, you have said what needed to be said and demonstrated your willingness to live with the consequences, whatever they may be.

As much as your own rule of independence should come into play, I do not believe that success as a facilitator should require that you change or "reform" powerful people. Having some positive influence and correcting the record will itself be a significant accomplishment. Instead, your primary goal is to facilitate, mediate, and, yes, absorb pain, so that important work continues to get done and business goals are achieved.

Powerful People Need Mediation

A final aspect of facilitating business for powerful people can be classified as mediation. Powerful people can leave those who are not used to them shell-shocked and unwilling ever to deal with them again; conversely, powerful people can be turned off by someone who approaches them the wrong way.

Seeing both sides of the story and empathizing with each party is the work of a good mediator. Mediators are in a unique position to present the other side of a story in the right way and manage emotions. They can be the constructive catalyst for a compromise by helping to develop options that resonate with the parties' preferences and avoid no-go zones.

If what is contemplated is a really bad deal, however, "mediation" may allow the project to die elegantly. That type of facilitation does not require any manipulation at all. All you need to do is let the parties communicate with each other or pass along their proposals as-is, and the problem will likely take care of itself. For example, you may see a proposal for a project you consider distracting or out of touch with established business goals, and you notice that it does not push the right buttons, or even that it pushes the wrong buttons. Under other circumstances, you might have intervened to increase the chances of approval. However, in this case, you let it go through unedited, and the powerful person will conclude that it does not have any merit.

> *Sometimes, the task is to facilitate failure of an idea.*

Your mediation can occur between the powerful person and outside parties (such as customers, suppliers, investors, and parties to a merger or acquisition) or internal ones who have some power, like a board of directors or senior executives. In other instances, you may have to mediate between departments or between the head office and subsidiaries.

When you are mediating internal conflict, the first step is always to listen and let each side know that you have understood. If you are perceived as an agent for the other side, you will get nothing done. In some instances, you will have to work hard to overcome that bias—for instance, if a local subsidiary looks at you as a person from headquarters. Only after that has been done can you point out some of the real constraints and make one side see the other side's perspective. You can then help the parties look for creative options to get both sides as much as possible of what they want. Your contribution in such a situation goes much further than resolving the issue at hand. As a facilitator, you can set the stage for improved relationships across organization boundaries.

POWERFUL PEOPLE TEND TO WORK BEST IF THEY HAVE CONTROL

In the case of larger-than-life people and others like them, however, mediation also has its clear limits. Some powerful people are just not cut out for a partnership or compromises. They simply work best when they have absolute control. As a result, a lot of work invested in the arrangement can be wasted when a highly controlling leader starts to notice that the other partner has his or her own vision, goals, and ways of doing things—and more often than not, the leader will find it hard to adjust. Therefore, when you are involved in a discussion about a joint venture or similar project, you may not be doing anyone any favors if you use your skills to smooth over differences. It may be much easier if everyone sees the incompatibility early on. For skilled facilitators, managing differences is second nature, but at some point, it will be better just to let the parties on each side see exactly whom they are dealing with.

What to do when . . .

. . . you have been chosen to be the messenger of bad news

You have been chosen as the messenger of bad news to the powerful person. The news could be that the deal has been lost, the job cannot be done, or the powerful person's request has been denied. You fear that the messenger might be shot.

That fear is justified. Therefore, first ask, "Why me?" The messenger of bad news should always be the person with the best relationship. There is opportunity as well, however. If you deliver the news, you are taking on a task no one else wants to do or is able to do. That can earn respect.

In the actual conversation, start with a preparatory sentence, but get to the point quickly: "I'm afraid I have some bad news. We have lost the rezoning application for the new facility." Then, try to get to options: "We can appeal, or we can look at an alternative location. [Ideally, have one ready.]" The powerful person will likely be looking to blame someone: "Maybe we have the wrong lawyers, architects, consultants." This is not the time to be defensive. Whether or not blame is justified, do not appear to be more invested in a relationship than in the powerful person's success. Simply agree: "Maybe we do; I can look at some alternatives." Otherwise, you risk provoking an explanation of why people are to blame, which can easily spiral out of control. Leave that discussion for another day.

At the moment, the key is this: present the bad news for what it is, keep reasons to a minimum, focus on alternatives, and give the powerful person as much control as possible. Discuss other aspects once everyone has calmed down. Especially when keeping the same team members on board is the right thing to do, it is better to have the powerful person realize that and want to convince you why you do not want to change the team.

Advise Those Who Like to Act

I present research, options, and opinions to her [Oprah Winfrey]. We discuss them and she makes the decisions.

—JEFF JACOBS, FORMER PRESIDENT
AND CHIEF OPERATING OFFICER, HARPO PRODUCTIONS

P eter Drucker has pointed out that advising and deciding are distinct activities. They are both very necessary and require different people. He explained that "a great many people perform best as advisors, but cannot take the burden and pressure of the decision. Other people, by contrast, need an advisor to force them to think, but then they can make the decision and act on it with speed, self confidence, and courage."[1] Powerful people can fall into the latter category in an even more pronounced way. They have a tendency to act because that's their bent and because they can. The thinking step can be easily skipped, although one should never underestimate the tremendous capacity for gut feeling. I have once heard "gut" described as a total body and mind response to the situation in front of a person; in the case of a person who has built a business from scratch or fought his or her way to the top, the person's brilliance, vast experience, and intuition make for a powerful mix.

Powerful People Have a Hard Time Getting Unbiased Advice

There can be no question that powerful people need unbiased advice. However, for a good many of them, especially those larger than life, it will be quite hard to get. One reason is that they are surrounded by people who seek their attention with an agenda of their own. Inner-circle executives, board members, financial and legal advisers, philanthropic fund-raisers, and even family members all have potential conflicts. This is not to say that all these people are scheming to accomplish selfish goals and ambitions, although some certainly will be. But it speaks to the fact that larger-than-life leaders have such an extraordinary impact on the personal and professional lives of others that, for better and for worse, many of those around and beneath them cannot focus on their best interests. Yet it is agenda-free advice that powerful people need most, whether they realize it or not.

The second factor preventing powerful people from getting the advice they need is that those around them may just be too afraid to raise difficult topics, let alone dispense advice. For example, advising a business founder that it is time to give serious thought to succession planning or, worse, stepping away so that the successor can prove his or her mettle is exceedingly difficult. It can even shake the foundation of the iconic leader's identity and in a very real way raises the specter that he or she may not be around

> Powerful people need agenda-free advice.

forever. This may indeed be a highly unpopular thought. We are told that Ted Rogers was serious when he said, "You can't run it from the grave, but you can try."[2]

Of course, my intention is not to pass judgment lightly. We can safely assume that most people at one point or another have told their boss what that person wanted to hear or have given "good advice" with an ulterior motive, whether the boss was larger than life or not. But the advice (and adviser) that will be effective and valued over the long term is the one that (and adviser who) leads to decisions that were based on a true understanding of interests, constraints, and different options.

LOYALTY IS A GOOD FOUNDATION FOR GOOD ADVICE . . .

Loyalty is a good foundation for becoming an influential adviser to the powerful. Loyalty has nothing to do with being a yes-man or -woman, but it gives the implicit assurance that the counselor wants what is best for the powerful person—in the context of a bigger picture.

Ted Rogers's experience provides great insight into who might make a good adviser to a strong-minded business founder. Despite all of his temperament, strong-headedness, and reputation for inducing fear, he valued sobering counsel. Rogers found his counselor in his stepfather, John Graham, a highly respected lawyer and businessman who served as chairman of Rogers Communications Inc. (RCI) and remained chairman emeritus until his death at age eighty-six. Graham had been a mentor for Rogers from his boyhood days; he had taught the thirteen-year-old Ted to keep meticulous financial records; he had provided the money and the connections to launch Rogers's career as a radio entrepreneur; and he had always been Rogers's most stalwart supporter. It was exactly this commitment to his stepson's success that provided the basis for sound advice. Graham always put Rogers's best interest first but at the same time kept "Ted and the company from going too far over the edge."[3] In reflecting on the role of his late stepfather, Rogers said that John Graham was the voice of conservatism and sober second thought and that "he provided me with what obviously Conrad Black never had."[4] An amazing insight from a larger-than-life entrepreneur about one of his peers.

Ted Rogers's testimony is not the only one that points to loyalty as a foundation for providing desperately needed critical advice. Earlier on, we mentioned Beate Baumann, the influential adviser to Chancellor Angela Merkel. We are told that Baumann is in a unique position to dispense controversial advice on unpopular topics. And she can do the advising in a remarkably straightforward manner that can at times be shocking to others in the chancellor's entourage. She may do so "because she only wants Merkel's success and nothing for herself."[5]

People who are loyal and understand the character of the powerful leader they work under make outstanding advisers. The best ones know their bosses better than they know themselves. Jeff Jacobs, who started out as Oprah Winfrey's lawyer and later on became president and chief operating officer of Harpo, Winfrey's production company, provides an outstanding example of great advice given by a loyal adviser.

While we are told that their business relationship eventually ended in controversy, Jacobs played a big role in Winfrey's business success. *Fortune* magazine called him "a little known power behind the media queen's throne."[6] And while he did hold an executive position, Jacobs described his job as Winfrey's counselor first and foremost: "I present research, options, and opinions to her. We discuss them and she makes the decisions."[7]

The counselor gave a critical piece of advice when it came to building Harpo Productions. Jacobs convinced Winfrey that she should establish her own company rather than be talent for hire, as most TV stars are. He pushed his advice hard and "helped Oprah see that she really could have control."[8] Most important, he sagely advised against going public—the thorn in the side of many powerful founders. He explained that if she maintained 80 percent ownership in a private company (the rest being owned by King World and Jacobs), she would not have to contend with scrutiny and disclosure requirements or have to answer to a board of directors. She would own it, and she would be in control.

That was great advice. Jacobs realized that full and outright ownership was what his boss really needed and wanted, even before she realized it herself. And he helped her see it. Winfrey would be the enterprise, with full protection against outside interference. This is a good place to note that outright ownership beats the vehicle of a public company with a dual-class share structure. Even if multiple voting shares do provide ultimate control, the public-company status invites activist shareholders and regulators to become a thorn in the side of the powerful person. Jacobs had it absolutely right. This counselor was worth his weight in gold.

> *Counsel will often be most effective if it is given by a loyal adviser who has every ambition to see his or her friend succeed.*

. . . BUT ADVISORS CANNOT BE TOO LAID-BACK

While I have stressed the value of a loyal adviser, we must keep in mind that an effective adviser must not be too laid-back either. In one of his frequent letters from his Florida jail, Conrad Black fondly remembers his adviser Cardinal Gerald Emmett Carter, then archbishop of Toronto. Black says he used to discuss "a good many subjects" with the cardinal, and he describes Carter as a friend and an "intimate whose counsel was only given when requested and was always wise."[9] In the same letter, Black remains defiant, some may say unrepentant, when he considers himself "unjustly indicted, convicted, and imprisoned, in a country I formerly admired (i.e., the United States)." We can only speculate whether or not the cardinal could have given Black better advice or should/could have been a firmer shepherd. But it is interesting that, as pointed out earlier, Ted Rogers did comment on the fact that Conrad Black did not have the kind of counselor that he, Ted Rogers, had.[10] By implication, we can argue that Carter did not fit the bill in Rogers's mind.

Effective counselors will therefore combine ambition for the interests of their powerful friend with an objective and independent view of what is needed. In other words, it would be reckless to misunderstand loyalty as a reason why you should not warn your powerful "friend" of clear and present danger. You may even have to paint a picture of what might happen if the powerful person goes down a certain path. Whether or not your warning will be heard or heeded is, of course, another matter, but loyalty demands that it be given.

THE FINE LINE BETWEEN RESPECT AND DEFERENCE

In *Confessions of a Trusted Counselor*, David Nadler advises counselors to talk to the chief executive officer as "you would to a colleague, not your boss." "If you talk and act like a subordinate," he says, "you'll be treated that way. Always."[11] As chairman of a large consulting firm, Nadler is certainly experienced and well versed on the topic of giving advice. But in the same piece, he also extols the virtue of the "enlightened" chief executive who welcomes frank discussions. That's where I believe we need a caveat. Some powerful people are in a league of their own and are to a large extent without peers. And there will be days when the last thing they are looking for is a frank discussion. Therefore, coming in with the attitude of a peer to a person who considers him- or herself peerless can easily backfire and be perceived as arrogant and condescending.

Remember that powerful people have radar-like perception. One of the most important questions to ask yourself, therefore, is whether, in the eyes of the powerful person, you have earned the right to act as a (peer) adviser. This will be a matter of your own background, experience, and track record as an adviser. These are practical considerations that deserve reflection before you act like a peer adviser. If there are doubts, there is nothing wrong with sticking to a lower-key approach.

Some Techniques for Low-Key Advice

As we have seen, asking questions is a good, low-key way of giving advice without giving advice. It also makes good sense to take a page out of Cardinal Carter's book and wait for the question "What do you think?" Even then, one should be careful not to blurt out controversial ideas.

If you do consider yourself to be a peer adviser, you may still have reason not to be lecturing too quickly. You may not fully understand the intricacies of the industry, the constraints of local business culture, or the history involved. Given any of these peculiarities, advice that could be sound in a different context may come off as amateurish. You may therefore want to think about phrasing your advice in the form of an indirect suggestion such as this: "In the United States, a strategy of X has proven effective, and some say it could work anywhere," or "Your competitors are following strategy X; would that work for you as well?" You can also hedge your bets more simply by leading with "from my limited perspective" or "I may not fully understand, but here is what one might consider." All of this gives plenty of room for retreat and allows an easing into the adviser role, especially for new or more junior executives or outside advisers who are not part of the organization's everyday affairs. None of this means you are a crouching underling. It simply means you are respectful, willing to admit that you don't know everything, and focused on what's effective so that your advice can be considered without hindrance.

Even board members who take their advice and oversight role seriously will not diminish their effectiveness by acknowledging, for example, that the founder is the founder and they are not. Showing humility, even if background and position would allow for a more peer-like demeanor, will go further than (real or perceived) arrogance in demonstrating the role of an equal when in fact there is a difference in experience and/or status. In other words, waiting until the powerful person bestows the role of sage adviser on you will be wiser than assuming you are entitled to it based on a formal title or position.

All of this cannot mean you approach the person in charge in a manner that suggests you are somehow awestruck by the person's presence. Yes, you can and must be respectful of the person's accomplishments, but you must always remain unawed in order to maintain perspective.

> *Humility always pays dividends, but you cannot afford to be awestruck.*

DON'T TAKE OVER TOO QUICKLY

In many instances, professional advisers are called in to become part of a project that requires their specialized expertise. Examples of such projects are union and other negotiations, strategic financial transactions, litigation, and dealings with governmental authorities. In smaller companies, these projects can take on major significance and require direct involvement of the owner, as they are not routine and present a major threat or opportunity for the organization. Especially if high-caliber advisers are brought in, they can easily exude an air of superiority.

In such situations, the outside (or inside) professional should start by considering carefully whether the powerful client wants him or her to take control of the project or simply provide the professional service. For example, Michael Wolff reports that Rupert Murdoch's general counsel, who joined News Corporation from an outside law firm, came to appreciate that Murdoch will not look to the experts to find out what to do.[12] In general, I believe lawyers and other high-profile consultants too quickly assume they can give peer advice or take over, and, as a result, they lose credibility before building the relationship.

Instead, outside advisers should recognize that leaders who are firmly in control may want to be directly involved in the process and/or put their unique stamp on it. As we have seen, it would be foolish to dismiss their unconventional ideas outright and give a lecture as to why they won't work. If a leader is truly in unfamiliar territory, a good starting point may be to provide a general education on the contemplated project (for example, principles and pitfalls of acquisition due diligence) to all the nonexpert participants. This will help everyone—including the person in charge—to be more effective and will establish the professional service provider's credibility without holding expert knowledge close to his or her chest. There is a great likelihood that a powerful leader will find such a 101 presentation interesting and educational. It will also make it easier to point out later why certain ideas may not work well (by referring back to previously established principles).

It may well be that after the general education, the powerful person will still want to keep control and run the process his or her way. If at all possible, you should work with people like this, adapt to them, and make things work their way. The reason is that, for high-profile leaders, the process is not just about getting things done but may be a reflection on their reputation, business culture, and values. They may even have the ambition to reform the way such processes are done. In any negotiation, for example, they will be inclined to get the deal done among businesspeople rather than negotiating through lawyers. Your role will be to equip them to do that, rather than to talk them out of it. In some instances, they may run out of steam as more pressing or more interesting matters emerge, and you can take the project off their hands at that time. In the meantime, you want to keep showing that you are a team player, open to ideas, and make things work in a way that suits your client's reality.

> *Earn the right to give counsel. Speaking too soon can easily backfire.*

A COALITION OF ADVISERS

A technique to consider when adding weight to a recommendation is to assemble a group of people who, under normal circumstances, may have competing agendas. The fact that the members of this group have overcome their differences shows that the matter is important and has been considered thoroughly. Be warned that such coalition building has to be done carefully, as it can easily create the impression of ganging up or conspiring and, as a result, backfire. The incentive for pursuing such a course of action is the tremendous power in taking the moral high ground

> *Enlisting the support of others for your ideas can make for highly effective counsel, especially when you have to overcome turf issues. But beware of creating a perception of ganging up.*

and having put the organization's interest ahead of one's own turf. Therefore, if you are, for example, advising that your company should start up a new group for advanced research or a similar activity, it will be much more credible if you propose that the new team report to another colleague, if that's what is best. Your main demonstrated interest should be that the job gets done, not that your "empire" is growing.

SPEAK THEIR LANGUAGE, AND USE THE RIGHT FRAME

This insight just confirms the fact that the best and most authoritative advice will be rooted in the firm's overall strategy and the powerful person's own values and principles. As explained in earlier rules, it is always best to listen and understand first and not patronize powerful people based on your "expert" knowledge. Nothing would drive them crazier! Instead, giving careful consideration to properly framing your advice will increase its effectiveness. As Jeffrey Pfeffer puts it in *Managing with Power*, what looks reasonable, or ridiculous, depends on the context—on how it is framed.[13] Therefore, it will be good to know what the powerful person is thinking before you offer up your own opinions; knowing that allows you to frame the advice in a way that fits with the person's ideas, views, and interests—even the latest fad. Furthermore, it helps you use their language and vocabulary, rather than expert jargon.

> *Finding out first what the powerful person thinks can make counsel much more effective. It allows you to frame your advice in the best way possible.*

Remember: Advice Is Just That

In the end, you have to remember that advice is just that—advice. You offer your best insight, you put it forward in the clearest and most effective way, and you point out the consequences of it not being followed. But once effective counsel has been given, it is up to the powerful person to accept or reject it. It is not your role as counselor to make the decision. The leader of the business, the troops, or the party, whichever the case may be, remains responsible for that. The leader has the bigger picture and arguably the greater insight, and he or she will use it. If you feel a powerful person is dead wrong after you have put forward your point with clarity and emphasis, you may still decide to take it upon yourself to forestall what you perceive to be a looming disaster. Just understand that if you do so, you will be taking on a different role, that of a counterweight, which we will explore in the next rule.

LET POWERFUL PEOPLE DO THEIR THING

There may be another reason for why you shouldn't be too unhappy when your advice is not taken. There are some things that powerful leaders will just have to experience for themselves. And that's when it is wisest to step back and let them do their thing.

A great example occurred in the mid-1990s, when Frank Stronach developed an idea of "government by jury." His thinking was that the flaw of Canada and democracies in general is that they are mismanaged because they are run by political rather than economic reasoning. Based on that rationale, Stronach developed a variation of the classic Greek democracy whereby a computer would select a "jury" of citizens at random to replace the Canadian senate (which is the upper house of parliament). This chamber of citizens would vote in secret on legislation and would make better decisions because political motives, such as reelection, would be replaced by practical economic reasons that more accurately represent the view of ordinary citizens.[14] Frank Stronach's advisers let the idea run its course;[15] ironically, one of them eventually accepted an appointment to the—unchanged—senate.[16]

> *Sometimes it may be best just to step back and let powerful people do their thing.*

Especially when no harm is done, it is sometimes best to just let powerful people go ahead with a controversial idea and learn from their own experience. That may be the only advice they accept anyway.

NEVER SAY, "I TOLD YOU SO"

A final warning to advisers is to beware of "I told you so." Wanting to be right is a very human emotion, especially if someone has used power to shut down your ideas. But we must control this emotion and withstand the temptation.

This lesson was learned the hard way by John Hoskyns, one of Margaret Thatcher's most able advisers. Shortly after Thatcher came to power, Hoskyns coauthored the *Stepping Stones* report, which became the blueprint for the "Thatcher revolution." Hoskyns's communication strategy played an important part in giving a well-articulated and effective voice to Thatcher's assault on Britain's socialist legacy.[17] That fight became very real when the Iron Lady started her collision course with the powerful miners' union led by Arthur "King Coal" Scargill. Hoskyns had warned his boss that taking on the coal miners would require a massive battle plan, especially now that the fearsome Scargill had taken over, yet nothing was done. As a result, when the unions challenged the Tory government in 1981, Thatcher was forced to capitulate. Following the humiliation, Thatcher went to war and wrestled the miners and Scargill to the ground in an epic battle. Alas, John Hoskyns, who had identified the threat and the need to brace for battle early on, was not part of it when it finally happened. While he never said, "I told you so" explicitly, we are told that his sentiments were clear enough. Hoskyns was excluded from discussing the miners issue after the 1981 defeat and resigned from his adviser post soon thereafter.[18]

What to do when . . .

. . . you are being put on the spot

You are sitting in the conference room during a discussion of a strategic initiative. A colleague is presenting a strategic initiative such as an investment in a new local office, a joint venture, or a new product line. You have no idea how the powerful person feels about the proposal when, out of the blue, you are asked for your opinion.

Especially if you are new to the organization, be careful not to blurt out your first impression and opinion too early, even if you think the proposal is a harebrained idea. However, you do not want to appear indecisive either. The best strategy therefore may be to ask a question.

While you may have specific questions based on what has been presented thus far, several generic questions are useful in many situations: (1) Do we have the right people to lead/manage the project? (2) Do we have a plan B if our projections/expectations are derailed? (3) What other options did you consider before settling on this proposal? (4) What are our competitors doing? (5) Are there any risks (ideally specific ones, such as currency fluctuations, security, unexpected delays, and intellectual property) that require more analysis?

You can lead into your question by saying something like "I can see the merits of the project and the opportunity it presents."

RULE 14

Know When (and Whether) to Put On the Brakes— if You Can

Going to extremes has a place in leadership— the problem comes when those extremes go beyond what the situation dictates.

—BOB KAPLAN AND ROB KAISER, *THE VERSATILE LEADER* [1]

Powerful people are a relentless force in the pursuit of their goals and ambitions and when provoked by what they consider incompetence or obstacles in their path. Once that force has gathered momentum, it is hard to stop. Sometimes, however, someone needs to put on the brakes. You may have to put on the brakes to get what you need to get your job done, to preserve the interests of a powerful leader's organization or ultimate objective, or even to protect powerful people from themselves.

In their book *The Versatile Leader*, Bob Kaplan and Rob Kaiser point out that "in any walk of organizational life, those individuals who go way out of bounds will probably forever need a counter-weight."[2] While going to extremes has a place in leadership, problems do arise "when those extremes go far beyond what the situation dictates."[3] In a way, Kaplan and Kaiser's insight describes the default mode of many powerful people, certainly those who are larger than life. These individuals can and will be relentless, no matter what.

As the Name Suggests: A Counterweight Needs Weight

Skill and courage certainly are involved if you want to be a counterweight. But the first thing you need is the actual weight, and you should have a very clear idea where the weight comes from and whether it is actually sufficient. When you are assessing your potential for filling this role, there is absolutely nothing wrong with coming to the conclusion that you are too light for the job. In fact, it is a sign of great wisdom. The greatest danger lies in thinking you are a counterweight when in fact you are not.

> Don't try to act as a counterweight unless you have the "weight" to do it.

CREDIBILITY: AN IMPORTANT INGREDIENT OF BEING A COUNTERWEIGHT

Therefore, you need a clear idea where your weight as a counterweight comes from and whether or not it is heavy enough. In that sense, I would think it almost impossible to do the job from day one, especially where a larger-than-life person is involved—unless, of course, you have a formal power base, as we will see a bit later in this chapter.

One of the most impressive performances of a counterweight has been provided by Marshal Zhukov. It is an example of competence, credibility, and courage. By promoting Zhukov to commander of the western front in 1941, his boss, Joseph Stalin, had solved his most pressing leadership problem. Upon receiving word about how weak the defenses really were, Stalin informed Zhukov that the previous man in charge, General Ivan Konev, would be held responsible and be handed over to a military tribunal. Zhukov knew what this meant: Konev would be shot. Instead of keeping his head down, however,

Zhukov told Stalin that such action would change nothing. What is more, it would probably further demoralize the troops—exactly what had happened after the shooting of one of Konev's predecessors. Zhukov argued that Konev was an intelligent man and could prove useful. The commander in chief grudgingly relented.

Zhukov's intervention was credible. For him, the mission and the cause always came first, and he had proven to be ruthless and merciless when it came to punishing cowards. Thus, he carried the weight to be "bluntly saying unpleasant things," as Stalin commented later.[4] Konev was spared and ended up performing well as deputy front commander. Zhukov had managed to put on the brakes with life-saving results for his subordinate, acting toward an eventual success for his boss and the salvation of Mother Russia.[5]

> *Don't throw your weight around needlessly. Your goal is to act in the powerful person's best interest, not to antagonize him or her.*

LOYAL INSIDERS CAN BE EFFECTIVE COUNTERWEIGHTS

Zhukov's example shows that a loyal insider can be an effective counterweight, even when working for a larger-than-life tyrant. Zhukov did not have any power base bestowed by another authority—though, as we will see, those can be helpful.

In the situation of a publicly traded corporation, governance experts typically look for a formally independent director (or better, an independent chairperson) to be the counterweight to an all-powerful chief executive. If the chief executive is also a major or controlling shareholder, this will be, of course, a formidable challenge. Accordingly, the experts are critical of a chairperson being "related" (i.e., having a material business or personal relationship) with the chief.

The chairman succession at Rogers Communications is a case in point. As reviewed earlier, Ted Rogers demanded the resignation of Gar Emerson, who had replaced John Graham, Rogers's stepfather, in the chairman's position. Emerson, a highly respected lawyer and one of Canada's foremost governance experts, had been a Rogers director for seventeen years and chairman for thirteen of those years. While the catalyst was a relatively minor controversy, Caroline Van Hasselt surmises that there had been a different problem: Emerson had started to act more like the independent chairman he was, rather than being a stalwart supporter of Ted Rogers.[6] Thus, when Alan Horn, Rogers's right-hand man, replaced the independent Emerson, some commentators saw this as "asking the fox to guard the hen house."[7]

However, I do not believe that this conclusion is always compelling. As we have seen, formal independence does not always equate to effectiveness, nor does its absence mean there cannot be an effective counterweight. On the contrary, it appears that while a closer personal or business relationship will negate or at least cast doubt on independence as defined by governance principles and regulation, it is the very ingredient that can make a counterweight effective. Everybody would have agreed that John Graham was the right person to keep Ted Rogers on course, yet as Rogers's stepfather, Graham did not technically pass the independence test. And while Gar Emerson is well respected, he was no longer around to get anything done at Rogers. Similarly, we can note that Marshal Zhukov was hardly independent from his boss.

There are quite a few additional examples of people who worked for powerful bosses and made very effective counterweights, even though theoretically they had to be concerned about their jobs. As president and chief operating officer of Enron (and even before), a tough, disciplined, and detail-oriented Richard Kinder was an effective counterweight to Kenneth Lay. Some believe that Enron would still be in existence if Kinder hadn't left the company to build an energy empire of his own.[8]

Quite remarkably, the value of these "internal" counterweights is not lost on outside stakeholders, such as lenders and investors. When Graham Savage resigned as Rogers's chief financial officer, investors reacted with great concern that the company had lost "the financially conservative counterweight to the founder's infectious enthusiasm," especially as Rogers Communications was carrying a huge mountain of debt.[9] On the urging of its key lenders, Ted Rogers had to soothe investor concerns and promise restraint in a press conference.[10]

Conversely, we can note cases of an "independent" chairperson being less effective. For example, the independent supervisory board chairman Klaus Liessen was not the counterweight to Ferdinand Piëch that some Volkswagen executives had hoped for. In a story surfaced by the weekly *Der Spiegel*, the executives complained in a letter to the chairman that Piëch with his controlling leadership style was running a global company as a "fiefdom."[11] Piëch offered to "speak personally" with anyone who might have a problem, but not surprisingly, no one took him up on his offer. Openly challenging the master of the power game was probably a bad idea to begin with, and Liessen, independent or not, was not going to stop him. The conclusion is clear: relationship does matter.

Additional Weight Helps

The position and heft of an internal counterweight is greatly enhanced when they are imposed by outsiders and necessitated by a crisis that even the most positively thinking powerful person cannot ignore. Such was the case in the early 1990s, when as part of their rescue package, the banks insisted that Donald Trump take on a chief financial officer. As Gwenda Blair tells the story, Steve Bollenbach took on the role and embraced a task that was new in the world of Donald Trump: someone else would be casting a highly critical eye on the Trump empire and Donald Trump's deals.[12] As Blair points out, Bollenbach limited conflict to where it was necessary, accepted his boss's personality, and refrained from seizing all of Trump's assets in one fell swoop. Instead, he took a firm hand where it mattered most and was not afraid to resort to a measure of brinkmanship. He boldly employed a "too big to fail" strategy, exploiting the fact that Donald Trump's name was a key component of asset valuation. One by one, he started releasing nonessential assets in return for concessions, and on occasion, he put in place highly visible "restrictions" that in practice did not amount to much. He adapted to his boss, who insisted on remaining in charge, and positioned him well in the negotiations.[13] Thus, with Bollenbach's help, Donald Trump made it through the crisis.

Bollenbach's success highlights some key components of effective work as a counterweight. First, Bollenbach was competent and had earlier "workout" experience and exposure to business legends (in the person of the reclusive shipping magnate and billionaire Daniel Ludwig). Second, while he did have weight, Bollenbach did not throw it around but rather appreciated and accepted his boss for who he was. Third, he knew how to take full advantage of his boss's strengths and positioned him well with outsiders. In particular, he told creditors that they would gain nothing if they pushed things over the edge. Fourth, he did not fight every battle. Far from it. But he did fight those that brought him maximum benefit on the outside and cost him the least on the inside. Finally, while doing all of this, Bollenbach displayed an impressive amount of courage and sheer chutzpah.

I believe that the lesson about not throwing your weight around (at least not more than you have to) has broader application. When you take on the position as a counterweight with some formal power, there may be an expectation that you step in right away. Maybe you are a new director on a board with outside shareholder backing. Maybe you join a company as an executive with the expectation that you will effect some change, as when a chief financial officer is hired to bring in financial discipline. While you may have been brought in by the boss, you will likely have some powerful colleagues who would prefer to maintain the status quo. Yes, it may be your job to lead the charge for change, and some people will not come along unless they have to. But others will be sitting on the fence and watching. For them, a firm but respectful approach will go a long way. You will make it more difficult for your opponents to complain and easier for your supporters to take your side.

At the same time, when you are the counterweight to an internal equal, you must be sure you will not be considered a pushover. For that, the energy to withstand conflict is critical and will pay dividends. I lived through one situation to learn that lesson. I had been invited to a meeting with a powerful colleague who had members of his team present. The meeting was held on his turf, far away from my home base. The colleague exhibited aggressive behavior, and the discussion started to deteriorate. Everybody was watching what was going on. To maintain credibility, I had no alternative but to engage and push back. Years later, one of the participants told me that this episode had been a defining moment for him and that he accepted my credibility. Of course, he had had the good sense to stay out of it while the battle was unfolding, but in that instant, not giving ground had definitely been worth it.

SPOUSES AS COUNTERWEIGHTS

Spouses can be excellent counterweights. Ted Rogers's marriage to Loretta lasted from their wedding day in 1963 until Ted's death parted them in 2009. Loretta was Ted's staunchest ally and acted as his sounding board. While she was not vocal at board meetings, she did not hesitate to speak her mind at home, and she established early on that Ted's legendary temper was not welcome at home: "When you are prepared to be civilized, I will speak to you."[14] Spoken like a true counterweight.

Colin Powell provides his thoughts on the topic when he reflects on his graduation from the command and general staff college at Fort Leavenworth, Kansas, where he finished number two in a class of more than twelve hundred officers. Although Powell was proud of his accomplishment, his wife, Alma, put him in his place by simply saying, "That's nice, but I always expect the best of you anyway." Powell goes on to acknowledge the value of an "unawed wife as good for keeping your head size constant."[15] Needless to say, the same applies

> *Don't become an accelerator when a counterweight is what's needed.*

to "unawed husbands." Likewise, when he received his promotion to general—which, it should be said, earned him more praise from his wife—the army chief of staff, General Bernard Rogers, warned the group of freshly minted army generals that some of their careers would stall out, because "their wives will start acting as if they got the promotion." The prediction, Powell says, did not go unfulfilled.

Thus, we can conclude that some spouses act as an accelerator when a counterweight is needed. In fact, this is a phenomenon that we have to beware of more generally. There will always be some who get the powerful person going, to deflect from their own problems or for other reasons. You must have a keen eye for accelerators.

Yes, everyone needs encouragement, and powerful people are no exception. The truth is, however, that where power and success abound, there will hardly be a shortage of cheerleading. Unfortunately, much less attention will be paid to keeping one's feet on the ground.

EXPERTS AS COUNTERWEIGHTS

While our main interest has been people who have power based on their position and domineering personality, that position of power can also be based on expertise. In particular, an expert can come to dominate the situation when he or she is the only expert in the room and no one can pose a challenge. In a situation like this, you may be reluctant to counter the expert, because the risk is simply too great.

This is particularly of concern if the expert has an interest in the outcome of the decision. For example, if there is a question whether or not to go forward with a financial transaction, the investment banker may have a special interest based on the potential of earning a transaction fee. If there is a question of whether to fight or settle a lawsuit, the advice of legal counsel may be influenced by the fact he or she would manage the litigation. And if the question is whether to promote from the inside or hire from the outside, an executive search consultant may not be the best adviser. Of course, good advisers will provide the advice that is in their client's best interest. But the situation may require the counterweight of a second opinion. And if it is not your decision to make, you may want to suggest or ask whether or not that second opinion might add value.

Of course, it can be delicate and expensive to have experts tripping over each other. But there are ways to address both concerns. For example, you can ask a third-party expert to provide an education on the general principles of the contemplated business at hand. That could be a simple fee for service, as when a legal firm provides a general overview of litigation in a foreign jurisdiction. Or you could ask a consultant to join the team—a retired manager with applicable expertise, for example. This latter approach can even save you some costs in the long run, especially when you can carve out a defined role for that person.

If you happen to be the established professional service provider, you should embrace additional experts who are joining the team temporarily or permanently. Anything you do to reject them or anything that makes you look defensive will immediately call into question your motives. If you're serving on an existing team and believe the additional third-party help is overkill, it will be best to let your clients come to that conclusion themselves.

Lodging Complaints

As we saw in the episode involving the "management revolt" at Volkswagen and the letters of complaint to the chairman of the board earlier in this chapter, officially complaining about a powerful person is risky business. For one, the powerful person in question may have even more power than you expected, or the "higher authority" receiving the complaint may side with the person complained about simply because of his or her (perceived) value to the organization.

The question is therefore whether it ever makes sense to complain (to a board or to the powerful person's boss, if he or she has one) if you feel you do not carry enough weight to take on the powerful person directly on an issue. In my view, such an instance would be rare. If the issue is simply one of management style and business judgment, it is appropriate to say you don't have the ability or responsibility to pursue the point. In this situation, it makes little sense to get involved in a process that will most likely backfire. In fact, I think it was naive for the Volkswagen managers to believe they could dislodge Ferdinand Piëch by sending letters of complaint. Even if a powerful person is not larger than life and not the boss of the enterprise, the person will not easily be shaken by complaints. In the case of a middle management boss, therefore, it will be easier to speak with a trusted insider—a human resource manager, for example—

Conduct an unemotional assessment of the situation before lodging complaints about powerful people.

who could start pursuing the issue if similar complaints are received from others. But even in this instance, it will always be wise to keep your emotions in check so that you do not say or write anything that looks unprofessional. Any complaint should be put into the context of the best interest of the company and the team, rather than a wounded ego, and it should reflect your mature ability to deal with conflict and controversy.

However, you cannot abdicate your responsibility for your own actions ("the powerful person made me do it"), and you have to keep your own independent judgment. Let's say it again: you are responsible for your own actions. Never become involved in anything that will damage your reputation and question your integrity. If you feel compelled to lodge a complaint in such an instance, you should do so without malice and fully prepared to accept the consequences.

What to do when . . .

. . . you disagree with a business decision made by the powerful person

The boss has made a decision to hire, fire, or promote someone in a critical position; to abandon or expand a market or product line; or to cancel a big project. You happen to disagree with the decision.

Decide first whether this is simply a business decision or a question of right and wrong that has a legal/ethical component. In both cases, you must first let the boss know that you understand the decision and the reasons for making it. Depending on the boss's communication style, this may involve verbal paraphrasing, writing a memo, or even doing some implementation/preparatory work on the decision. The message is that you have listened and do understand. In the case of a business decision, you can remind the boss that you know he or she is the boss and that you will accept and support the decision, no matter what. All you are asking is to present your thoughts. This approach will put the boss in the best position to listen to you. There is no need to be defensive. Then make your case, possibly with support from others. But don't try to convince the boss right there and then. Getting him or her to rethink the decision is a much more realistic goal and already a big win.

When legality or ethics is a factor, stay clear of making express or implied accusations as much as you can while approaching the powerful person with your concern. Say, for example, "Here is how someone who wants to harm you may interpret your/our actions." Remember that it may be very hard for the powerful person to see the problem; people who attain power have overcome obstacles and concerns all their life. No matter what you do, however, do not become involved in activities that are illegal. It is not worth it, and even with best intentions, the powerful person may not be able to protect you—or may even turn around and say that he or she did not understand the issue and leave you on your own.

Of course, much will depend on the nature of the issue, but here are some points to consider: (1) Entrust the situation by talking to a person who has a fiduciary duty, like a general counsel, outside counsel, or board member; that person can assess whether your concern is valid and can assist with explaining the problem to the powerful person. (2) Assess whether it is acceptable simply not to participate in the matter or whether you have a duty to report the matter. (3) Simply disagreeing may not be sufficient, depending on your position and the nature of the issue; you may have to resign. It is true that some of these options are scary, but there are a lot worse things that can happen than losing your job.

Coach with Caution

**Never criticize those above you directly. Err
on the side of subtlety and gentleness.**

—ROBERT GREENE, *THE 48 LAWS OF POWER*[1]

Afinal role we may play for a powerful person is that
of a coach. Originating from the world of sports and
morphing into society at large in the form of a life
coach, coaching has become quite popular in the
business world. It has been recognized as a key component to helping people develop into more effective leaders. Very often, one's
boss is expected to provide coaching, but it can be delivered by
outside professionals as well.

Assess Coachability at the Outset

Only rarely does a larger-than-life leader engage a professional outsider in a formal coaching engagement. After all, the person in
power is already successful and got to that exalted position by following his or her own instincts. The suggestion that such a person
would have to "reinvent" him- or herself may sound trendy and
progressive but will easily run into rough waters when it starts to
get translated into concrete change. Also, leaders who are larger
than life may question what they can actually learn from the

coach, even though impressive credentials and client references will certainly help overcome that obstacle. Nonetheless, even if a powerful client were to engage you as a professional outside coach, you may find that your protégé is simply not coachable, and you should give careful consideration as to whether you are prepared to take on the assignment. A hard look at the psychology of powerful people, a tremendous amount of empathy, and a realistic assessment of what can and cannot be achieved would be critical before you jump in. The conclusion that the job simply cannot be done would be a sign of wisdom and strength, rather than a lack of confidence in your abilities.

A successful professional coaching relationship is more likely with candidates who are not in the larger-than-life category, such as senior managers or even chief executives. They may have a greater desire to develop and improve because their career progression and success depend, at least to some extent, on the assessment of others. The opportunity—and the promise—to help them improve that assessment is a powerful incentive to accept outside help. Also, they are typically facing more constraints, obstacles, and challenges and will therefore be more open to seek coaching assistance to become even more successful. But even in this scenario, coachability is an issue that should not be underestimated. This is particularly the case where the coaching assignment is given by the protégé's superior, who will be expecting to see results. Of course, improvement in a "difficult case" will demonstrate the coach's value, but it will always be preferable to at least start out with a more manageable assignment in order to build a track record.

> *Carefully assess the powerful person's coachability, especially if you are a formally appointed outside coach.*

Package Coaching Differently

Acknowledging the obstacles to success does not mean that powerful people, even those who are larger than life, cannot benefit from coaching or that it should not be provided. For such people, it just has to be packaged differently. In my experience, coaching will be provided most effectively by people who have an otherwise official role that is normal and expected. People in these roles will be executives, board members, professional service providers, and other advisers whose actual coaching will be under the radar.

Even after starting to work as a professional business coach, I have found in quite a few instances that taking on a formal role with the client company has provided an effective platform on which to coach powerful people. For example, as a business coach, you could become a member of an advisory board (or even public company board if you are a coach with a strong and relevant business background). This position will provide clout for coaching members of management or even a chief executive. A midlevel or even senior manager will likely value the attention from a board member and will more readily perceive your thoughts and insights as relevant. In addition, you will have a better big-picture view of the business to put your business coaching into the right context. Some purists may feel that such an arrangement divides the coach's loyalties between the protégé who receives the coaching and the client who pays the bills. But there is always the potential for such a perceived conflict, and it will be up to you to manage your relationships in such a way that you are trusted by everyone involved. In fact, taking messages back and forth in an appropriate manner will often become an important part of making a coaching assignment succeed.

When you are coaching a powerful person, the actual coaching work may encompass many of the actions that have already been reviewed in previous rules. There will be a great need for empathy and diplomacy, there will be counsel, and you may even become a counterweight. However, it will be helpful to review coaching as its own category of activity, as it reveals some further aspects of effectively engaging and influencing powerful people.

Be Very Careful with Formal Performance Feedback

An important aspect of coaching is to provide feedback. Sports coaches love video footage that allows a play-by-play analysis. In the business world, a foundational practice is the employment of so-called

360-degree feedback instruments. Superiors, peers, and subordinates answer a series of questions and provide ratings across a battery of dimensions related to strategic ability, leadership style, and results orientation. In the case of a powerful business leader, the "superiors" who provide feedback will likely be board members. The coach then communicates a summary of the feedback, including graphs, charts, and some actual feedback commentary. This method protects the anonymity of specific feedback providers.

While this all sounds good in theory, it has plenty of pitfalls in practice. Powerful chiefs are highly sensitive to criticism and easily fall into the mode of "Who do they think they are?" Even if anonymity is "guaranteed," the powerful person may go to great lengths to find out who said what.

An example of this second pitfall is an episode where Colin Powell provided some "performance feedback" to Norman Schwarzkopf. When the Desert Storm commander asked Washington for more troops, some members of the National Security Council felt that this request was simply the delaying tactic of a general hesitant to fight. In the meeting, someone made the snide remark, "Thank you, General McClellan," an allusion to George McClellan, President Lincoln's reluctant commander of the Army of the Potomac.[2] When Powell passed along the jibe—in order to goad Schwarzkopf, as he said later[3]—the commander grew even angrier. He demanded to know who had made the comment and was ready to set that person straight, right then and there. While Powell says he concealed his source, Schwarzkopf himself recounts later that the comment had been made by a civilian adviser.[4] Whether or not he got an actual name is unclear, but you can be sure he tried.

When you work with the commanding person in your life, you have to remember that you will likely not have the stature of a Colin Powell. Your supreme leader may insist that you reveal your source. Hiding behind such justifications for secrecy as "an in camera meeting" (a meeting of board members without the chief executive present) or "the confidentiality of the process" will not always work. And again, such a reaction is by no means the exclusive domain of larger-than-life characters. I have even seen a senior professional executive (granted, he saw himself as larger than life) become obsessed with the commentary section in his 360-degree review and fixate on tracking down the source of feedback he considered unjust and offensive.

In my experience, two considerations will help you mitigate the risk of excessive and obsessive feedback tracing. First, if you are passing along informal "coaching comments" based on feedback from others, you must be ready for the fact that you may have to reveal your source or face the consequences. This is a critical insight, as there will be people who will seek to use you to deliver feedback to an autocratic leader that they are not prepared to give directly. You absolutely cannot expect that this powerful person will accept your insistence on confidentiality. If you feel that you cannot reveal your source, you must be prepared for this to be the end of the assignment. Always think about that before you share your feedback or insight, however helpful it may be. There always is the option to aggregate insight over time and provide direct feedback yourself when you observe a similar issue. Now the feedback comes from you and your observation, and there is no source to reveal.

The second consideration is to administer a formal, written feedback exercise with much care. You must consider that individuals who have always been the boss, especially those in the larger-than-life category, may have never had any formal performance feedback in their life. Again, while they might readily agree to collecting it, the world may look very different when they actually receive it. Their expectation of what they might receive may be completely out of sync with what they actually get—to the point that I would counsel against such an exercise altogether. When you go through with the formal report, you must realize that the way things are said can easily allow conclusions with regard to the identity of the author. This is especially the case if feedback providers are an international group. A nonnative speaker will be easily detected, and so will a person from a different English-speaking geography. In a U.S. context, for example, a British accent

> *Think twice before employing formal feedback mechanisms.*

will show up in writing as much as it can be heard. If you are the one managing the feedback process, you should give serious thought to "sanitizing" feedback comments that may have an offensive edge; there is rarely a risk that criticism will be missed or overlooked.

Further, you may want to rewrite the entire open-feedback section in order to harmonize the language: standardize the spelling on the convention in your region, change any unusual words, and in general bring the commentary into a common style. All of these steps will help avoid the hunt for an offensive source and allow the focus to be on the actual feedback content. Feedback purists may disagree with my suggestion, but here it is nonetheless. It is a tough world out there.

Ad Hoc Feedback Will Be Much More Effective

Given the risks and complications associated with formal feedback sessions, informal feedback at the right moment will be much more effective. The earlier example, in Rule 8, of John H. Tory giving Ted Rogers feedback on his temper remains the gold standard. We should note that Tory provided his feedback as an executive working for the larger-than-life boss. He just incorporated coaching into his job description.

One more thought about the right time for feedback: You should consider the right time with the broadest parameters, rather than just waiting for the right moment. John Tory's "feedback coaching" came at a time when Rogers was more advanced in years and had supposedly mellowed,[5] keeping in mind of course that mellowness with Rogers was a relative concept. We do not know how Rogers would have reacted to such coaching in his younger years. In other instances, you may be dealing with a powerful leader in the making, and that person may be open to coaching, while the accumulation of more power and success may eventually close that window.

In some instances, powerful people themselves may be soliciting the ad hoc feedback. This may come, for example, in a rare moment of quiet reflection. But even then, one would be well advised to tread carefully. As in other moments discussed, when you seem to have a green light to speak freely, don't fall into the trap of reciting everything you always thought was wrong with the powerful person. Even if the environment is relaxed and the request is genuine, you still should proceed with great caution. The quiet moment can give way to an outburst of indignation in a split second. Keep your guard up at all times!

Become a Sounding Board

An important technique in coaching is to act as a sounding board. This requires patience, attention, and strong listening skills, all of which are the hallmarks of a great coach. As a coach, you are well advised to let the "client" do the talking, even if you think you have the solution. Questions for clarification and other active-listening techniques are better than opinions, because the purpose of the exercise is to allow the powerful person to crystallize his or her ideas. Acting as a thought organizer by writing down the person's thoughts in an organized fashion is an effective way of helping him or her get clarity and provides an opening for inserting additional ideas and thought. Remember that powerful people are often more open to their own ideas than those of others; this critical insight cannot be underestimated.

Use Task Preparation as a Key Opportunity for Coaching

Coaching becomes particularly valuable when it occurs in the context of a critical task. Preparing for a board meeting, a shareholders' meeting, or a major negotiation with customers, unions, or other stakeholders provides the backdrop for discussing options and rehearsing answers. The immediate need to get something done will often increase coachability at least to a minimal level. A full-blown crisis may actually present the biggest opportunity for coaching. It is the occasion where you help the powerful person think through issues, generate alternatives, anticipate objections, and sometimes even change the game.

This lesson can be learned best from none other than "Dr. Phil," referring to an example that occurred when he was still known as Phil

McGraw. The story reveals a master coach. On April 16, 1996, Oprah Winfrey presented a show titled "Dangerous Foods," which dealt with the mad-cow scare that had gripped Britain and was threatening to invade the United States.[6] One of Winfrey's guests was a gentleman from the Humane Society of the United States, who explained that the human form of mad-cow disease could make "AIDS look like the common cold."[7] According to the expert, the reason was that every year in the United States, one hundred thousand sick cows were slaughtered, ground up, and used for feed. A disgusted Winfrey exclaimed, "Cows should not be eating other cows. . . . They should be eating grass." The audience roared in approval, and cattle prices dropped on the trading floor of the Chicago Mercantile Exchange. Within six weeks, various cattle groups had banded together to sue Winfrey in what became known as the "Amarillo, Texas, beef trial."

Winfrey quickly realized that more than money was at stake. The ranchers were attacking her entire credibility as a television personality, so she mounted a vigorous defense. The case was tried in Amarillo, Texas, hardly a hotbed of vegetarians. Both sides had lined up impressive legal teams and were ready to bring in notable scientists who would get into sophisticated explanations. That's when trial consultant Phil McGraw asserted himself.

The Oprah Winfrey team could not win a shoot-out among dueling experts in the beef town of Amarillo. Rather, the members of the jury needed to know that if they voted to take away Winfrey's right of free speech, someone would come along and vote to take away theirs. Based on McGraw's advice, Winfrey delivered a stunning courtroom performance. Her attorneys quickly jumped on the bandwagon, declaring that Winfrey represented a "shining light" for millions of Americans and that her show was a symbol for the right of the people to have free speech. The jury voted in her favor. Winfrey went on to remain Oprah, and Phil McGraw went on to become Dr. Phil with his own television show produced by Harpo Studios. His masterful coaching had clearly elevated his client's game. Winfrey delivered the speech in a way that only she could, but the coach had provided the foundation and the right frame for it.

While there will not always be a crisis, you can always work to frame the situation as preparation or even wait until preparation becomes necessary, so that you avoid coaching "out of the blue" or being perceived as criticizing the powerful person for no apparent reason. For example, when, as mentioned in Rule 12, Colin Powell thought Ronald Reagan needed coaching on how to interface with Mikhail Gorbachev, Powell did so in the context of preparing for the next meeting. He convinced the president to rely on talking points that he could use as an intelligent launch pad for his warm and engaging style. This proved to be the right formula, and offering it was more diplomatic than criticism after an evident lack of preparation.[8]

One of the reasons why coaching is so powerful in the context of task preparation or crisis response is that it leaves no doubt that the coach is on the protégé's side, rather than trying to criticize him or her. The coach is a friendly helper who is there to assist in solving real and present problems, not an armchair critic with some vague concepts of self-improvement. This immediate-reality context makes it much easier to explain (again) that the overall goal is to make the leader more effective. I have seen this as a helpful discussion with managers who were perceived as too domineering and harsh with their subordinates. One of the managers' critical paradigms was that they had a choice between being "nice" or getting things done. Over time, they understood that those were not trade-offs. The goal of the coaching was not to make them into nice managers who miss their targets but into effective managers who deliver and get the most out of their people. They came to understand that there was no trade-off. The coach was not sent by the head office to improve their manners but to help them become better leaders.

> *Crisis and task preparation are key opportunities for coaching.*

Use the Debriefing

Another technique for embedding coaching into a specific business issue that holds the powerful person's attention is the debriefing, also known as the postmortem. The debriefing can be a regular practice—after management or board meetings, for example—or ad hoc after the conclusion of a business project, customer visit, or similar occasion. When you use the debriefing as a coaching opportunity, you should give ample time to reviewing all kinds of things that worked well or that could have been done differently.

While debriefing, it would be a mistake to prevent the powerful person from talking first or to jump into issues pertaining to the powerful person right away. Gauging the temperature of the discussion, you can then ask the boss whether he or she would do something differently next time. That question puts the emphasis on "what can we all learn from this?" rather than on performance feedback. (Of course, powerful people themselves will not be shy to voice their assessment in the form of a performance evaluation or worse.) As a follow-up question, you can ask whether something should be done immediately as a result of the debriefing. In one instance, the powerful person in the room came to the conclusion that he had treated some shop floor staff members too harshly during a site visit. The workers had created a new kind of fixture, and the chief executive had zeroed in on its shortcomings. As a result of the debriefing, the executive sent the workers a note thanking them for their initiative and explaining that discussion of how things can always be improved was part of the never-ending quest to achieve excellence. The workers were happy to get the message and put the "mentoring" they had received into context.

This context of task preparation, debriefing, and other business-related discussions confirms that the role of coaching is not reserved to an éminence grise who might be called upon to provide sage advice. Anyone who is part of the project can contribute, as long as it is done with humility and diplomacy.

You should use similar techniques to coach people who help you engage the powerful superiors in your life. Reviewing the rules of engagement before the meeting, preparing and anticipating questions, organizing business arguments, and examining the boss's perspective on an issue are part of the ongoing coaching and reinforcement of effectively dealing with a powerful person. After the commander in chief has left, you should ask the team to stay for a debriefing. You can effectively teach what worked well and what should have

> *Practice the art of becoming an active sounding board. Crystallize and organize thoughts.*

been done differently when the object lessons have just been provided. These debriefing sessions should happen whether or not the meeting was successful; we can learn from both success and failure.

Coaching for a New Role

There is a great opportunity for coaching when people make a power shift that moves them into a larger or different role. There is a wide range of scenarios: an executive is promoted to a higher level of responsibility; a chief executive officer is appointed from within as a result of an internal succession process; a manager has received an expatriate assignment, which brings the first real exposure to operating in a foreign culture and making things happen in an unfamiliar environment; or a professional executive has obtained a first assignment to a board of directors. All of these transition points will make the powerful person open to looking for insight.

In situations like this, coaches (whether unofficial/internal or official/external) may be surprised to find how quickly their suggestions are picked up. In other words, powerful people under these circumstances may actually do what you tell them without the usual challenge. In these instances, it becomes even more important to refrain from thinking out loud, or you must be really clear when you are doing so.

> *A power shift can be a fantastic coaching opportunity. Use the window as long as it is open.*

In the opposite situation, you may sometimes advise powerful people when they have to deal with a downshift in power. This can happen to retired senior executives who become consultants or join boards. They may have become used to having all the power, and now they have to work as part of a team. Coaching will be valuable to them, but it must be done while respecting the powerful-person paradigm—i.e., with humility, diplomacy, and respect.

Finally, coaching will be exceedingly valuable and difficult when the task is to prepare a larger-than-life leader for a whole new role. Examples would be an initial public offering where the owner for the first time interacts with an "independent" board or a succession where the founding chief executive moves into the role of chairperson. In these situations, it is your job to adapt to the leader who has taken on the new role—if you are the successor or new independent board member, for example. The reason is that if the powerful person does not like his or her new situation, the person may use his or her power to reverse it. For example, Marriott's new chief executive officer, Arne Sorenson, knew he had to adapt his chief executive role to Bill Marriott Jr., who was taking on the role as chairman. "Accepting the role of the family" at the hotel chain was a big part of that adaptation.[9] It was certainly more effective than explaining the difference between a chairperson and a chief executive officer and expecting that someone like a famous hotel owner with a proud history would conform.

If you can help powerful people do some adapting themselves, you are doing them (and everyone around them) a great service. You just have to remember that, in the case of individuals who have always had all the power all their life, coachability will be low, and setbacks must be expected. But even baby steps will mean huge progress from the perspective of a powerful person.

What to do when . . .

. . . others present their ideas to the powerful person

If you are working closely with the powerful person, you will likely become aware of others who are presenting their ideas to that person. Such ideas could take the form of an internal proposal, a sales pitch for a product or service, a job interview, or any kind of sensitive conversation.

You will likely have considerable insight into the best time and place and the best way to present the information. This insight gives you tremendous influence. You have to decide whether you want to help the person submitting the idea or simply let the other person do his or her own thing. Here are some considerations for making that decision: If you provide too much coaching to the person presenting his or her idea, you deprive the powerful person of making his or her own assessment. If you provide too little, extraneous factors can derail an otherwise valuable project. Also, some people will reject coaching (they think they know better), and they should be on their own. Those who ask for and appreciate help will by and large deserve it, because they realize that putting their best foot forward requires thorough preparation.

Use Your Own Power Well

If you want to test a man's character, give him power.

—ABRAHAM LINCOLN

Now that you have thought about how to influence (other) powerful people, one question remains: What do you do if *you* have the power? You may not be a domineering, larger-than-life character, or at least you may not see yourself as such. If you are a manager, department head, or government official, you may actually feel that your exercise of power is quite reasonable and constructive and that people by and large like working with you and for you. However, this may not be the case, and you may never know. Powerful people have a tough time getting accurate feedback. If people who work for you laugh at your jokes, for example, the reason may not be that you are incredibly funny. The reason may simply be that you are the boss or they want something from you that only you can give.

Another problem may be that you turn into a different person when you are stressed or that you have become a different person over time. You may have started out as approachable and participatory when you received your promotion, but you have become more difficult to deal with as you have risen through the ranks or become comfortable in your new position. And just before you dismiss this point, think of this: management professor Jean Lipman-Blumen asserts that the most exemplary leaders are not immune to abusive of overbearing behavior. She even discovered leadership "toxicity" in Mother Teresa![1] If a revered (future) saint is not exempt from being criticized for the way she uses her power, neither are you and I.

Therefore, even if you have but a small amount of power relative to corporate tycoons and decorated generals, you should think about how you are exercising the power you do have and how others around you are seeking to influence you. That's why I have included a chapter that will help you make better use of your own power.

Get Clarity of Purpose

If you want people to help you, you must let them know what you are trying to achieve. As we have seen, the pursuits of powerful businesspeople cannot be explained by monetary goals, at least not exclusively. Ted Rogers is one powerful person who explicitly articulated his ambition beyond money as a driver to build a multibillion-dollar corporation from scratch. His drive to make money, he believed, was not nearly as strong as the emotional drive to restore his father's reputation as a leader in communications. He believed that the primacy of emotional drive over the desire to accumulate wealth applied as a universal principle. To make his point, Rogers referenced the Canadian immigrant experience, in which people work hard to prove to their parents in the Old Country that they can achieve success. Thus, construction workers become land developers, and factory laborers become owners. What drives them is much more than money: "What drives them [i.e., the immigrants] is that emotional need to prove to their parents, whether they are still alive or not, that they have achieved something in their name. The same applies to me."[2]

Even if you are not an entrepreneur but have goals that are set by a company for you, there is still a great need for clarity. For example, if you are a sales manager, you should have a clear idea whether you are trying to increase sales volume or get a higher price. If you want to build a world-class finance department or other operation, you need a clear idea as to what exactly that would look like. Or maybe you want to be the lowest-cost provider of a service, and you need clarity as to what are essentials versus frills.

Don't wait until you start writing your memoirs or you're preparing for retirement to articulate your purpose and what really drives you. Taking the time now to identify and communicate what you are trying to achieve makes much more sense. To find the answer, first ask yourself: Is the purpose you are intuitively pursuing really the purpose you want? If you are part of an organization, do your priorities fit with the overall organizational strategy? In other words, are you aligned?

Second, embrace the notion that clarity of purpose allows you to communicate to your team and others what is expected of them. Don't make your expectations a secret for people who are part of your inner circle. Especially in larger organizations, this may not eliminate the need for translating high-level vision statements into concrete action plans, but it will make the job of the translators much easier, because they can relate assignments and initiatives to a big picture that is known to everyone.

Of course, you may run into a problem if the purpose is not entirely noble or rational, or if it keeps changing. But even then, an exercise in articulating the purpose is of value. Just as powerful people cover a huge trajectory of personal development and occasionally reinvent themselves, you may want to recalibrate yourself during midlife or may have to adjust to changing realities, even if you have not built a multibillion-dollar empire from scratch. Whether you are articulating your purpose or redefining it, you can get some help in a way that meets at least some sort of minimum standard of nobility. The key is to keep it real, as

> *Ask yourself: What exactly are you are trying to achieve, and how can others help you get there?*

you will gain more by authenticity than by contrived nobility. Not everyone aspires to be a role model of social responsibility, and at least you can avoid disappointment and cynicism.

Articulate How Best to Work with You and for You

We have seen earlier, in Rule 7, how critical it is to understand a powerful person's style of communication and information absorption. Using the right style not only gives you influence, it also helps you do a better job for the boss. That's why you should make it easy for your people to help you. The most basic understanding relates to whether you prefer written briefings or oral updates. Beyond that, there may be a whole raft of unwritten "rules" that people should not have to learn the hard way when dealing with you. These expectations relate to communication, involvement, conduct, results, formalities, informalities, and much more. Think about completing sentences like "Nothing bothers me more than _____" or "I really like it when _____." If you do this exercise with someone who knows you well, you can put together a helpful set of dos and don'ts.

More broadly, this description may include what kinds of people will do well working with you and other powerful people in your organization. Some expectations may, of course, look quite unreasonable, and, as we know by now, that may be par for the course. But it is still better to have your wishes and preferences laid out with some clarity than to leave people in shock when it's too late.

> *Articulate what it takes to work with you—not only so others are aware, but also so you are sure that you know what suits you (and your organization's culture).*

This clarity can go a long way toward avoiding misunderstandings, employment casualties, and just plain agony. We looked, for example, at John Doddridge, who joined Magna International after a successful career as a professional manager at Dana Corporation. He clearly drew incorrect conclusions from the fact that he was hired as chief executive officer. In a case like this, the stated job requirement of "being able to work with a hands-on chairman/founder" would have given a clear indication of what to expect. The succession at Marriott mentioned earlier, in Rule 15, is a good example to emulate. The new chief executive took the position while "accepting the role of the family."[3]

Build the Team Around You

No matter how much power you have, you won't be able to do your job alone. In fact, the more power you have, the more likely it is that you will have to rely on a team of people. As we have seen, a great team of people is an indispensable asset when you are dealing with other powerful people in your life.

Of course, you need the right skills on the team while covering necessary functional expertise, such as sales, operations, and finance. When you are assembling a board of directors, the matrix of required skills may include industry background, mergers and acquisitions, knowledge of regulatory environments, risk management, and similar director-type qualities. However, these skills are limited to "professional competency," which is a necessary but not nearly sufficient quality of engaging powerful people. You should also ask yourself whether you need and have someone who becomes your complementor, counselor, coach, and even counterweight. Perhaps one person can assume all or most of these roles, but not necessarily.

When explaining the success of Ted Rogers's "high-wire act," Rogers's biographer Caroline Van Hasselt identified reasons beyond Rogers himself: a diverse team with diverse tasks; a spouse (Rogers's wife, Loretta) who was his "staunchest ally and sounding board"; and people who watched Rogers's back, raised the money, kept the bankers at bay, built the cable franchises, and made the cable systems work. And, of course, John Graham, Rogers's stepfather, managed Ted Rogers. Graham, together with key directors, provided sound advice and either put on the brakes or encouraged Rogers on the right track. Alan Horn, who later became chairman, "protected the family's wealth before moving into the CFO's chair."[4]

> *You need more than subject-matter experts. You need people who can coach, provide counsel, be a counterweight, and clean up the occasional mess.*

Rogers was surrounded by a well-rounded group of people who were needed to manage the business and the man. It is telling that Rogers's wife gets first mention. And even if your power base is more modest, the right team of people will make a big difference in your success and become a key element in enlarging your sphere of influence.

Decide What You Should and Should Not Do Yourself

Powerful people like to be involved in the details of their operations. We have seen how Bill Marriott Jr. shows up in the kitchens of his hotels, how Rupert Murdoch appears at the most unlikely times in his newsroom, and how Ferdinand Piëch visits the night shift in his engine design group. My personal favorite is Ted Rogers spending his Sunday afternoon in the call center, listening to unhappy customers.

While those habits can be dismissed as micromanagement, they do add a unique intensity that permeates the enterprise. And there are things that you as the powerful person can do better than anyone. Only Ted Rogers could pull the million-dollar stunt with Angelo Drossos, only Frank Stronach could market the turnaround of a hitherto unknown auto parts producer to investors in the United States, and only Conrad Black could bedazzle Margaret Thatcher with amazing details on the history of the Tory Party in Britain. In your world, you may be the sales manager who calls up the angry customer, the finance manager who speaks with the investor, or the operations manager who pitches the expansion proposal to the chief executive. There are things that you'd better not delegate.

But we have also seen that, in other circumstances, much is to be gained from the powerful person staying away. Andrew Knight settled a strike with one of the toughest unions in the England by keeping Conrad Black out of the picture. And there are other instances where the powerful person's presence can be counterproductive. We do not want these leaders in a price negotiation meeting with a customer, where they can be asked for immediate discounts and concessions. We do not want them in a termination meeting, where we are trying to focus someone on moving on. That's when powerful people should know they cannot add value and should trust their capable helpers to get the job done.

But in other instances, your people need the freedom to act, and your presence may even become counterproductive. If, as a big-picture marketing-oriented leader, you want (or must) introduce financial and operational discipline into your department, someone needs to have some freedom to implement it. You must not allow those who dislike the discipline to snipe under the cover of creative conflict. Nothing will get done.

Therefore, you should think about what is best to leave for others to do. This is not an exercise in learning to delegate more, nor a suggestion that you stay out of the business or make a wholesale change to your management style. In all likelihood, those actions won't work anyway. Rather, I am suggesting an exercise in intentionally understanding and agreeing that certain activities or (parts of) projects are

> *Even if you are hands-on, decide what is better done by others.*

better left alone, at least for a time. Keeping that freedom to operate as specific as possible and making sure there is good communication to avoid surprises will make it easier to stick to the plan.

Put in Place an Acceptable Feedback and Appeal Mechanism

Powerful people prefer decisions over debate. They are people of action. But the brutal reality is not that simple: Powerful people brim with ideas that would be impossible to implement in their totality. They are often brilliant but sometimes not. They may challenge their people to do the impossible, but there are some insurmountable constraints in the real world. And even the best ideas may need refinement to work. Furthermore, there actually may be situations where other people have good ideas of their own.

Therefore, you should recognize that disagreement and debate can actually contribute a lot. The reason is that the purpose and value of debate is not just to stop great ideas in their tracks but to look at options and alternatives, mitigate potential risks, stimulate imagination, or simply to make things better. Someone who disagrees is not necessarily negative per se and may be just as interested in seeing the venture succeed. Even the Catholic Church instituted the *advocatus diaboli* (devil's advocate) as someone who would have the right and the responsibility to oppose the canonization of saints.

You should therefore think about institutionalizing some kind of process of disagreement and feedback that is acceptable to you.

The easiest would be to make debate a mandatory component of the decision process, so no decision is made unless there has been disagreement. If that's not possible, you could assign someone to act as a facilitator who collects "other ideas" and feedback, communicating it in an appropriate manner. The advantage of such an institutionalized appeal is that it avoids overly heated debate in the tension of the moment. It also allows for the collection of facts on which to base the discussion. Most important, giving the mechanism a "name" makes it easier to remember that the practice is accepted.

> Giving your feedback mechanism a name will help ensure that it gets used.

Decisions would therefore be subject to appeal and would become final only after that appeal had been heard. Once the matter had been reviewed and decided, however, the expectation would be that everyone, including the dissenters, would fully support its implementation.

Don't Overstress Your People

Powerful people are intense, demanding, and highly stress inducing. If that's you, you will probably say you do not expect more from others than you expect from yourself. However, this reciprocity of expectations does not mean that stress levels are the same. The differentiating factor may just be that you do not have yourself to deal with! And even if you have surrounded yourself with people who are extra stress resilient and whose mettle has been tested, they can still be worn down over time or if personal and work stresses relentlessly converge.

You should therefore have a basic awareness of how people are doing in their private lives. Show genuine concern, but don't pry. Also, be aware that your people may need a break at some point. This can be as simple as a *real* vacation or as significant as a different assignment or sabbatical. You should be absolutely clear that this need is not a sign of weakness; it a sign of human nature and of the fact that loyal helpers take their jobs seriously and literally "to heart." A periodic check of health—physical and emotional—should be de rigueur and, if possible, even mandated. I once worked with a powerful person who would ask me at the beginning of our periodic meetings how I was doing and how my family was doing. The inquiry was genuine; he actually did want to know how I was doing. And it made a world of difference.

> *Even if you do not demand more from others than you demand from yourself, the impact may be harsher than you think.*

Deal with Succession

When it comes to leaving a lasting personal legacy as a larger-than-life business founder, the person who must come to mind immediately is Milton S. Hershey. Not only does the Hershey name remain foremost on North Americans' minds when it comes to chocolate bars, but his legacy continues to live on in his "model community" in Hershey, Pennsylvania. The most notable component is the Milton Hershey School, a residential school for needy children, which celebrated its centennial in 2009.

In 2002, however, many felt that the Hershey legacy was gravely threatened. The Milton Hershey School Trust, which holds the controlling interest in the famous chocolate company for the benefit of the school, had a plan to sell the stock, which was worth as much as $10 billion, to the highest bidder. The big global companies that dominated the candy business (Nestlé, Cadbury Schweppes, and Kraft) were in a buying mood, and the members of the trust's board felt they had a fiduciary duty to diversify the trust's wealth.[5] They had, however, totally underestimated the spirited campaign of Pennsylvania politicians and workers to stop Chocolate Town, USA, from falling into the hands of rapacious foreigners with no care for its heritage."[6] The coalition of politicians, workers, and local townspeople forced a U-turn in the trust board's decision by using the key argument that "if Milton Hershey were alive there's no way he'd want the Hershey Trust to sell the company."[7] If Milton Hershey's goal was to leave a legacy that would keep alive the question "What would Milton Hershey do?" he certainly succeeded.

I am not advocating that you expect to rule from the grave. Not at all. But there is something to be said for legacy. And especially larger-than-life owners must realize that if they don't decide and plan for succession of ownership and leadership, someone else will do it for them. In particular, their life's work may fall into the hands of foreign enterprises or other owners who have a much different agenda. But hard realities also must be faced. If there ever was the need for a staunch ally, an empathetic sounding board, and a dash of cold and sober second thought, this is where it arises. Powerful people must be very careful in thinking these things through and getting the right people to help them do it. The transition of ownership is *the* issue where many would-be counselors have their own interests.

> Indispensability is a myth, and everyone will have to move on at some point. Make it your own choice!

Succession is an important issue if you are not larger than life. It would be completely wrong to consider yourself indispensable in your position as a means to securing your power base. If you want to move ahead, you have to think about who will take your place. Once you have identified potential candidates, you must give them room to prove themselves and to build their credibility as viable successors. If you don't, the company will look for potential successors in other parts of the organization or think about outside succession. It may be harder than you think to see someone else take over with a whole new agenda and direction, especially if you have invested a large part of your life in your job. Even if your plan is to retire or move into a whole new direction, it is a significant source of satisfaction to have left your responsibilities in good hands. And that's to say nothing of the fact that it will provide a lot of comfort to the powerful people who may be conducting your next job interview!

What to do when . . .

. . . you are building your team

You have achieved a position of power and responsibility. You own your business, or you are the chief executive of a publicly traded corporation, the head of a local subsidiary, the head of a department, or otherwise in charge of a group of people. You intuitively know that building a strong team is a key to your success.

Even if you are completely in charge, you should seek accountability. If you own your own business, think of forming an advisory board, or consider your spouse to be an accountability partner. You need people in your professional life who want to see you succeed but do not need or depend on you for their own success. As you build your team, think of "team" in the broadest possible sense, not just including people who work for you. The broader team could include board members, external professionals, peers, counterparts in other parts of the organization, and mentors (a former boss is a great choice). Make sure your team covers all the expertise you need; there is nothing wrong with having people who are smarter than you working for and with you. Go beyond subject-matter expertise and covering of job functions to include people who provide counsel, cover over weaknesses, moderate the impact of your forceful personality, and can act as a counterweight. Realize that you need all of them.

Powerful People Need People Who Don't Need Them

Leadership is influence.

—JOHN C. MAXWELL, *THE 21 IRREFUTABLE LAWS OF LEADERSHIP* [1]

Working with powerful people can be an exciting and rewarding endeavor. It allows you to become part of great accomplishment, bold challenges, and unique experiences. The constant drama will provide an environment where there is never a dull moment. Honing your ability to influence powerful people will become an even more important skill as power structures become diffuse in a global business context. People who don't need titles and positions to get things done and who can move a project forward even if they are not in charge (or not fully in charge) will be in great demand. It is no accident that Norman Schwarzkopf received more accolades for his skills as a diplomat than for his skills as a general.

The analysis of effectively working with and influencing powerful people leads to three overarching conclusions:

» A strong relationship is essential. Your relationship must be strong enough that it can survive the intensity, the ups and downs, and the twists and turns. A strong relationship does not just happen. And it certainly does not happen as a result of spending some nice leisure time together. A working relationship requires work. As we have seen, that requires you to get your (regular) job done, communicate well, and understand and appreciate the powerful person and what he or she is trying to achieve. These are generalities, and throughout this book, I have filled in the blanks with more specific rules and examples.

» You must be willing and able to adapt. Most powerful people are who they are, and they will not change. At the very least, you must be ready to accept the fact that they will not change just because you are telling them they should. Therefore, it is up to you to adapt to them. You have to make the relationship work. You have to find out what is effective and what is not. There are rules for doing so, and there is trial and error. Of course, there cannot be too much of the latter, because error may lead to getting out the door.

» Finally, you need to maintain your independence. You have to remain your own person, even or especially when working with a larger-than-life character. Your independence is not just necessary for yourself. It also is a key requirement for effectively helping the powerful person. Independence ensures that your advice is based on that person's interest, rather than someone else's agenda, including your own. It also ensures that you are prepared to move on when your help is no longer needed or when your best contribution is no longer perceived as good enough. Your skill in influencing powerful people will open up many opportunities elsewhere.

Powerful leaders have no shortage of people who need the job, need the money, need the trappings, and need the glory. These needs can help those in power push people harder to accomplish remarkable feats and achieve great things. But these needs can also lead those in power to push so hard that people become less effective and less productive. Therefore, for their sake and yours, what powerful people need most of all are people who do not need them. I strongly believe that if you are that kind of person, you will meet a real need, do a better job, and get further ahead.

Notes

RULE 1

1. Adam Lashinsky, "Steve Jobs: CEO of the Decade," *Fortune*, November 23, 2009, p. 90.
2. Klaus Brinkbäumer and Thomas Shulz, "Der Philosoph des 21. Jahrhunderts" ("The Philosopher of the 21st Century"), *Der Spiegel*, April 26, 2010, p. 67.
3. "Murdoch Demands Pay for Content," *Business Week*, December 1, 2009, at http://www.businessweek.com/technology/content/dec2009/tc2009121_423109.htm.
4. Richard Siklos, *Shades of Black: Conrad Black, His Rise and Fall* (McClelland & Stewart, 2004), p. 144.
5. Gordon Pitts, "Ted Rogers Dies at 75," *Globe and Mail*, December 2, 2008.
6. Caroline Van Hasselt, *High Wire Act: Ted Rogers and the Empire That Debt Built* (Wiley, 2007), p. 225.
7. Ted Rogers with Robert Brehl, *Relentless: The True Story of the Man Behind Rogers Communications* (HarperCollins, 2008), p. 162.
8. Adam Lashinsky, "The Decade of Steve," *Fortune*, November 23, 2009, p. 96.
9. Peter Elkind, "The Trouble with Steve," *Fortune*, March 17, 2008, pp. 91, 94.
10. Wayne Lilley, *Magna cum Laude: How Frank Stronach Became Canada's Best-Paid Man* (McClelland & Stewart, 2006), p. 112.
11. Ibid., p. 200.
12. Ibid., p. 246.
13. Jean Lipman-Blumen, *The Allure of Toxic Leaders: Why We Follow Destructive Bosses and Corrupt Politicians, and How We Can Survive Them* (Oxford University Press, 2004), p. 145.
14. Jeffrey Pfeffer, *Managing with Power: Politics and Influence in Organizations* (Harvard Business Press, 1993), p. 166.
15. Ibid., pp. 166–167.
16. Michael Wolff, *The Man Who Owns the News: Inside the Secret World of Rupert Murdoch* (Broadway Books, 2010), p. 23.

17. Rogers, *Relentless*, p. 79.

18. Kitty Kelley, *Oprah: A Biography* (Crown Publishers, 2010), pp. 209–210.

19. Lilley, *Magna cum Laude*, p. 181.

20. Kelley, *Oprah*, p. 444.

21. Sally Bedell Smith, *In All His Glory: The Life and Times of William S. Paley and the Birth of Modern Broadcasting* (Random House, 2002), p. 18.

22. Rogers, *Relentless*, p. 24

23. Rita Stiens, *Ferdinand Piëch: Der Automacher* (Econ Taschenbuch, 2001), p. 125.

24. Ibid., p. 113.

25. Lilley, *Magna cum Laude*, p. 9.

26. Van Hasselt, *High Wire Act*, p. 464. Rogers had said earlier that he was in charge of the department of discontent and called himself the Chief Agitator.

27. Marc Gunther, "Marriott Gets a Wake-Up Call," *Fortune*, July 6, 2009, p. 62.

28. Elkind, "The Trouble with Steve," p. 91.

29. Greg Keenan, "GM's Board Scuttles Magna's Deal for Opel," *Globe and Mail*, November 3, 2009.

30. Blema S. Steinberg, *Women in Power* (McGill–Queen's University Press, 2008), p. 236.

31. Conrad Black, "Tutor Has His Reward," *National Post*, November 14, 2009.

32. "Conrad Black Is Given Bail in Fraud Case," *New York Times*, July 20, 2010, www.nytimes.com/2010/07/20/business/media/20black.html.

33. Colin Powell with Joseph E. Persico, *My American Journey* (Ballantine, 2003), p. 492.

34. Rick Atkinson, *Crusade: The Untold Story of the Persian Gulf War* (Mariner, 1994), p. 68.

RULE 2

1. Sally Bedell Smith, *In All His Glory: The Life and Times of William S. Paley and the Birth of Modern Broadcasting* (Random House, 2002), p. 20.

2. Ibid., p. 13.

3. Peter Elkind, "The Trouble with Steve," *Fortune*, March 17, 2008, p. 91.

4. Matt Hartley, "Apple Results Overshadowed by Jobs' Health," *Globe and Mail*, January 22, 2009.

5. Wayne Lilley, *Magna cum Laude: How Frank Stronach Became Canada's Best-Paid Man* (McClelland & Stewart, 2006), pp. 177–178.

6. Dacher Keltner, Deborah Gruenfeld, and Cameron Anderson, "Power, Approach, and Inhibition," *Psychological Review* 110, no. 2 (2003), pp. 276–277.

7. Lilley, *Magna cum Laude*, p. 15.

8. Katie Hafner, "Steve Jobs's Review of His Biography: Ban It," *New York Times*, April 30, 2005; http://www.nytimes.com/2005/04/30/technology/30apple.html.

9. Bedell Smith, *In All His Glory*, p. 20.

10. Richard Siklos, *Shades of Black: Conrad Black, His Rise and Fall* (McClelland & Stewart, 2004), p. xiii.

11. Peter Elkind, "The Trouble with Steve," *Fortune*, March 17, 2008, p. 94.

12. Ted Rogers, *Relentless: The True Story of the Man Behind Rogers Communications* (HarperCollins, 2008), pp. 245–266.

13. Blema S. Steinberg, *Women in Power* (McGill–Queen's University Press, 2008), p. 278.

14. Betsy Morris, "What Makes Pepsi Great?" *Fortune*, February 19, 2008.

15. Keltner, Gruenfeld, and Anderson, "Power, Approach, and Inhibition," pp. 276–277.

16. Siklos, *Shades of Black*, p. 350.

17. See the excellent analysis by Deborah A. DeMott, "Guests at the Table?: Independent Directors in Family-Influenced Companies," *The Journal of Corporation Law* 33, no. 4, pp. 819–841; see also *Report of Investigation by the Special Committee of the Board of Directors of Hollinger International Inc.* (Breeden Report), August 30, 2004, at http://www.sec.gov/Archives/edgar/data/868512/000095012304010413/y01437exv99w2.htm.

18. "In Full: Conrad Black Verdict," *BBC News*, July 14, 2007, http://news.bbc.co.uk/2/hi/business/6270162.stm.

19. Ralf Neukirch, "Ich, Merkel" ("I, Merkel"), *Der Spiegel*, June 22, 2009, p. 34.

20. Jim Collins, *Good to Great: Why Some Companies Make the Leap and Others Don't* (HarperBusiness, 2001), p. 46.

21. Alex Altman, "Tim Cook: The New Steve Jobs?" *Time*, January 16, 2009.

22. Information complied from Bedell Smith, *In All His Glory*; and Holocomb Noble, "Frank Stanton, Broadcasting Pioneer, Dies at 98," *New York Times*, December 26, 2006.

23. Information compiled from Colin Powell with Joseph E. Persico, *My American Journey* (Ballantine, 2003); Rick Atkinson, *Crusade: The Untold Story of the Persian Gulf War* (Mariner, 1994); Gerald Parshall, "Powell and Schwarzkopf," *U.S. News & World Report*, March 16, 1998; and other sources.

24. Otto Preston Chaney, *Zhukov*, Revised Edition (University of Oklahoma Press, 1996), p. xix.

25. Malcolm Mackintosh, Foreword, in Chaney, *Zhukov*, p. xvi.

26. Carol Hansell, *Corporate Governance: What Directors Need to Know* (Thomson Carswell, 2003), p. 3.

27. Caroline Van Hasselt, *High Wire Act: Ted Rogers and the Empire That Debt Built* (Wiley, 2007), pp. 433–434.

28. Ronald Daniels and Edward Iacobucci, "Some of the Causes and Consequences of Corporate Ownership Concentration in Canada," in *Concentrated Corporate Ownership*, ed. Randall Morck (Chicago: University of Chicago Press, 2000), pp. 81–103.

29. DeMott, "Guests at the Table?" p. 821.

30. Siklos, *Shades of Black*, p. 188.

31. Ibid., p. 407.

32. Jean Lipman-Blumen, *The Allure of Toxic Leaders: Why We Follow Destructive Bosses and Corrupt Politicians, and How We Can Survive Them* (Oxford University Press, 2004), p. 181.

33. Ibid., p. 162.

34. Detlev Vagts, "CEOs and Their Lawyers: Tension Strains the Link," *Harvard Business Review*, March–April 1981, p. 6.

35. Michael Maccoby, "Narcissistic Leaders," *Harvard Business Review*, January 2004, p. 98.

36. Michael Wolff, *The Man Who Owns the News: Inside the Secret World of Rupert Murdoch* (Broadway Books, 2010), p. 69.

RULE 3

1. Ted Rogers with Robert Brehl, *Relentless: The True Story of the Man Behind Rogers Communications* (HarperCollins, 2008), p. 62.

2. Ferdinand Piëch, *Auto.Biographie* (Hoffmann & Kampe, 2002), p. 161.

3. Ibid.

4. Ibid., p. 163.

5. Ibid., p. 162.

6. Wayne Lilley, *Magna cum Laude: How Frank Stronach Became Canada's Best-Paid Man* (McClelland & Stewart, 2006), p. 228.

7. Rogers, *Relentless*, p. 229.

8. Robert B. Cialdini, *Influence: The Psychology of Persuasion* (Harper, 2006), p. 167.

9. Rogers, *Relentless*, p. 230.

10. "Piëch Was Always in the Driver's Seat," *Automotive News Europe* 76, no. 5982, p. 32.

11. Michael Wolff, *The Man Who Owns the News: Inside the Secret World of Rupert Murdoch* (Broadway Books, 2010), pp. 237–238, with a detailed account of such a visit.

12. Mark Gunther, "Marriott Gets a Wake-Up Call," *Fortune*, July 6, 2009, p. 62.

13. John Brodie, "The Business of Style," *Fortune*, September 1, 2008, p. 53.

14. Sally Bedell Smith, *In All His Glory: The Life and Times of William S. Paley and the Birth of Modern Broadcasting* (Random House, 2002), p. 407.

15. Colin Powell with Joseph E. Persico, *My American Journey* (Ballantine, 2003), p. 321.

16. Mike Ramsey and Sara Gay Forden, "Three Strikes You're Out: After Two Previous Owners Failed, Fiat Is Likely Chrysler's Last Chance," *National Post*, September 18, 2009.

17. Ibid.

18. Caroline Van Hasselt, *High Wire Act: Ted Rogers and the Empire That Debt Built* (Wiley, 2007), p. 183.

19. Rick Atkinson, *Crusade: The Untold Story of the Persian Gulf War* (Mariner, 1994), p. 4.

RULE 4

1. "Bill Paley often fired people without warning": Sally Bedell Smith, *In All His Glory: The Life and Times of William S. Paley and the Birth of Modern Broadcasting* (Random House, 2002), p. 400. "An awful lot of people going through [Ted Rogers's] revolving door in twenty years": Caroline Van Hasselt, *High Wire Act: Ted Rogers and the Empire That Debt Built* (Wiley, 2007), p. 192.

2. Thomas Watson, "His Way or the Highway," *Canadian Business*, May 23, 2005, pp. 38–45.

3. Alex Altman, "Tim Cook: The New Steve Jobs?" *Time*, January 16, 2009.

4. Wayne Lilley, *Magna cum Laude: How Frank Stronach Became Canada's Best-Paid Man* (McClelland & Stewart, 2006), p. 302.

5. "Tobin Resigns from Magna Group," *CBC News*, August 20, 2004, http://www.cbc.ca/canada/story/2004/08/20/tobin_magna040820.html#ixzz13BZOrBNd.

6. Derek DeCloet, "The Cost of Playing Back-Up to Stronach," *Globe and Mail*, August 12, 2008.

7. Ibid.

8. Lilley, *Magna cum Laude*, p. 300.

9. Ibid., p. 189.

10. Ibid., p. 192.

11. David D'Alessandro, *Executive Warfare* (McGraw-Hill, 2008), p. 22.

12. Ibid., p. 23.

13. Lilley, *Magna cum Laude*, p. 62.

14. Ibid., p. 204.

15. Ibid., p. 57.

16. Rita Stiens, *Ferdinand Piëch: Der Automacher* (Econ Taschenbuch, 2001), p. 134.

17. Kitty Kelley, *Oprah: A Biography* (Crown Publishers, 2010), p. 264.

18. William D. Cohan, "The Rise and Fall of Jimmy Cayne," *Fortune*, August 18, 2008, pp. 91, 94.

19. D'Alessandro, *Executive Warfare*, p. 46.

20. Michael Wolff, *The Man Who Owns the News: Inside the Secret World of Rupert Murdoch* (Broadway Books, 2010), p. 300.

21. Ibid., p. 163.

22. Ibid.

23. Rick Atkinson, *Crusade: The Untold Story of the Persian Gulf War* (Mariner, 1994), p. 95.

RULE 5

1. Colin Powell with Joseph E. Persico, *My American Journey* (Ballantine, 2003), p. 492.

2. Caroline Van Hasselt, *High Wire Act: Ted Rogers and the Empire That Debt Built* (Wiley, 2007), p. 192.

3. Peter Elkind, "The Trouble with Steve," *Fortune*, March 17, 2008, p. 91.

4. Rita Stiens, *Ferdinand Piëch: Der Automacher* (Econ Taschenbuch, 2001), p. 120.

5. Van Hasselt, *High Wire Act*, p. 193.

6. Alex Altman, "Tim Cook: The New Steve Jobs?" *Time*, January 16, 2009.

7. Sally Bedell Smith, *In All His Glory: The Life and Times of William S. Paley and the Birth of Modern Broadcasting* (Random House, 2002), p. 394.

8. Otto Preston Chaney, *Zhukov*, Revised Edition (University of Oklahoma Press, 1996), p. 167.

9. Claire Berlinski, *"There Is No Alternative": Why Margaret Thatcher Matters* (Basic Books, 2008), pp. 296–297.

10. Ibid., p. 297.

11. Powell, *My American Journey*, pp. 267–268.

12. Ibid., p. 268.

13. Stiens, *Ferdinand Piëch*, p. 134.

14. Daniel Goleman, *Social Intelligence* (Bantam, 2007), p. 177.

15. Peter Frost and Sandra Robinson, "The Toxic Handler: Organizational Hero—and Casualty," *Harvard Business Review*, July/August 1999, pp. 96–107.

16. Ibid. Authors quote research conducted by Andre Delbecq, of the Leavey School of Business at Santa Clara University, and Frank Friedlander, of the Fielding Institute in Santa Barbara, California.

RULE 6

1. Dacher Keltner, Deborah Gruenfeld, and Cameron Anderson, "Power, Approach, and Inhibition," *Psychological Review* 110, no. 2 (2003), p. 266.

2. Quoted by Caroline Van Hasselt, *High Wire Act: Ted Rogers and the Empire That Debt Built* (Wiley, 2007), p. 193.

3. Colin Powell with Joseph E. Persico, *My American Journey* (Ballantine, 2003), pp. 309–310.

4. Rick Warren, *The Purpose Driven Life* (Zondervan, 2007), p. 17.

5. Wayne Lilley, *Magna cum Laude: How Frank Stronach Became Canada's Best-Paid Man* (McClelland & Stewart, 2006), pp. 227–228.

6. Adam Lashinsky, "The Genius Behind Steve: Could Operations Whiz Tim Cook Run the Company Someday?" *Fortune*, November 10, 2008.

7. Lilley, *Magna cum Laude*, p. 336.

8. Otto Preston Chaney, *Zhukov*, Revised Edition (University of Oklahoma Press, 1996), pp. 202, 237.

9. "Never outshine the master. . . . Make your masters appear more brilliant than they are and you will attain the heights of power." Robert Greene, *The 48 Laws of Power* (Penguin Books, 2000), p. 1.

10. Richard Siklos, *Shades of Black: Conrad Black, His Rise and Fall* (McClelland & Stewart, 2004), p. 344.

11. Peter Oborne, "The Ballad of Connie and Babs," *Spectator*, January 24, 2004.

12. Bruce Peltier, *The Psychology of Executive Coaching* (Routledge, 2009), p. 167.
13. Erich Eyck, *Bismarck and the German Empire* (Norton, 1964), p. 58.
14. Ibid., pp. 57, 60.
15. Rosanne Badowski, *Managing Up* (Crown Business, 2004), front cover.
16. Ibid., pp. 24–26.
17. Account from Dick Cheney reported by Colin Powell in *My American Journey*, p. 492.

RULE 7

1. Dale Carnegie, *How to Win Friends and Influence People*, Revised Edition (Simon & Schuster, 1981), p. 18.
2. Daniel Goleman, *Social Intelligence* (Bantam, 2007), pp. 88–89.
3. Jeffrey Pfeffer, *Managing with Power: Politics and Influence in Organizations* (Harvard Business Press, 1993), p. 173.
4. Betsy Morris, "What Makes Pepsi Great?" *Fortune*, February 19, 2008.
5. Alfons Frese, "Wer ist Ferdinand Piëch?" ("Who is Ferdinand Piëch?"), *Der Tagesspiegel*, March 6, 2006, at www.tagesspiegel.de/zeitung/Fragen -des-Tages;art693,1894347.
6. Frank T. Gallo, *Business Leadership in China* (Wiley, 2008), p. 61.
7. In an interview with Sonia Alleyne, "Oprah Means Business," *Black Enterprise*, June 2008, pp. 116, 126.
8. Nanette Byrnes and Roger Crockett, "Ursula Burns: An Historic Succession at Xerox," *Bloomberg BusinessWeek*, May 28, 2009.
9. Colin Powell with Joseph E. Persico, *My American Journey* (Ballantine, 2003), pp. 492–493.
10. Wayne Lilley, *Magna cum Laude: How Frank Stronach Became Canada's Best-Paid Man* (McClelland & Stewart, 2006), p. 161 with further references.
11. Ibid., p. 164.
12. I would like to thank John Doddridge, who shared his perspective on the story beyond what has been published.
13. Ferdinand von Schirach, "An der Seite des Verbrechers" ("On the side of the criminal"), *Der Spiegel*, August 17, 2009, pp. 132, 134.
14. Lilley, *Magna cum Laude*, p. 312.
15. Robert H. Mnookin, Scott R. Peppet, and Andrew S. Tulumello, *Beyond Winning: Negotiating to Create Value in Deals and Disputes* (Belknap, 2004), p. 62.

16. Peter Drucker, *Classic Drucker* (Harvard Business School Press, 2008), pp. 6–7.

17. Lilley, *Magna m Laude*, p. 313.

18. Marc Gunther, "Marriott Gets a Wake-Up Call," *Fortune*, July 6, 2009, pp. 62, 66.

19. "Piëch Was Always in the Driver's Seat," *Automotive News Europe* 76, no. 5982, p. 32B.

20. Rick Atkinson, *Crusade: The Untold Story of the Persian Gulf War* (Mariner, 1994), p. 234.

21. Ibid.

22. Erich Eyck, *Bismarck and the German Empire* (Norton, 1964), p. 74.

23. Michael Wolff, *The Man Who Owns the News: Inside the Secret World of Rupert Murdoch* (Broadway Books, 2010), p. 277.

RULE 8

1. Betsy Morris, "What Makes Pepsi Great?" *Fortune*, February 19, 2008.

2. Kathleen Eisenhardt and L. J. Bourgeois, "Politics of Strategic Decision Making in High-Velocity Environments: Toward a Midrange Theory," *Academy of Management Journal* 31, no. 4 (1988), pp. 737, 743.

3. Jeffrey Pfeffer, *Managing with Power: Politics and Influence in Organizations* (Harvard Business Press, 1993), p. 18.

4. Blema S. Steinberg, *Women in Power* (McGill–Queen's University Press, 2008), p. 243.

5. Pfeffer, *Managing with Power*, p. 173.

6. Caroline Van Hasselt, *High Wire Act: Ted Rogers and the Empire That Debt Built* (Wiley, 2007), p. 193. She quotes the late Bob Francis's widow, Marilyn.

7. Sally Bedell Smith, *In All His Glory: The Life and Times of William S. Paley and the Birth of Modern Broadcasting* (Random House, 2002), p. 404.

8. Ted Rogers with Robert Brehl, *Relentless: The True Story of the Man Behind Rogers Communications* (HarperCollins, 2008), p. 161.

9. Ibid.

10. Ibid., pp. 160–161.

11. David D'Alessandro, *Executive Warfare* (McGraw-Hill, 2008), pp. 21–22.

12. Bedell Smith, *In All His Glory*, p. 405.

13. Van Hasselt, *High Wire Act*, p. 226.

14. Rick Atkinson, *Crusade: The Untold Story of the Persian Gulf War* (Mariner, 1994), pp. 269, 270.

15. Ibid., p. 344.

RULE 9

1. "The Daily Stat," *Harvard Business Review*, July 8, 2010.
2. Dacher Keltner, Deborah Gruenfeld, and Cameron Anderson, "Power, Approach, and Inhibition," *Psychological Review* 110, no. 2 (2003), p. 271.
3. David d'Alessandro, *Executive Warfare* (McGraw-Hill, 2008), pp. 161–162.
4. Ibid., p. 162
5. Daniel Sankowsky, "The Charismatic Leader as Narcissist," *Organizational Dynamics* 23, no. 4 (Spring 1995), pp. 57, 59.
6. Sally Bedell Smith, *In All His Glory: The Life and Times of William S. Paley and the Birth of Modern Broadcasting* (Random House, 2002), p. 400.
7. Ibid., p. 471.
8. Otto Preston Chaney, *Zhukov*, Revised Edition (University of Oklahoma Press, 1996), p. 373.
9. Claire Berlinski, *"There Is No Alternative": Why Margaret Thatcher Matters* (Basic Books, 2008), p. 326.
10. Michael Friscolanti, "Conrad Black's Codefendants Found Guilty," *Maclean's*, July 30, 2007.
11. Ibid.
12. Herbert P. Bix, *Hirohito and the Making of Modern Japan* (Harper Perennial, 2001), pp. 42–43.
13. D'Alessandro, *Executive Warfare*, p. 217.
14. Ralf Neukirch, "Ich, Merkel" ("I, Merkel"), *Der Spiegel*, June 22, 2009, p. 35.
15. Jim Collins and Jerry I. Porras, *Built to Last: Successful Habits of Visionary Companies* (HarperBusiness, 2004), p. 121.

RULE 10

1. Ferdinand Piëch, *Auto.Biographie* (Hoffmann & Kampe, 2002), p. 187.
2. "Machen Sie etwas anderes" ("Do something different"), *Der Spiegel* 26, June 24, 2002, p. 26.
3. "Piëch will von Lustreisen nichts gewusst haben" ("Piëch claims he did not know about pleasure trips"), *Welt Online*, January 9, 2008, www.welt.de/wirtschaft/article1533526/Piech_will_von_Lustreisen_nichts_gewusst_haben.html.
4. Adam Lachinsky, "Apple: The Genius Behind Steve," *Fortune*, November 24, 2008, p. 73.
5. Graham Sharman, "The Logistics of the Gulf Campaign," *McKinsey Quarterly*, 1991, no. 4, pp. 37–39.

6. H. Norman Schwarzkopf with Peter Petre, *It Doesn't Take a Hero* (Bantam, 1993), pp. 396–397.

7. Colin Powell with Joseph E. Persico, *My American Journey* (Ballantine, 2003), pp. 193–194.

8. Caroline Van Hasselt, *High Wire Act: Ted Rogers and the Empire That Debt Built* (Wiley, 2007), p. 164–165.

9. Sally Bedell Smith, *In All His Glory: The Life and Times of William S. Paley and the Birth of Modern Broadcasting* (Random House, 2002), pp. 403–404.

10. Ted Rogers with Robert Brehl, *Relentless: The True Story of the Man Behind Rogers Communications* (HarperCollins, 2008), p. 130.

11. Powell, *My American Journey*, pp. 282–283.

12. Wayne Lilley, *Magna cum Laude: How Frank Stronach Became Canada's Best-Paid Man* (McClelland & Stewart, 2006), pp. 147–149.

13. Ibid., p. 150.

14. Richard Siklos, *Shades of Black: Conrad Black, His Rise and Fall* (McClelland & Stewart, 2004), pp. 140–141.

15. Ibid., p. 141.

16. Ted Rogers made the story the opener for his autobiography, *Relentless*, pp. 1–5.

17. Van Hasselt, *High Wire Act*, p. 170.

18. Powell, *My American Journey*, pp. 379–380.

RULE 11

1. Adam Lachinsky, "Apple: The Genius Behind Steve," *Fortune*, November 24, 2008, p. 73.

2. Nanette Byrnes and Roger Crockett, "Ursula Burns: An Historic Succession at Xerox," *Bloomberg BusinessWeek*, May 28, 2009.

3. Sally Bedell Smith, *In All His Glory: The Life and Times of William S. Paley and the Birth of Modern Broadcasting* (Random House, 2002), p. 391.

4. Kitty Kelley, *Oprah: A Biography* (Crown Publishers, 2010), p. 180.

5. Dacher Keltner, Deborah Gruenfeld, and Cameron Anderson, "Power, Approach, and Inhibition," *Psychological Review* 110, no. 2 (2003), p. 271.

6. Michael Wolff, *The Man Who Owns the News: Inside the Secret World of Rupert Murdoch* (Broadway Books, 2010), pp. 282–283.

7. David Carr and Tim Arango, "A Fox Chief at the Pinnacle of Media and Politics," *New York Times*, January 10, 2010, http://www.nytimes.com/2010/01/10/business/media/10ailes.html?_r=1&pagewanted=print.

8. Bethany McLean and Peter Elkind, *The Smartest Guys in the Room: The Amazing Rise and Scandalous Fall of Enron* (Portfolio, 2003), p. 24.

9. Ibid., p. 25.

10. Ibid., p. 99.

11. Byrnes and Crockett, "Ursula Burns."

12. "Rogers Shares Dip After Founder's Death," *CBC News*, December 2, 2008, cbc.com.

13. David A. Nadler, Beverly A. Behan, and Mark B. Nadler, *Building Better Boards: A Blueprint for Effective Governance* (Jossey-Bass, 2005), p. 31.

14. Bedell Smith, *In All His Glory*, p. 471; and McLean and Elkind, *The Smartest Guys in the Room*, p. 91.

RULE 12

1. Rick Atkinson, *Crusade: The Untold Story of the Persian Gulf War* (Mariner, 1994), p. 68.

2. Peter Frost and Sandra Robinson, "The Toxic Handler: Organizational Hero—and Casualty," *Harvard Business Review*, July/August 1999, p. 96.

3. Betsy Morris, "What Makes Pepsi Great?" *Fortune*, February 19, 2008.

4. Indra Nooyi, Chairman and CEO, PepsiCo, "Capitalism Is Great for Economic Recovery" (address delivered to the Economic Club of Washington, D.C., May 12, 2009).

5. Colin Powell with Joseph E. Persico, *My American Journey* (Ballantine, 2003), p. 207.

6. H. Norman Schwarzkopf with Peter Petre, *It Doesn't Take a Hero* (Bantam, 1993), p. 231.

7. Wayne Lilley, *Magna cum Laude: How Frank Stronach Became Canada's Best-Paid Man* (McClelland & Stewart, 2006), p. 272.

8. Frost and Robinson, "The Toxic Handler," p. 96.

9. Claire Berlinski, *"There Is No Alternative": Why Margaret Thatcher Matters* (Basic Books, 2008), p. 47.

10. Caroline Van Hasselt, *High Wire Act: Ted Rogers and the Empire That Debt Built* (Wiley, 2007), p. 364.

11. Ibid.

12. Atkinson, *Crusade*, p. 68.

13. Sally Bedell Smith, *In All His Glory: The Life and Times of William S. Paley and the Birth of Modern Broadcasting* (Random House, 2002), pp. 407–408.

14. Powell, *My American Journey*, pp. 362–363.

15. Frost and Robinson, "The Toxic Handler," p. 96.

RULE 13

1. Peter F. Drucker, *The Essential Drucker* (Harper, 2008), p. 222.
2. Caroline Van Hasselt, *High Wire Act: Ted Rogers and the Empire That Debt Built* (Wiley, 2007), p. 431.
3. Ibid., p. 362.
4. Ibid., p. 433.
5. Ralf Neukirch, "Ich, Merkel" ("I, Merkel"), *Der Spiegel*, June 22, 2009, p. 35.
6. Patricia Sellers, "The Business of Being Oprah," *Fortune*, January 4, 2002, pp. 50–64.
7. Kitty Kelley, *Oprah: A Biography* (Crown Publishers, 2010), p. 215.
8. Ibid.
9. Conrad Black, "Why I Became a Catholic," *National Post*, September 29, 2009.
10. Van Hasselt, *High Wire Act*, p. 433.
11. David Nadler, "Confessions of a Trusted Counsellor," *Harvard Business Review*, September 2005, p. 73.
12. Michael Wolff, *The Man Who Owns the News: Inside the Secret World of Rupert Murdoch* (Broadway Books, 2010), p. 147.
13. Jeffrey Pfeffer, *Managing with Power: Politics and Influence in Organizations* (Harvard Business Press, 1993), p. 190.
14. I had the opportunity to listen to Frank Stronach's idea personally when he explained it in a keynote speech at a business gala. For a written reference, see Wayne Lilley, *Magna cum Laude: How Frank Stronach Became Canada's Best-Paid Man* (McClelland & Stewart, 2006), p. 167.
15. Lilley, *Magna cum Laude*, p. 167.
16. Ibid.
17. Claire Berlinski, *"There Is No Alternative": Why Margaret Thatcher Matters* (Basic Books, 2008), p. 45.
18. Ibid., p. 208.

RULE 14

1. Bob Kaplan with Rob Kaiser, *The Versatile Leader* (Pfeiffer, 2006), p. 131.
2. Ibid., p. 130.
3. Ibid.
4. Otto Preston Chaney, *Zhukov*, Revised Edition (University of Oklahoma Press, 1996), pp. 165–166 and pp. 147, 375.
5. Ibid.

6. Caroline Van Hasselt, *High Wire Act: Ted Rogers and the Empire That Debt Built* (Wiley, 2007), p. 438.

7. When Alan Horn, Rogers's right-hand man, replaced the independent chairman Gar Emerson, David Beatty, the head of the Canadian Coalition for Good Governance, commented, "You are asking the fox to guard the hen house." Van Hasselt, *High Wire Act*, p. 435.

8. According to a report in *Fortune*, P. Anthony Lanniee, a former Kinder Morgan executive who later became general counsel of oil and gas exploration company Apache Corporation, said, "I am in the camp that believes Enron would still be in existence if Rich had been running the company. It would have looked very much like it did in the early 1990s: an asset-based company." Doris Burke, "The Anti-Enron," *Fortune*, November 24, 2003, p. 178.

9. Van Hasselt, *High Wire Act*, p. 358.

10. Ibid., p. 359.

11. Hans Leyendecker, "Fast immer gewinnt Piëch"("Almost Always Piëch Wins"), November 14, 2007, available at http://www.sueddeutsche.de/wirtschaft/661/424420/text.

12. Gwenda Blair, *Donald Trump: Master Apprentice* (Simon & Schuster, 2008), p. 169 and following.

13. Ibid., pp. 179–181.

14. Van Hasselt, *High Wire Act*, p. 66.

15. Colin Powell with Joseph E. Persico, *My American Journey* (Ballantine, 2003), p. 244.

RULE 15

1. Robert Greene, *The 48 Laws of Power* (Penguin Books, 2000), p. 181.

2. Rick Atkinson, *Crusade: The Untold Story of the Persian Gulf War* (Mariner, 1994), p. 112.

3. Colin Powell with Joseph E. Persico, *My American Journey* (Ballantine, 2003), p. 485.

4. H. Norman Schwarzkopf with Peter Petre, *It Doesn't Take a Hero* (Bantam, 1993), p. 420.

5. Caroline Van Hasselt, *High Wire Act: Ted Rogers and the Empire That Debt Built* (Wiley, 2007), p. 192.

6. The whole story is told in more detail by Kitty Kelley, *Oprah: A Biography*, (Crown Publishers, 2010), pp. 315–324.

7. Ibid.

8. Powell, *My American Journey,* p. 364.

9. Mark Gunther, "Marriott Gets a Wake-Up Call," *Fortune,* July 6, 2009, p. 62.

RULE 16

1. Jean Lipman-Blumen, *The Allure of Toxic Leaders: Why We Follow Destructive Bosses and Corrupt Politicians, and How We Can Survive Them* (Oxford University Press, 2004), p. 6.

2. Ted Rogers with Robert Brehl, *Relentless: The True Story of the Man Behind Rogers Communications* (HarperCollins, 2008), p. 249.

3. Mark Gunther, "Marriott Gets a Wake-Up Call," *Fortune,* July 6, 2009, p. 62.

4. Caroline Van Hasselt, *High Wire Act: Ted Rogers and the Empire That Debt Built* (Wiley, 2007), p. 467.

5. Michael D'Antonio, *Hershey: Milton S. Hershey's Extraordinary Life of Wealth, Empire, and Utopian Dreams* (Simon & Schuster, 2007), p. 4.

6. Stephen Foley, "Hershey Would Make a Perfect Fit for Demerged Cadbury—but Is It for Sale?" *The Independent,* March 29, 2007.

7. D'Antonio, *Hershey,* p. 7.

A FINAL RULE

1. John C. Maxwell, *The 21 Irrefutable Laws of Leadership* (Thomas Nelson Publishers, 1998), p. 17.

Index

About the Author

Dirk Schlimm is a corporate director, an executive coach, and principal of Jenoir Management Consultants. He serves as an adviser to business owners and executives and works with leadership teams in North America, Asia Pacific, and Europe to increase their alignment and effectiveness. Dirk also teaches a regular session on "Engaging Powerful People" at the Rotman Directors' Education Program (University of Toronto).

For fourteen years, Dirk worked as a senior executive at Husky Injection Molding Systems, a global technology leader in the capital equipment industry. At Husky, he was responsible for communicating and implementing company values across operations in the Americas, Europe, and Asia; developing governance practices; facilitating the relationship of a successful entrepreneur, a public company board, professional management, and external stakeholders; as well as leadership development and change management.

Dirk is an experienced negotiator in a variety of contexts, including dispute resolution as well as agreements with major corporations and government. In his work on strategy development, CEO succession, and change management, Dirk had the opportunity to work with Peter Drucker, Michael Porter, and Jim Collins as management consultants.

Dirk completed his post-graduate clerkship in judicial service with the Court of Appeals in Cologne, Germany. He is a Konrad-Adenauer-Scholar and earned his doctorate in international law from the University of Konstanz, Germany. His work on lender liability toward financially troubled borrowers under German and U.S. law has been published by Lloyd's of London Press. Dirk also holds a law degree from the University of Bonn, Germany. In addition, he studied international and comparative law at the universities of Geneva, Switzerland, and Trento, Italy, and he is a graduate of the Rotman Directors' Education Program in Toronto.

Dirk speaks English, French, and German. He and his family live in Toronto, Canada.